THE ACCOUNTS OF THE BRITISH EMPIRE

T0362041

To Andrea

The Accounts of the British Empire

Capital Flows from 1799 to 1914

MARIO TIBERI

Translated from Italian by
Judith Turnbull

Routledge
Taylor & Francis Group

LONDON AND NEW YORK

First published 2005 by Ashgate Publishing

Reissued 2018 by Routledge
2 Park Square, Milton Park, Abingdon, Oxon OX14 4RN
711 Third Avenue, New York, NY 10017, USA

Routledge is an imprint of the Taylor & Francis Group, an informa business

First issued in paperback 2018

A Library of Congress record exists under LC control number: 2004057368

Notice:
Product or corporate names may be trademarks or registered trademarks, and are used only for identification and explanation without intent to infringe.

Publisher's Note
The publisher has gone to great lengths to ensure the quality of this reprint but points out that some imperfections in the original copies may be apparent.

Disclaimer
The publisher has made every effort to trace copyright holders and welcomes correspondence from those they have been unable to contact.

ISBN-13: 978-0-815-39739-7 (hbk)
ISBN-13: 978-1-138-62261-6 (pbk)
ISBN-13: 978-1-351-14800-9 (ebk)

Contents

List of Tables

The Accounts of the British Empire

Acknowledgements

I am very grateful to all the people who have helped to improve my work; among them I would like to mention Nicola Acocella, Alberto Bagnai, Francesco Carlucci, Anna Maria Cetta, Giorgio Gagliani, Silvia Gentili, Raffaele Principe, Claudio Rotelli, and Ernesto Volpe di Prignano.

A special thank you is due to the two referees whose suggestions have produced some significant changes to the Italian edition of the book. Nevertheless, I remain ultimately responsible for what has become the final result of this collaboration.

Maria Teresa Madeo has been incredibly helpful in providing the CRC for the publisher.

Last but not least, thanks are also due to the Italian institutions that have given financial support for this research: Consiglio Nazionale delle Ricerche, Ministero per l'Università e la Ricerca Scientifica and Fondazione Caripe.

Introduction

The following work forms part of a long research project which has examined the history of the British Empire until the First World War from a very particular point of view. It aims to trace the evolution of the economic system of Great Britain on the basis of information gathered from the country's balance of payments. Given the limited amount of data available, the balance of payments has been reconstructed from estimates made by the various scholars who have focused their attention on this topic. Within this field of study, the author has already published (see final bibliography) short monographs dealing with the balance of trade and invisible items which illustrate to some extent the role played at that time by the British economic system in the world economy.

In fact, as far as the balance of payments is concerned, these monographs confirmed the absolute and relative importance of export and import flows from and to Great Britain in comparison with the amount of international trade made by other countries in the period under examination. Alongside these standard movements, there emerges another distinctive element of British international trade, namely the phenomenon of re-exports, whose unusual dimensions were one of the signs of Britain's significant presence in numerous intermediary functions, both commercial and financial. Indeed, Britain's invisible earnings, with the currency flows derived from re-exports, together with those provided by the intense activity of the merchant navy and companies involved in business services, counterbalanced at least in part the continuous trade deficits which characterized the British economy from about the middle of the 19th century.

Other sources of foreign currency were represented by income of various types (profit, interest, dividends, rents) accruing from the stock of wealth held abroad by people resident in Great Britain. This income became more and more substantial, as the positive balances in the current account enabled the country to accumulate other financial and real assets abroad.

During the study of the trends of Great Britain's current account in the balance of payments it has become evident that the most significant, though not the only, variable of the British imperial presence was the volume of foreign investments. Some authors have estimated some of these items as part of a wider project to determine the amount of British foreign assets. This is particularly true of those researchers, among them Hobson and Imlah, who applied the so-called indirect method to measure Britain's international investments. This well-known method is based on the aggregation of a country's annual balances on current account, which is obviously a preparatory stage for the measurement of the total wealth owned abroad.

Even though the application of this method is particularly suited to this research, it seemed right and proper to take into account the estimates of the quantitative dimension of international investments made by other authors who have adopted alternative methods.

The second method, favoured by Giffen and Hirst, involves the capitalization of annual income earned from British financial and real investments abroad. The amounts of these flows were officially registered in the *Report of the Commissioners of His (Her) Majesty's Inland Revenue*, though the documentation is limited and starts at the end of the 1870s.

Other scholars, like Crammond and Paish, followed original, but similar, procedures. Yet others, like Segal and Simon first, and Davis and Huttenback more recently, concentrated on the direct findings of assets owned by British citizens abroad, relying on the information drawn from different sources on securities issued annually on financial markets.

In spite of the variety of methods, the different length of the period under examination, the limited availability of data and the large number of authors, it has been possible to determine the historical series of flows and stocks of Britain's foreign investments. The estimates made with different methods do not converge totally, although a comparison of the proposed values can establish a certain pattern in the course of time which appears to be fairly sound empirically speaking. However, there have been some dissenting opinions, which at times have fuelled their very own scepticism about this convergence considered by some, including Platt, to be rather suspicious.

This book intends to explore the vast literature on this subject, proposing in particular in the last chapter an unprecedented review of the results obtained so far and of their reliability. This is not intended as the last word in the debate, but hopefully it will act as a useful reference for those who want to continue the discussion in the future.

The quantitative dimension of Britain's international investments was the most important aspect of this historical phenomenon that dominated world events, economic or otherwise, for more than a century. Certainly it was not the only aspect, as demonstrated by many scholars who have worked on other themes connected with the expansion of the British economy abroad; indeed, the author himself hopes to dwell upon these themes later on.

Chapter 1

The Prevalence of the Indirect Method

1.1 Introduction

An essential element for any qualitative valuation of the role played by Great Britain in events, economic or otherwise, in the period leading up to the First World War is the computation of the size of its foreign investments as both annual and accumulated flows, so that the total value of the stock can be calculated. Naturally there are other indicators that can help to establish the comparative positions of various countries, such as income, exports, imports, terms of trade, etc. Apart from the fact that these variables are always strictly dependent on capital movements in ways and degrees that vary according to the kind of movements in question, it can be argued that investment abroad always implies a degree of interference by one economic system in another.

The question of making an accurate measurement will always be a problem, even when there is an abundance of both official and unofficial data available, as at present. However, any attempt to trace the historical course of the internationalization of British investments is immediately complicated by a lack of information from sources of the period. In view of the remark passed by Hobson, an expert on the subject, that 'the origin of the present gigantic efflux of capital must be sought deep in the past',[1] it is, indeed, unfortunate to note how the path of knowledge meets increasingly long shadows the further we move back in time.

There have been many attempts to track the evolution of investments made abroad by residents in Great Britain. In some cases these works have been sporadic investigations, though usually they have concentrated on specific moments in recent British history, which, for various reasons, have been of particular interest to scholars wanting to further their understanding of the international accounts of the country.

Although a number of methods have been adopted for this estimate, there are basically three main approaches:[2] 1) the first, called the indirect or residual method,[3] consists in aggregating the balances on current account, which are generally measured on a yearly basis; 2) the second is based on the accurate capitalization of the various types of income (profits, dividends, interest and rent) annually accruing to the citizens of a country from abroad; 3) finally, the third, also called the direct method,[4] relies on the cataloguing of financial and real assets held abroad, starting with those that are most easily identified, such as securities issued on the market.

The choice of method made by scholars has been influenced by the availability of data and the objectives of the research, though in some cases the same author has applied more than one criterion to give greater reliability to his estimates.[5]

It should be pointed out, however, that no choice had been possible between the three methods of measurement until the last decades of the 19th century, when more data on international capital flows and their relative returns gradually became available. For the earlier period, the method aggregating the balances on current account was, and still is, practically the only alternative, because at least the data on the flows of goods and the volumes of shipping was kept in official sources and can be used as basic information for the construction of the current account.

It is well to remember that an increased amount of data was also to be made available by official sources over the following decades. For example, the balance on current account was first published by the Board of Trade in 1923, whilst the balance of payments, which also contained capital movements, became official only after the Second World War.[6]

The first of the three methods mentioned above to be applied to determine the annual series of Britain's foreign investments before the First World War was the so-called indirect or residual method,[7] which consists in measuring the balances on current account. Indeed the case of Great Britain, which recorded regular surpluses in these balances and was a great national creditor towards the rest of the world in the 19th century, illustrates very clearly how the balances on current account, net of the movements of bullion (principally gold), represent the potential value that could be used to accumulate profitable assets for British residents abroad, whether they were real or other kinds of assets with different maturity dates, short term or otherwise. However, to determine the overall volume of foreign investments or, in disaggregated terms, of direct and portfolio investments, additional elements are needed in order to construct the aggregates desired. Consequently, to estimate the stock of foreign investments at any particular date, the simple sum of annual balances has to be accompanied by strong assumptions, such as the absence (or neutralization) of gains and/or losses on capital account and the insignificance of amounts of capital finally repatriated.[8]

The application of this method depends on both the reliability and the availability of data on the single items on both the credit and the debit sides of the balance on current account, which together will produce the final balance used to measure the capital owned abroad. And the further back in time the first substantial traces of this accumulation are to be found, the greater the degree of discretion needed in the estimate of certain items in the balance. Negligence or lack of attention in the reconstruction of any of these items can make the estimation of the balances on current account in the initial years of the series a very delicate question; given the length of the period examined that sometimes extends over more than a century, an error may give rise to an increasing distortion in the total sum of capital invested abroad that is calculated at annual intervals.

In order to appreciate these difficulties, we first have to bear in mind that only from 1854 onwards can the official data on the principal components of Britain's balances on current account, that is the exportation (and re-exportation) and importation of goods, be considered as fairly accurate, since prices applied to physical quantities had become more reliable.[9]

Before this year, only the figures for exports had acquired an aura of respectability, because they had been registered by law as values declared by exporters for accounting purposes from 1798, whereas imports and re-exports were measured with the so-called 'official' prices that were completely out-of-date and sometimes even held over from the previous century. As a result the trade balance was clearly distorted and almost consistently showed consecutive surpluses for the years from 1801 to 1841. From 1842 onwards, however, it was to change its plus signs into minus signs in an almost equally consistent manner with a more correct evaluation, for exports at least, thus giving rise to small trade deficits. These were due to a falling trend in the current export prices from the beginning of the 1820s, which clearly invalidated the surpluses arising from the swollen evaluation of exports when they were measured at official prices and not at the prices declared by exporters.[10]

This rather imprecise picture of Britain's trade accounts in the first half of the 19th century could not provide a valid basis for an estimate of the current accounts and subsequently of the evolution of the country's foreign investments. Therefore, it became absolutely essential for the computation of these estimates to correct the so-called official measurements, which meant going back in time as far as possible, starting from 1853.[11]

The problem was first tackled in a systematic way by Schlote[12] and then by Imlah,[13] although they were pursuing very different academic interests. Schlote wanted to analyse the trend of British foreign trade over a long period of time (1700-1930) and used data that had been adapted from measurements that were clearly unsound, whilst Imlah shared the same objective, but considered it to be only an intermediary stage on the way to measuring the evolution of Britain's stock of foreign capital, which was eventually to be achieved in a much more extensive work.[14]

Both writers adopted a very similar methodology which made use of the series of flows of foreign trade published in documents from government sources, such as the *Annual Statement* for the years 1854-1869. These flows were measured, in one case, according to the old mixed criterion of exports at current prices and imports (and re-exports) at official prices. In the other case, all the flows were measured in various ways at current prices according to the innovation introduced into accounting in 1854. A comparison of the two measurements was then used to take the estimates back in years by calculating the balances with the current prices that had been 'constructed' on the basis of the double measurement at current prices and official prices between 1854-1869.[15]

Thus the most significant part of the current account has sufficient reliable documentation available covering the period from 1796-1913 that Imlah was working on, although some estimates refer to about half the period of time under consideration.

In any case interest in the invisible items in the current account grew among British historians, not so much as a result of academic and intellectual involvement in an important economic topic, but rather as a worried response to what had been brought to light by data on the movement of goods, that is the systematic trade deficits reported officially in the figures of the *Annual Statement* from 1854 onwards.[16]

Indeed the various contributions made after the 1870s aimed to identify the currency flows that Britain could draw on to finance its unfavourable trade balances, rather than to complete the picture of the balance on current account in order to determine the total amount of capital accumulated abroad. Nevertheless anyone who was particularly interested in this picture was still able to make good use of the results obtained by others.

One component of the invisible items included all the currency inflows resulting from the many business services accompanying trade, such as brokerage, commissions, insurance, stamp duties, etc., in various combinations and under different names. An important point that needs to be noted is that, in view of the obvious difficulties involved in obtaining a direct estimate, scholars have preferred to calculate these items by applying percentages to the values of the goods exchanged, which has led to an accentuation of evaluation errors already made in the estimation of these values.[17]

There was also concern about the accuracy of the estimates proposed for another component of the invisible items strictly connected with trade. These were earnings from shipping and related services which, regardless of any uncertainty about their precise evaluation, produced substantial currency flows. This was to be expected, of course, in view of the fact that Great Britain is an island and was a great sea and commercial power whose ships were widely used for the transport also of its imports. In this case the lack of data applied specifically to the formation of prices (freights, tariffs, fees, etc.) to be paid on the volume of imported and exported goods, which, conversely, was sufficiently documented in official sources.

There have been many more or less rigorous attempts to reach estimates of the net earnings of these items reported in the literature. However, it should be stressed that, in the case of the indirect method of evaluating foreign investments, the measurement of some significant items of currency flows has basically been left to the discretion of the experts.[18]

The vast research carried out on this topic has brought to the fore other economic data that has since been included in the estimates of balances on current account constructed by various authors. These include emigrants' remittances, colonial duties (especially those paid by the Indian government), diamond movements, expenditure on war, tourism and diplomatic representation, etc. Generally these factors have neither the continuity nor the quantitative consistency to warrant a separate mention, unlike the income earned by Great Britain from foreign investments, which deserves to be considered amongst the relevant invisible items because it has both these characteristics.

It was only from the 1870s that the *Report of the Commissioners of His (Her) Majesty's Inland Revenue*[19] began the publication of official data on capital income from abroad. Although the quality of its evaluation gradually improved, it was always to appear partial, not only for the presence of various forms of evasion, but also for the difficulty involved in identifying specific incomes when they were not directly linked to the ownership of bonds or shares.

These flows of foreign currency, which were obviously net inflows given the creditor position of Great Britain in relation to other countries, raise the question of the interdependence between the sum of these inflows and the sum of the accumulated capital that produced it (see note 2). Indeed, in attempts to measure the accumulated capital by means of the indirect method, the annual capital income has to be determined by hypothesizing an average rate of return on the stock of existing investments at the beginning of each year. The size of the stock is calculated by totalling the annual series of the balance on current account and also, for the first years of the series, by means of a hypothetical value attributed to the capital accumulated abroad up to that date (see section 1.5.4).

This brief analysis of the various items in the current account of the balance of payments should have revealed the uncertainty hanging over the values of both the flows and stock of British foreign investments obtained by applying the indirect or residual method. This does not take anything away from those who, at various times, have been engaged in the arduous task of quantifying phenomena which are at least partially unknown from a statistical point of view, in spite of the clear evidence to the contrary in the real world.

1.2 The first tentative measurements

The specialist literature of the period did not show any great interest in the quantitative evolution of Britain's foreign investments. In fact, only a few occasional notes about them were furnished from time to time until the 1870s[20] when, as we have already seen, there was a particular rush of enthusiasm on the part of scholars in response to the significant deficits in Britain's trade balance.[21]

But then there followed the publication of numerous contributions trying to define in accounting terms the components of what today we would call Britain's balance on current account with more or less complete and careful calculations.[22] In point of fact, some authors simply showed the existence of a favourable balance on the account, admittedly in a convincing manner, but they did not quantify all the items. This was possible, first of all, because of the substantial reduction in the annual trade deficits that emerged immediately when all the invisible items arising from the movement of goods were taken into consideration, although the estimates were inevitably subject to approximations.

These items, which generally brought favourable currency flows, were not able to convert the negative sign of the British trade balances on their own, but nevertheless managed to reduce the size of the deficits considerably, so much so that the estimates which indicated a favourable balance on the current account with the inclusion of other invisible items now seemed convincing.

The work of McKay in this field was exemplary. In a letter to *The Economist* he indicated a series of items which gave rise to figures which, taken as a whole, could be deducted from imports on the one hand and added to exports on the other (discounts, freight, insurance, porterage, storage, stamp duties, commissions, wharfage, brokerage, profit on foreign trade), thus making it possible to reduce substantially the unfavourable trade balances for the years 1858-1876.[23]

Naturally, attributing precise values to these items that refer to large aggregates and to a rather broad temporal horizon may be questionable,[24] but any doubts about these valuations cannot blot out the actual existence of significant sources of currency inflows for Great Britain. Moreover, similar doubts have also been raised about the estimates based on the application of an overall percentage to correct downwards for imports and upwards for exports, as many scholars have done.[25]

Our attention will now focus on the works of two authors in particular, Seyd and Shaw-Lefevre (see note 22), both of whom tackled the question of Britain's international accounts as pioneers of the indirect or residual method. In fact, they both estimated the balance on current account of their country and, as a consequence, its foreign investments over a number of years, albeit very gradually and with a few gaps.

The word 'gradually' has been used to show an element common to both authors, who made the measurements of the items that correspond to today's balance on current account in two phases at a time when the instruments of national accounting had not yet been established.[26] In line with the work of other colleagues, they first extracted a partial balance not only for trade, but also for the services strictly connected with commercial activities (freight, brokerage, commissions, etc.) and then corrected this balance by taking into consideration other currency movements to faithfully reflect the trend of Britain's international accounts with the rest of the world.

Apart from the similarity in their methods, Seyd and Shaw-Lefevre followed quite distinct paths. Seyd considered the period 1854-1877[27] and proceeded with adjustments to the elements of total imports and exports using a procedure that was as fast as it was disconcerting. Instead of patiently identifying the items to be subtracted from imports and added to exports with different percentages, as Newmarch[28] had done for example, Seyd chose to use just one percentage on the side of exports.[29] However, he wisely used a percentage of 12 per cent from 1854 to 1868 and ten per cent from 1869 to 1877, thus taking into account the declining trend in freight and commissions.[30]

Next Seyd dealt with the question of income accruing from what he called 'international wealth', in which he included 'the capital value of the total of our shipping property', that is 'ships anchored in our harbours, at sea, or in foreign ports'.[31] Obviously the problem that Seyd had to face was how to compute the series of values of this income since there was still not enough satisfactory information, official or otherwise, at that time[32] and for the first year of the series there was the additional difficulty of having to estimate the stock of capital for the end of the previous year, from which the relative flow of income was to be calculated.

His approach to this problem was fairly correct, although it is supported only by sketchy information about the numerous difficulties that he had to overcome in order to account for the currency movements for so many years.[33]

Seyd believed an acceptable estimate of Britain's international wealth for 1816 to be between £100-200 million. Such a wide margin in Seyd's evaluation was gradually narrowed down as he moved towards the more precise figure of £600 million for the stock in 1854, the year in which he started his estimate of capital earnings that were calculated by applying a rate of return of about six per cent.[34]

Table 1.1 Annual real balance of trade and presumed annual income from external investments; the remaining balance increasing or decreasing such investments, 1854-1877 (millions of pounds)

Year	Annual balance of goods	Annual international income	Balance*	
	-	+	+	-
1854	23	37	14	
1855	13	39	26	
1856	17	41	24	
1857	24	34	10	
1858	8	38	30	
1859	5	40	35	
1860	26	46	20	
1861	39	49	10	
1862	40	50	10	
1863	28	51	23	
1864	37	52	15	
1865	26	54	28	
1866	28	48	20	
1867	22	50	28	
1868	40	56	16	
1869	35	58	23	
1870	35	65	30	
1871	19	67	48	
1872	9	67	58	
1873	29	63	34	
1874	43	62	19	
1875	64	60		4
1876	94	60		34
1877	117	60		57

*The column of figures under the plus sign (+) indicates the balances amounting to £521,000,000 in the aggregate which increased international wealth from £600,000,000 in 1854 to £1,121,000,000 in 1874. The balances under the minus sign (-) reduced the international wealth to £1,026,000,000 at the end of 1877.

Source: Seyd (1878), Table II.

Although this is the only other item taken into consideration by Seyd, the amount of these earnings produced a favourable balance on current account for the years between 1854 and 1874, while for the last three years (1875-1877) he reported only a reduction in the trade deficit, corrected as indicated above with the percentage added to exports. According to the canons of the indirect method, these balances on current account obviously influenced the amount of Britain's foreign investments that reached their maximum level of £1,121 million at the end of 1874.[35] Seyd's work, although steeped in approximations and reticence, made a noteworthy contribution, as shown by the final results listed in Table 1.1, to the establishment of the indirect method of estimate and more generally to our knowledge of some important aspects of the British economy in the mid 19th century.[36]

The path followed by Shaw-Lefevre, although identical in its method to Seyd's, differed in some significant aspects. In the first place, his estimates covered a period of just twelve years, from 1865 to 1877, a choice which was not explained and certainly was not in line with his introductory notes in which he intended 'to call attention to the progress made by the country during the past decade–since the year 1867'.[37]

Table 1.2 Annual balance on Great Britain's current account, 1865-1877 (millions of pounds)

Year	1 Estimated interest on government and other public loans	2 Estimated remittances including traders' profits	3 Total of columns 1+2	4 Difference between value of net imports and exports*		5=3-4 Probable amount of investments in foreign securities**
				+	-	
1865	28	25	53		19	34
1866	30	25	55		19	36
1867	32	26	58		15	43
1868	34	27	61		31	30
1869	36	28	64		21	43
1870	39	28	67		21	46
1871	42	31	73		4	69
1872	46	31	77	8		85
1873	51	31	82		12	70
1874	56	31	87		26	61
1875	60	32	92		47	45
1876	62	32	94		77	17
1877	65	32	97		97	
Total						579

* The values below represent, respectively, unfavourable (-) and favourable (+) balances.
**It is assumed that these investments were made at 6 per cent.

Source: Shaw-Lefevre (1878), Tables A and B in the *Appendix*.

Furthermore, Shaw-Lefevre fully accepted Newmarch's criterion of deducting five per cent from imports and adding ten per cent to exports (see note 28) to calculate the first part of the current account, and so here another distinction can be drawn between Shaw-Lefevre's and Seyd's series.

For the other invisible items, he took another important step closer to the real situation by including amongst currency inflows both the Indian government's transfers of various kinds (armed forces, provisions, pensions and wages)[38] and profits obtained from brokerage. On the whole, these items were quite significant, as Table 1.2 shows. In addition to these, Shaw-Lefevre included movements corresponding to capital income that he had clearly calculated at six per cent, as Seyd had in fact done, but he did not give any hints about his source of information on the quantity of capital stock invested abroad at the end of 1864, on which the flow of interest for 1865 was calculated.[39]

Reading Shaw-Lefevre's work gives the impression, however, that he was particularly drawn to the figure that Giffen, an authoritative expert of the time, had estimated as the movement of capital income for 1875 (see below, Table 2.1). In a certain sense Shaw-Lefevre's series seems to rely on that figure, even if he did revise it noticeably.[40]

Table 1.3 Synthesis of Great Britain's balance on current account, according to Seyd's (S) and Shaw-Lefevre's (S-L) estimates, 1865-1877* (millions of pounds)

Year	Corrected trade balance		Income from overseas investments		Other inflows	Balance on current account			
	S	S-L	S	S-L	S-L	S		S-L	
	+	+ -	+	+	+	+	-	+	-
1865	26	19	54	28	25	28		34	
1866	28	19	48	30	25	20		36	
1867	22	15	50	32	26	28		43	
1868	40	31	56	34	27	16		30	
1869	35	21	58	36	28	23		43	
1870	35	21	65	39	28	30		46	
1871	19	4	67	42	31	48		69	
1872	9	8	67	46	31	58		85	
1873	29	12	63	51	31	34		70	
1874	43	26	62	56	31	19		61	
1875	64	47	60	60	32		4	45	
1876	94	77	60	62	32		34	17	
1877	117	97	60	65	32		57	–	

* The data is presented in this table according to the criteria adopted today in the accounting of the balance of payments.

Source: Tiberi (1988), Table 9.

Both Seyd and Shaw-Lefevre's researches represent a truly valid source of information, both for their method and contents, and therefore deserve to be illustrated further as in Table 1.3,[41] which summarises their empirical results for the years that overlap in their estimates. Significantly, there emerges a general concordance in their estimates of the final capital stock. In fact, by using the quantity calculated as the initial stock for the end of 1864, as indicated in note 39, and adding the annual totals together, a figure of more than £1,000 million can be calculated for the stock by the end of 1877.

We are effectively dealing with two valid examples of the measurement of the flow of Britain's foreign investments, even though they both reveal one of the weaknesses of the indirect method, that is the difficulty of identifying the initial stock of capital, which, as we have seen, was dealt with in different ways in the two works.

Hence on the basis of the information reported so far, the stock of British overseas investments at the end of 1877 can be set, according to Seyd's estimate, at £1,026 million and Shaw-Lefevre's estimate at £1,046 million.

1.3 Hobson's systematic research: 1870-1913

The great momentum given to the knowledge of Britain's international accounts by scholars at the end of the 1870s was followed by a long period in which no similar concurrent contributions appeared.

The indisputable verdict on the solidity of the country's position in relation to foreign countries, which was confirmed by a further specific article by Giffen,[42] perhaps curbed interest in the subject. The fact remains that very few new research works on the evolution of British investments abroad can be found in the literature for about two decades and of course this was also true for the application of the indirect method that had produced Seyd's and Shaw-Lefevre's important results (see section 1.2).

In the last decades of the century, in fact, there were only a few isolated examples of quantitative analyses of Britain's international position based on the connection between the balance on current account and foreign investments. However, they were intended to determine the flows, not the stock, of capital.

One of these that is worth mentioning for its informative nature is the brief, but clearly presented balance on current account which appeared under the entry 'Commerce' in Palgrave's *Dictionary of Political Economy*.[43] As Palgrave[44] pointed out, the data, which was calculated in an approximate way, referred to the year 1890 and indicated a favourable balance on current account of £20 million that could then be used to boost foreign investments.[45]

A positive impulse to improving our quantitative knowledge also came from the *Report of the Commissioners* which documented the progress made in the fight against the evasion of Income Tax on the earnings from capital invested abroad and gave a more detailed presentation of these earnings.[46]

It should also be remembered that it was in this period that Bastable made an important contribution towards a definition of the structure of the so-called 'debt/borrowing equation', which corresponds to the set of current transactions and long term capital movements, known nowadays as the 'basic balance of payments'.[47]

At the beginning of the 20th century there was a revival of the debate on the question of trade policy that divided experts into two blocs; the traditional position of free traders, which had ruled supreme from the 1840s onwards, was now being challenged by the supporters of protectionism, of which Joseph Chamberlain had become the political exponent.[48]

Now the economic events that alarmed protectionists were not, as in the 1870s, the supposed deficits in the balance on current account, but rather the unsatisfactory trend of British exports that were coming under greater pressure from the exports of new industrializing countries, even in those markets that had always been controlled by British companies. In fact, as illustrated by numerous empirical research works that were stimulated by the debate, the trend of the country's exports was not inferior to its imports at the turn of the century (1899-1903). However, as imports had structurally been of greater value than exports for some time, even a similar growth rate for the two aggregates still resulted in a negative increase in the absolute value of the trade balance.

The emphasis placed on this result was probably created by exaggerated criticisms, because in the following years the trend of the value of goods entering and leaving led to levels in the trade balances comparable to those experienced in the early 1890s.[49]

The interest of scholars in the quantitative aspects of the international position of Great Britain had a certain repercussion on the specific question of foreign investments and the income that was derived from them. Consequently, numerous works were published that gave greater recognition to the attempts to measure in ways other than the indirect or residual method, which will be discussed later (see chapter 2).[50]

In this climate, brimming with enthusiasm, but also tinged with an inappropriate bias at times, an extensive volume was published by Hobson, who most decisively placed the phenomenon of foreign investments at the centre of both his theoretical and empirical analysis, as suggested by the very title.[51]

Hobson's approach followed in the wake of the tradition started by Seyd and Shaw-Lefevre, which had also been followed occasionally by other authors in the course of the years, and corresponded to the application of the so-called indirect or residual method. Indeed the approach of this work is announced in the title of the main chapter on the empirical part,[52] which established the term 'balance of trade' that was to be used for many years by many authors and by official sources to refer to the international accounts of Great Britain.[53] It should not be forgotten, however, that Hobson also recommended, and actually made use of, the direct method, though without the analytical support of the principal estimate that was made with the indirect method (see note 66).

Hobson's book presented two new important features with respect to the earlier estimates made with the indirect method: the greater completeness of the items quantified in the balance on current account and the length of the period under consideration, 1870-1912.[54]

For the import and export of goods, his only references were data published in the *Annual Statement*, though he observed that, given the procedure adopted to collect the information, 'intentional deception is probably unimportant; but errors due to carelessness and ignorance cannot be entirely eliminated'.[55]

Unlike Seyd and Shaw-Lefevre, Hobson put the value of the movement of goods alongside the transfer of gold and silver bullion and coins according to the praxis at that time. To some extent he gave more importance to the objective physical analogy between the two movements than to their different economic natures. In fact, the movements of bullion were linked less to the limited function of goods, as played by gold and silver in industry and the crafts, than to the function as a means of payment or of transfer of wealth. Today these movements would be placed most appropriately amongst the balance of financial transactions.[56]

Some omissions concerning his data, at times just for brief stretches, at others covering the whole period (diamonds, the sale of old and new ships, etc.), were accounted for by Hobson with other estimates (in the case of ships), but in some cases the data was simply confirmed (as in the case of diamonds).

As far as the long list of invisible items is concerned, the author adopted various solutions. He eliminated some items from the accounts where estimates could not be made or had irrelevant values to be quantified, as in the case of tourist and postal expenses, believing they would be compensated to some extent by currency inflows and outflows. Wherever possible he used official sources, at least in part in such cases as remittances from emigrants, financing of the British colonial apparatus by the Indian government and expenses to cover the cost of Britain's diplomatic and military presence in the world. And he also made very careful estimates of the volume of the flows when he considered it necessary. Furthermore, there were three other items of significant value that challenged the researcher's talent in Hobson, namely, earnings from the transport by ship of both passengers and cargo, payments for all kinds of 'financial and other services performed on behalf of foreign countries'[57] and income from capital invested abroad.

As far as freights and earnings from services connected with transport (assistance, victualling, provisioning, etc.) were concerned, he had to move on very treacherous terrain, because the information that could be obtained was only a limited part of the total amount that was necessary for an adequate measurement.[58]

Hobson suggested three possible valuation criteria for the year 1907, from which three different, but not too divergent, values were obtained and he chose the intermediate figure. The value estimated was £90 million which corresponded to more than 1/6 of the total exports in the year being considered. It is therefore an absolutely respectable figure within the context of Britain's currency earnings.

Hobson's approach was certainly scrupulous, but an air of uncertainty hangs over his estimate for 1907, which unfortunately becomes more intense as the series of those earnings was gradually constructed over the whole period.[59] In the absence of analytical data, the series could be determined only by using the fragmentary information available, which was rather inadequate to capture the variations in fares, technology, efficiency, tonnage, the presence of British shipping, etc. Once again, Hobson was concerned about filling the gaps that were particularly relevant in the early years he examined. He did so by constructing his own indices or by using those elaborated by others,[60] by introducing reasonable criteria of equivalence between steam ships and sailing ships, hypothesizing plausible changes in their respective cruising speed, etc. It is right to point out, however, that the overall results, although imprecise, do not necessarily overestimate Britain's currency earnings. For example, Hobson himself indicated a certain underestimation in his own estimates for the early 1870s in comparison with those proposed authoritatively by Giffen.[61]

Giffen's reputation was again confirmed by his estimates of the currency flows resulting from the above mentioned 'financial and other services' conducted principally, but not entirely, on the London market by operators resident in Great Britain. In this case the figure used by Hobson as a starting point was the estimate of £18 million for the flows which Giffen had calculated for 1899 by applying a rate of 2.5 per cent to the total value of imports and exports. Hobson took this figure and introduced an adjustment to the percentage, thus taking into account the trend of the official discount rate in the years covered in his series. The reason for this procedure seems to be that this rate served as a reference parameter for those who were engaged in foreign trade and for those who operated in financial markets.[62]

Even the last item of a certain quantitative importance, that is the income from capital invested abroad, posed something of a problem for Hobson. Some valuable help for this item, which included profits, dividends, interest and rent, came from the data published in the *Report of the Commissioners*, which accounted for these earnings, although incompletely, in so far as they had been assessed for an eventual levy through Income Tax. However, this valid documentation has limitations too. To start with, the figures began to acquire a clear accounting identity only in the data for the financial year 1877-1878 onwards. Furthermore, these figures continued to be partial, because obviously they did not include earnings which evaded taxation or were taxed though considered unidentified as they were mixed up in an aggregate under the broader name of 'Businesses, professions, etc., not otherwise detailed (including salaries of employés)'.[63]

Just a few years before Hobson, the same situation had already been dealt with by Paish when he adopted a very particular method (see section 2.3) to determine the stock of Britain's foreign investments.[64] By drawing on the various documents that were available on the life of firms working in particular sectors whose income escaped detection, according to indications provided by the *Report of the Commissioners*, Paish had fixed the sum of unidentified income at £58 million. This amount corresponded to little more than 40 per cent of the total flow of earnings estimated at £140 million for the year 1907.[65]

Hobson constructed a series by extending to the whole period the composition of the 1907 flow divided into identified and unidentified income (60 per cent and 40 per cent respectively) on the basis of the data on identified income that appeared annually in the *Report of the Commissioners*. Any doubt about this simplification is legitimate and Hobson himself expressed concern, especially as the starting data of identified income given in the *Report of the Commissioners* was unsatisfactory even for the first years of his estimate.[66]

Nevertheless, by collecting this more or less reliable information, Hobson was able to present the most complete analysis of the international accounts of Great Britain before the First World War and of the sum of the annual flows of the country's foreign investments, as shown in Table 1.4,[67] that had ever been produced by a scholar at that time.

Table 1.4 Great Britain's balance of payments and export of capital, 1870-1913 (millions of pounds)

| | Credits | | | | | | | | Debits | | | |
| | Visible exports | | Invisible exports | | | | | Import of capital | Visible imports | | Invisible imports | Export of capital |
Year	Goods	Gold and silver bullion	New ships	Shipping earnings	Commissions, insurance, and banking charges	Government services, remittances and old ships[1]	Income from investment abroad		Goods	Gold and silver bullion		
1870	244.1	18.9	1.0	39.5	11.0	6.0	44.0a		303.3	29.5		31.7
1871	283.6	33.8	1.0	50.0	12.0	6.2	46.0a		331.0	38.1		63.5
1872	314.6	30.3	2.0	51.0	15.5	6.4	48.0a		354.7	29.6		83.5
1873	311.0	28.9	3.0	60.5	17.2	6.6	50.0a		371.3	33.6		72.3
1874	297.7	22.9	2.0	57.5	14.6	6.8	52.0a		370.1	30.4		53.0
1875	281.6	27.6	1.0	53.5	13.5	7.0	49.5		373.9	33.3		26.5
1876	256.8	29.5	1.0	56.0	11.8	7.2	46.5	3.4	375.1	37.1		
1877	252.3	39.8	1.0	55.5	12.7	7.4	47.5	15.4	394.4	37.2		
1878	245.5	26.7	2.0	57.5	13.6	7.6	47.0	1.3	368.8	32.4		
1879	248.8	28.6	3.0	52.5	11.3	7.8	47.3		363.0	24.2		12.1
1880	286.4	18.9	3.0	52.5	13.3	8.0	49.5		411.2	16.3		4.1
1881	297.1	22.5	5.0	49.0	14.8	8.2	50.5		397.0	16.9		33.2
1882	306.7	21.0	5.0	51.5	16.8	8.4	52.5		413.0	23.6		25.3
1883	305.4	16.4	6.0	54.0	15.8	8.6	55.8		426.9	17.2		17.9
1884	296.0	22.0	4.0	50.0	13.6	8.8	57.0		390.0	20.4		41.0
1885	271.5	21.8	2.0	46.0	12.6	9.0	64.0		371.0	22.0		33.9
1886	269.0	21.0	2.0	45.5	12.4	9.2	73.0		349.9	20.4		61.8
1887	281.3	17.1	3.0	46.0	13.5	9.4	77.5		363.2	17.8		66.8
1888	298.6	22.6	4.0	52.5	14.3	9.6	82.5		387.6	22.0		74.5
1889	315.6	25.1	9.0	62.0	16.0	9.8	86.0		427.6	27.1		68.8
1890	328.3	25.2	7.0	57.0	18.3	10.0	91.5		420.7	34.0		82.6
1891	309.1	37.2	5.0	56.1	15.5	10.2	90.0		435.4	39.6		48.5
1892	291.6	28.9	4.0	52.3	13.2	10.4	91.0		423.8	32.3		35.3
1893	277.1	33.1	4.0	52.0	13.7	10.6	91.0		404.7	36.7		40.1

Table 1.4 (continued)

Year											
1894	273.8	27.8	4.0	52.0	11.8	10.8	88.0	408.3	38.6		21.3
1895	285.8	31.7	5.0	50.2	11.9	11.0	90.5	416.7	46.7		22.7
1896	296.4	45.2	7.0	54.0	13.6	11.2	92.5	441.8	38.8		39.3
1897	294.2	49.6	7.0	57.7	14.0	11.4	93.0	451.0	48.8		27.1
1898	294.0	52.2	8.5	65.5	15.8	11.6	98.5	470.5	58.4		17.2
1899	320.3	35.5	9.1[3]	64.5	18.0	11.8	99.0	485.0	45.3		27.9
1900	345.8	32.0	8.5	76.3	20.2	12.0	99.0	523.1	39.5		31.2
1901	338.7	26.0	9.1	60.0	19.1	12.2	103.0	522.0	32.2		13.9
1902	343.4	26.1	5.8	60.0	18.3	12.4	105.0	528.4	31.4		11.2
1903	356.1	39.2	4.2	64.5	20.0	12.6	108.0	542.6	39.0		23.0
1904	366.6	46.3	4.4	66.0	19.2	12.8	108.5	551.0	45.6		27.2
1905	402.2	45.4	5.4	72.5	19.4	13.0	121.5	565.0	51.6		62.8
1906	452.0	61.5	8.6	85.0	25.3	13.2	130.0	607.9	63.3		104.4
1907	508.0	67.8	10.0	90.0	29.9	13.4	140.0	645.8	73.1		140.2
1908	446.1	63.3	10.5	79.0	20.9	13.6	146.0	593.0	56.5		129.9
1909	463.6	60.0	5.8	83.0	21.6	13.8	153.5	624.7	66.5		110.1
1910	525.4	64.7	8.7	95.0	26.7	14.0	166.0	678.3	71.4		150.8
1911	551.2	57.0	5.7	110.0[4]	26.3	14.2	171.0	680.1	63.0		192.3
1912	591.9	64.9	7.0	156.0[4]	29.9	14.4	176.0	744.6	69.5		226.0
1913[5]	623.8	62.1	11.0	110.0	30.0	25.0	200.0	768.7	74.0	20.0[6]	189.2

1. A miscellaneous item because it includes old ships that should appear under visible exports.
2. Estimated figures in the absence of specific information from the *Report of the Commissioners*.
3. From 1899 onwards the data appeared in the *Annual Statement*, whereas the figures for the years 1870-1898 were estimated.
4. These figures are probably exaggerated because they do not take sufficient account of the 1911 strike and are influenced significantly by an exceptional increase in freight rates in 1912.
5. Official values from the *Annual Statement* and Hobson's estimates revised (see note 54).
6. Hobson did not provide estimates for the years 1870-1912.

Source: Hobson (1921), Table on p. 146; (1963), *passim*.

Apart from any remarks that can be passed about the method and specific application adopted by Hobson, there is one important omission in his work that needs to be pointed out. His work did not include a separate estimate of Britain's capital stock invested abroad on the eve of the First World War. It would certainly have been a very difficult task to estimate the stock at the beginning of the period being studied, that is 1870, and then to add the annual flows of foreign investments to this figure in order to calculate the stock in 1913. Hobson only managed to sidestep this problem by adopting the technique of working backwards in his construction of the series of capital earnings.

It should be noted, however, that the sum of these flows for the period 1870-1913, as Tables 1.4 and 4.1 show, corresponds to a total amount of £2,524 million.

1.4 Schooling's eccentric elaboration: 1880-1910

Schooling's attempt to measure the international accounts of Great Britain from 1880 onwards deserves a special mention, because he came to a conclusion that was quite unique among all the authors working with a certain systematic approach, and, perhaps, for this very reason it is worthy of particular attention.[68] In fact, he concluded his work on the estimation of Britain's balance on current account by indicating a persistent deficit for the whole period he had considered, that is from 1880 to 1910. This happened as a result of the evaluation criteria Schooling adopted for some of the invisible items;[69] on the one hand, he omitted an item of currency earnings from 'financial and other services' provided by British companies which could easily have been identified,[70] as well as the remittances of the Indian government and, on the other hand, he used modest estimates for two fundamental items, that is shipping and income from foreign investments.

For the first, Schooling judged other estimates, such as Giffen's and the Board of Trade's,[71] to be too high and followed an approach that we have seen in Seyd, who considered the merchant navy as a kind of foreign investment (wealth) and consequently first and foremost as a provider of profits. Naturally, attributing a monetary value to these investments required the use of discretional adjustments to the more or less official estimates which were circulating at the time. Schooling then decided to calculate an annual profit rate of five per cent, perhaps rather overcautiously for this amount. Finally, he put the overall estimate of currency inflows under this item and, as the annual profits were calculated, he multiplied them by five. This calculation produces, therefore, a ratio of one to four between these entries and the value of British shipping capital,[72] which is quite low in comparison with other estimates.

As far as capital income is concerned, Schooling limited himself to considering only the series of so-called identified income following the terminology proposed in the *Report of the Commissioners* (see section 1.3) and therefore excluded the annual flow of unidentified income from the calculation of Britain's currency surplus, but he did so with fairly unconvincing arguments.[73] The size of this flow was relatively important, as can be seen from the indications contained in the *Report of the Commissioners* and from the estimates made by numerous contemporary scholars of Schooling, such as Crammond and Paish (see section 2.3).[74]

Table 1.5 Great Britain: Gross shipping earnings, profits from abroad, excess of imports, and amount of excess of imports *not paid for*, 1880-1910 (yearly averages during each decade, millions of pounds)

Decade	Gross shipping earnings	Profits from abroad	Gross shipping earnings *plus* profits from abroad	Excess of imports *less* 7 million for export of ships	Excess of imports *not paid for*
	A	B	C=A+B	D	D-C
1880-1889	25	39	64	97	33
1881-1890	25	42	67	95	28
1882-1891	26	44	70	98	28
1883-1892	26	47	73	101	28
1884-1893	27	49	76	102	26
1885-1894	27	51	78	107	29
1886-1895	28	52	80	112	32
1887-1896	29	53	82	118	36
1888-1897	30	54	84	126	42
1889-1898	31	55	86	135	49
1890-1899	31	56	87	141	54
1891-1900	32	57	89	149	60
1892-1901	33	57	90	155	65
1893-1902	34	58	92	161	69
1894-1903	34	59	93	167	74
1895-1904	35	61	96	171	75
1896-1905	36	62	98	173	75
1897-1906	37	65	102	176	74
1898-1907	38	68	106	175	69
1899-1908	40	71	111	171	60
1900-1909	41	74	115	170	55
1901-1910	42	78	120	168	48

Source: Schooling (1911), Table 101.

Table 1.5 reproduces the table prepared by Schooling with some marginal variations.[75]

At this point there only remains to recall the harsh opinion expressed by Stamp, an authoritative scholar, who stated that 'his whole treatment of the subject falls to pieces' and described Schooling's contribution as a research that had been unwittingly distorted by the great political passion of the scholar.[76] In fact, Schooling sided with the protectionist faction that had taken up the campaign against the prevailing free trade approach of Britain's trade policy at the beginning of the century (see section 1.3). In this context, the temptation to show a critical situation in the country's balance of payments had perhaps proved to be just too great for him.

1.5 The contributions of other scholars

1.5.1 The work of the Board of Trade: 1907, 1910, 1913
In the years following the First World War interest in the evolution of Britain's overseas relations was reawakened. This coincided with the growth of a more general interest in the question of international accounts throughout the world. The Economic and Financial Committee of the League of Nations intervened to solve the problem of the lack of documentation that had prevailed in almost all countries and in 1922 it unanimously passed a resolution that 'invite les Etats Membres de la Société des Nations à prêter leur concours à la Commission économique et financière en lui fournissant, avec le plus de détails possibles et aussi rapidement qu'ils le pourront, les informations que la Commission pourrait avoir à leur demander, notamment en ce qui concerne ses diverses publications et ses investigations sur le traitement équitable du commerce'.[77]

Apart from these international pressures, there also existed both new and old reasons why Great Britain wanted to extend the existing knowledge of phenomena that were of utmost importance for its own economic system, especially as it was so open to integration with the rest of the world. It was felt that, even if disequilibrium had been a constant feature of the British trade balance for decades, the size of the deficit that had grown from £134 million in 1913 to £669 million in 1919 warranted immediate and serious attention.

At the same time, the fact that the war effort had forced the country to frequently resort to international financing, especially from the United States, could not be ignored. Indeed, this had had an impact on one of the largest invisible items, that is income from assets owned abroad by British citizens. Moreover, these selfsame invisible items had always provided the currency inflows that had enabled Great Britain to compensate its trade deficits before the First World War (see section 1.3).

Hence a governmental body, the Board of Trade, undertook a more direct commitment towards international accounting by publishing 'tentatively and unofficially' Britain's balance of trade, which corresponds to the balance on current account in modern terminology.[78] Any reference made to the documentation provided by the Board of Trade focussing on the post-war years is warranted, firstly, because of the endorsement the authoritativeness and competence of the institution itself gave to the indirect method of measuring the annual variations in the stock of Britain's foreign investments and, secondly, because of the retrospective view given of some of the invisible items in the limited information presented in Table 1.6, even if only for the years 1907, 1910 and 1913.

On the first point, the Board of Trade's position was made explicit by the name chosen to denote the balance on current account: 'Income available for investment overseas', as this balance was regularly favourable, as other sources had shown.

As for the originality of the estimates made by the Board of Trade, the most important innovation was more a question of method than results and concerned the measurement of currency earnings from shipping. The Board preferred to adopt an average freight rate per ton multiplied by the total tonnage of the British merchant navy,[79] even for the main component of these earnings, as opposed to the three criteria proposed by Hobson (see section 1.3).

Table 1.6 Synthesis of Great Britain's balance on current account: 1907, 1910, 1913 (millions of pounds)

Year	1907	1910	1913
Net income from overseas investments	160	187	210
Net national shipping income	85	90	94
Commissions	25	25	25
Other services	10	10	10
Total 'invisible exports' on balance (B)	280	312	339
Excess of imports of merchandise and bullion (A)	142	159	158
Balance available for investment overseas (B-A)	138	153	181
New overseas issues on London market in year	91	207	198
New overseas issues on London market in following year	142	166	158

Source: Board of Trade (1923), Table on p. 386.

Alongside this basic value, however, other expenditure arising from the movement of ships (provision of coal, port dues, cost of stores and bunkers abroad) had to be taken into account, regardless of whether they were to be added or subtracted. The fact is that the Board of Trade recorded a total of £94 million for 'Net national shipping income' in 1913, the year before the First World War broke out. This figure does not actually differ very much from the calculation made by Hobson (see section 1.3), who was never quoted by the anonymous writers of articles published in the *Board of Trade Journal*. Nor are there any significant differences between the valuations of the Board of Trade and those of Hobson for the same shipping items in 1907 and 1910 or for the whole set of items on the current account for the years 1907, 1910 and 1913, as can be seen from a comparison of Table 1.6 with Table 1.4. However, it should be noted that the trade balances prepared by the Board of Trade differ from those calculated by Hobson, because the Board's took into account the movement of diamonds, which naturally gave rise to currency outflows, but was not formally recorded in the *Annual Statement* and was only mentioned in it among the information coming from other sources.[80]

One last point to be made about the Board of Trade's contribution emerges from the last lines in Table 1.6, which seem to suggest a close link between the balances on current account and the issues of new securities on the London Stock Exchange. This juxtaposition seems inappropriate because of the net and contradictory differences between the series of values and because of suggestions made in various passages of articles in the *Board of Trade Journal* about the existence of other financial markets, the frequent use of credit to place exports, the variety of investments overseas, the presence of investors from other countries on the London Stock Exchange, etc.

The ambiguity in the Board of Trade's presentation of data was later removed as a consequence of the comments made in a report edited by some government-appointed experts, who were charged 'to report on the existing estimates of the annual balance of payments, with particular reference to the power of this country to make overseas investments'.[81]

The report gave a clear explanation of the marked qualitative and quantitative differences between the two aggregates – the balance on current account and the new overseas issues on the London market – together with other useful ideas,[82] and suggested abolishing the presentation of the two variables and substituting the term 'Balance available for investment overseas' with 'Estimated total credit (or debit) balance on items specified above'.[83] This proposal was immediately accepted by the Board of Trade, as the tables published by the same body in its weekly journal showed over the following years.[84]

1.5.2 The limits of Jenks's estimates: 1854-1880

On the whole the importance given by Jenks to the quantitative aspects of Britain's investments overseas was marginal, bearing in mind his vast amount of research that endeavoured 'to set forth some of the principal ways in which the migration of capital has influenced the rise of an invisible empire of which London is the metropolis – the empire of British enterprise – the overseas extension of the British economic system'.[85]

He did, however, write a long note in his book about the estimate of 'Great Britain's export of surplus capital',[86] which he obtained by determining the balances on current account. The period under consideration, 1854-1880, is limited, on the one hand, by the beginning of more reliable data on trade movements published in the *Annual Statement* and, on the other, by the time deadline Jenks gave to his research.

Just as the Board of Trade had done, Jenks drew widely on the work of the experts of the time. We therefore find the well known names of Bourne and Giffen (see bibliography) among his sources, together with the solid information published in the *Annual Statement*. The only important adjustment that he introduced concerned the item 'Foreign trade profits'; Jenks corrected the evaluation proposed by Bourne by measuring it with the fixed percentage of five per cent on the annual total of British foreign trade.[87]

The set of data proposed by Jenks is presented in Table 1.7 in the form he himself chose.[88]

Jenks's decision to place the balance in a single column by aggregating all estimated items on current account, except for capital income from abroad, is slightly perplexing, especially in the absence of any further explanation. A similar procedure had already been followed by Hobson (see section 1.3), who had then disaggregated his balance into its components of currency inflows (income from capital invested abroad + foreign investments in Great Britain) and currency outflows (income paid on foreign investments + British investments abroad) and had finally used the balance with the other three components under consideration that were supposedly known in order to determine the last item, that is the export of capital (British investments abroad).[89]

Table 1.7   Balance of payments of Great Britain and the net movements of capital, 1854-1880 (millions of pounds)

Year	Import balance including bullion and ship sales	Net freight earnings	Foreign trade profits	Insurance, brokerage, etc.	Capital and interest balance
	1	2	3	4	5=2+3+4-1
1854	40.6[1a]	24.0	12.4	7.9	3.7
1855	34.0[1]	25.2	11.9	7.7	10.8
1856	34.1[1]	25.3	14.4	9.1	14.7
1857	33.5[1]	26.6	15.5	9.9	18.5
1858	33.7	27.4	14.0	8.9	16.6
1859	17.0	27.3	14.4	10.2	34.9
1860	49.9	27.4	17.3	10.6	5.4
1861	55.5	28.7	17.1	10.4	0.7
1862	61.1	29.6	17.4	11.3	-2.8
1863	54.9	32.2	18.8	12.6	8.7
1864	66.1	34.6	21.7	13.5	3.7
1865	57.5	36.5	21.8	13.1	13.9
1866	67.8	37.2	24.2	14.7	8.3
1867	57.8	37.3	22.8	13.5	15.8
1868	70.1	37.5	23.6	14.2	5.2
1869	61.6	37.6	24.2	14.2	14.4
1870	68.0	39.2	25.1	14.9	11.2
1871	50.4	41.2	27.7	17.2	35.7
1872	36.1	43.7	30.5	18.2	56.3
1873	61.0	45.7	31.3	18.6	34.6
1874	70.6	48.2	30.4	18.0	26.0
1875	96.1	49.8	29.8	17.9	1.4
1876	125.4	51.0	28.7	17.4	-28.3
1877	138.8	53.0	29.6	18.1	-38.1
1878	127.5	55.5	28.0	16.8	-27.2
1879	107.2	57.6	27.7	16.6	-5.3
1880	119.5[a]	59.8	31.7	18.3	-9.7

1. No official records were kept of bullion movements, 1854-1857 inclusive. The estimates of Giffen have been used.

a. There is no estimate available for ship sales in 1854. For 1880 the value has been estimated in the same proportion as for 1879, as Bourne's calculations did not reach this year.

Source: Jenks (1971), Table on p. 414.

Although Jenks's reluctance to embark on his own complex calculations is quite understandable, it is surprising that he did not use the information that was already available for the years 1854-1880 on the quite substantial income Great Britain was said to have earned from capital abroad. For example Seyd's and Shaw-Lefevre's estimates refer to a great part of the period he was studying (see section 1.2) and Hobson's calculations to the later years (see section 1.3).[90] Moreover, these same years were covered by the partial, but reliable data published in the *Report of the Commissioners*.

This incongruence in his work led Jenks to clearly underestimate the total stock of wealth accumulated abroad in the years considered. In fact, he spoke explicitly of £332 million for 1854-1874, a total that is significantly lower than the one reached in Seyd's and Shaw-Lefevre's estimates.[91] Consequently, the valuations proposed by Jenks cannot convincingly help to define the quantitative dimension of the phenomenon studied, although they obviously represent one of the many attempts made using the indirect method.[92]

It should be remembered, however, that Jenks won quite a reputation among those who adopted the direct method. His work, in fact, was based on a formidable archive of data on the events surrounding a great part of the financial assets issued by Great Britain in the period he studied. In this way Jenks actually made an early and valuable contribution, both in method and content, to a different current of research on Britain's foreign investments (see section 2.4).

1.5.3 Cairncross's adjustments to Hobson's series:1870-1913

Unlike Jenks, Cairncross considered the empirical results of the phenomenon of Britain's foreign investments to be an essential part of his research. His book, as the title suggests, consisted in a set of papers focussing on a few important aspects of the accumulation of capital, both at home and overseas, in the decades leading up to the First World War. These aspects were, namely, the possible presence of cyclical trends, the complementary or reciprocal crowding out of domestic and foreign investments, and a possible connection between migratory movements and capital transfers.[93]

Hence Cairncross needed to use empirical evidence elaborated both by himself and by others. As far as the annual amount of Britain's foreign investments was concerned, he took Hobson's estimate (see section 1.3) and proceeded to correct just two of the items that were, in fact, the two most substantial invisible items, that is 'Total shipping earnings' and 'Interest on foreign investments'.[94]

Cairncross used the term 'Total shipping earnings' because, unlike Hobson, he preferred to disaggregate the currency inflows from shipping into two parts: the first, the more important one, was made up exclusively of income from the British fleet and the second accounted for the expenses borne by foreign ships in British ports for port dues, bunker coal, loading and unloading, etc.

For the first part, Cairncross followed one of the three calculation methods used by Hobson when he had analytically constructed the items making up the receipts from shipping, that is costs (wages, insurance, repairs, port and deck charges, etc.) plus the net average profits of seven per cent on the value of shipping capital, valued at £150 million at the beginning of 1907, the year chosen by Cairncross as his base year.[95] He also stayed close to Hobson's estimates for the values attributed to the single items, except in three particular cases. The first was the cost of bunker coal, for which Hobson considered both British and foreign ships together, whilst Cairncross, as mentioned above, preferred to put the expenses incurred by non-British ships under a separate heading. In the second case, the profit rate on British shipping capital is higher than Hobson's five per cent. In the third case Cairncross quantified an item that Hobson had certainly noted, but had not evaluated, that is the fares paid by British passengers and subsidies awarded by their government. They constituted real and substantial earnings for shipping companies in Great Britain, but represented a kind of transfer within the country and were therefore irrelevant when identifying positive currency inflows.[96]

Cairncross also had to deal, as Hobson had done, with the problem of determining the series of his item 'Total shipping earnings' for the whole period he studied. He therefore elaborated two indices to take account of the variations in the freight rates and in the total tonnage of the British fleet. In this way he had all the elements necessary to build the series which he then had to add to the other series with more modest values for the expenditure of foreign ships in British ports to obtain 'Total shipping earnings'. These values were calculated by assigning an average expenditure per ton transported, which was higher for steam vessels than for sailing vessels and amounted to £10 million for the base year 1907.[97]

The final result led to a revision of Hobson's series with a decrease in the total amount attributed to Britain's currency earnings for this item between 1870 and 1913. For Cairncross the figure stood at about £2,340 million, as compared with about £2,800 million for Hobson (see Tables 1.4 and 1.8).

At this point it is worth remembering what, to all intents and purposes, appears to be an intellectual exercise. Cairncross put to one side the punctilious attitude he had adopted initially in tracing the evolution of the earnings from shipping and set about a completely different estimate guided by good common sense.

This time the estimate adopted a very similar ratio between the total shipping earnings and total foreign trade (imports + exports + re-exports), six per cent for 1913 and 5.5 per cent for 1936, when calculating the whole series of 'Shipping earnings' from 1870 to 1913, but the above mentioned payments made by foreign ships in British ports were left out. Cairncross made an upward adjustment to the proportion, that is $6^2/_3$ amounting to about 1/16 of all foreign trade, thus obtaining results that were not far from those reached by the more sophisticated procedure.[98]

The adjustment that Cairncross made to the series of income from foreign investments led to completely different conclusions as far as currency inflows were concerned. In this case Cairncross adopted the procedure followed by Hobson, which had in turn been adopted by Paish (see section 2.3), with the only significant and systematic difference to be found in the years from 1870 to 1885. The introduction of a fiscal measure, the Coupons Act of 1885, led to a reduction in tax evasion on foreign capital income and as a result there was a change in the rigid proportion between identified income (about 60 per cent) and unidentified income (about 40 per cent) estimated by Paish for 1907, which Hobson had extended to all the years initially examined (1870-1912).[99]

As a consequence Cairncross took steps to review what he called the 'Interest on foreign investments' for the years 1870-1885 with an upward correction to Hobson's estimate from about £807 million to more than £883 million. This resulted in an estimate for this item of about £3,980 million for Hobson and more than £4,050 million for Cairncross for the whole period, even allowing for what was said in note 99.

Table 1.8 Great Britain's balance of payments on income account and net export of capital, 1870-1913 (millions of pounds)

Year	Excess of imports	Total 'Shipping earnings'	Interest on foreign investment	Other invisibles (including ships)	Balance of payments on income account	Net export of bullion and specie	Net export of capital
	1	2	3	4	5=(2+3+4)-1	6	7=5+6
1870	59.2	37.9	42.0	18.0	38.7	-10.6	28.1
1871	47.4	40.9	45.0	19.2	57.7	-4.3	53.4
1872	40.1	43.9	48.0	23.9	75.7	0.7	76.4
1873	60.3	49.6	52.0	26.8	68.1	-4.7	63.4
1874	72.4	50.7	55.3	23.4	57.0	-7.5	49.5
1875	92.3	46.4	55.7	21.5	31.3	-5.7	25.6
1876	118.3	47.5	52.8	20.0	2.0	-7.6	-5.6
1877	142.1	50.7	54.0	21.1	-16.3	2.6	-13.7
1878	123.3	46.6	53.7	23.2	0.2	-5.7	-5.5
1879	114.2	47.0	53.8	22.1	8.7	4.4	13.1
1880	124.8	51.0	56.2	24.3	6.7	2.6	9.3
1881	99.9	55.8	57.4	28.0	41.3	5.6	46.9
1882	106.3	57.0	59.8	30.2	40.7	-2.6	38.1
1883	121.5	56.7	63.5	30.4	29.1	-0.8	28.3
1884	94.0	51.6	65.2	26.4	49.2	1.6	50.8
1885	99.5	46.3	69.1	23.6	39.5	-0.2	39.3
1886	80.9	45.2	73.0	23.6	60.9	0.6	61.5
1887	81.9	46.3	77.5	25.9	67.8	-0.7	67.1
1888	89.0	53.2	82.5	27.9	74.6	0.6	75.2
1889	112.0	63.7	86.0	34.8	72.5	-2.0	70.5
1890	92.4	60.0	91.5	35.3	94.4	-8.8	85.6
1891	127.1	58.7	90.0	30.7	52.3	-1.6	50.7
1892	132.2	51.0	91.0	27.6	37.4	-3.4	34.0
1893	127.6	50.4	91.0	28.3	42.1	-3.6	38.5

Table 1.8 (continued)

1894	134.5	50.8	88.0	26.4	30.7	-10.8	19.9
1895	130.9	48.6	90.5	27.9	36.1	-15.0	21.1
1896	145.4	52.6	92.5	31.8	31.5	6.4	37.9
1897	156.8	54.6	93.0	32.4	23.2	0.8	24.0
1898	176.5	62.0	98.5	35.9	19.9	-6.2	13.7
1899	164.7	59.3	99.0	38.9	32.5	-9.8	22.7
1900	177.3	68.7	99.0	40.7	31.1	-7.5	23.6
1901	183.3	58.0	103.0	40.4	18.1	-6.2	11.9
1902	185.0	58.6	105.0	36.5	15.1	-5.3	9.8
1903	186.5	62.6	108.0	36.8	20.9	0.2	21.1
1904	184.4	61.6	108.5	36.4	22.1	0.7	22.8
1905	162.8	68.8	121.5	37.8	65.3	-6.2	59.1
1906	155.9	78.2	130.0	47.1	99.4	-1.8	97.6
1907	137.8	82.5	140.0	53.3	138.0	-5.3	132.7
1908	146.9	73.5	146.0	45.0	117.6	6.8	124.4
1909	161.1	75.8	153.5	41.2	109.4	-6.5	102.9
1910	152.9	79.7	166.0	49.4	142.2	-6.7	135.5
1911	128.9	89.1	171.0	46.2	177.4	-6.0	171.4
1912	152.7	110.7	181.5	51.3	190.8	-4.6	186.2
1913	144.9	105.0	194.0	56.0	210.1	-11.9	198.2

Source: Cairncross (1975), Table 40.

Table 1.9 Hobson's and Cairncross's estimates of Great Britain's export of capital, 1870-1913 (millions of pounds)

Year	Estimates	
	Hobson	Cairncross
1870	31.7	28.1
1871	63.5	53.4
1872	83.5	76.4
1873	72.3	63.4
1874	53.0	49.5
1875	26.5	25.6
1876	-3.4°	-5.6°
1877	-15.4°	-13.7°
1878	-1.3°	-5.5°
1879	12.1	13.1
1880	4.1	9.3
1881	33.2	46.9
1882	25.3	38.1
1883	17.9	28.3
1884	41.0	50.8
1885	33.9	39.3
1886	61.8	61.5
1887	66.8	67.1
1888	74.5	75.2
1889	68.8	70.5
1890	82.6	85.6
1891	48.5	50.7
1892	35.3	34.0
1893	40.1	38.5
1894	21.3	19.9
1895	22.7	21.1
1896	39.3	37.9
1897	27.1	24.0
1898	17.2	13.7
1899	27.9	22.7
1900	31.2	23.6
1901	13.9	11.9
1902	11.2	9.8
1903	23.0	21.1
1904	27.2	22.8
1905	62.8	59.1
1906	104.4	97.6
1907	140.2	132.7
1908	129.9	124.4
1909	110.1	102.9
1910	150.8	135.5
1911	192.3	171.4
1912	226.0	186.2
1913	189.2	198.2
Total	2,524.0	2,417.0

° Years with an unfavourable balance on current account.

Sources: Hobson (1963), Table 1.4; Cairncross (1975), Table 1.8.

A synthesis of both the work of corroboration and revision made by Cairncross with respect to Hobson's reconstruction can be seen in Table 1.8.[100]

The other table, Table 1.9, reveals the considerable proximity between the estimates for the stock of foreign capital which the two authors believed to have been accumulated by British residents in the years 1870-1913 as a result of the trend in the current account of the balance of payments.

In point of fact, as far as Cairncross is concerned, it is possible to propose on his behalf an estimate of the total stock of British foreign investments for the end of 1913. In fact, he had presented an estimate of £785 million for the stock of these investments at the end of 1870 (see section 3.2), which, added to the value accumulated on current account between 1871 and 1913, leads to a stock of £3,173.9 million on the eve of the First World War.[101]

There are good reasons at a logical level why this can be considered an underestimation of the net wealth of Great Britain, even though foreign investments in the country were taken into account: for example, he did not include direct investments in the estimate of the stock in 1870 or an adequate upward revision of the other invisible items, when he was calculating the series of the balances on current account from 1870 to 1913. Nevertheless, the competence and the overall results of Cairncross's work should be given recognition.

1.5.4 Imlah's important retrospect: 1816-1913

As mentioned above, the long imperial phase of Great Britain's history until the First World War has engaged the interest of many scholars of various disciplines, including economic historians. Among these scholars Imlah inevitably holds an eminent position, especially when the focus of a book, as in this case, is directed on the evolution of British foreign investments in that period.

The main objective of Imlah's research was to provide adequate arguments to support the view he had of that phase. Even the very title of his most important work, in which he collected the results of research carried out over a number of years, intimated this view.[102] Indeed, Imlah defined that century of history as the period of the *Pax Britannica* because, in his opinion, 'Britain [...], mature in her nationalism and relatively free from constricting fears for her own security, and with parliamentary institutions, including freedom of speech and press [...], demonstrated the practical possibilities for orderly progress in organized human affairs'.[103]

Imlah's historical assessment does not concern us here,[104] but it is nevertheless appropriate to examine the extraordinary wealth of data he produced to show the 'economic elements'[105] in support of his position. At the centre of his empirical reconstruction lie Britain's foreign investments, whose trend was analysed year by year with an estimate of the country's balance on current account, since there was only a limited amount of information available (see section 1.2). The quantities which Imlah needed were obtained by patiently reconstructing all the plausible data. The result was, on the whole, the most significant contribution to our knowledge of the subject made by a scholar applying the indirect method.[106]

The balances on current account played an important part in this work and an acceptable statistical method had to be elaborated in order to project as far back in time as possible, even to 1796, for both imports and exports.[107]

For exports it was possible to refer to the series published in the official sources, which were based on the values declared by exporters. On the whole, they were considered to be reliable except for occasional errors, as these declarations might have been distorted downwards only during the Napoleonic Wars when duties *ad valorem* were imposed by the Convoy Act of 1798.[108] As a consequence only imports and re-exports needed to be estimated more homogeneously.

However, Imlah set 1816 as the starting point for the balance on current account because he believed, 'estimates of invisible income for the period of the Napoleonic Wars, and earlier, would be almost purely conjectural and subject to a wide and incalculable margin of error'.[109]

The only piece of data that violated this time limit and represented a contradiction of his previous statement was the net aggregation of the balances on current account fixed, in a purely circumstantial way, at ten million pounds and quite irrespective of every other analytical estimate of visibles and invisibles made for the preceding years. This was, in fact, the stock of capital on which the net currency inflow for 'Interest and dividends' was calculated for the year 1816, because Imlah had also put forward the hypothesis that 'all in all, the foreign capital placed in Britain may have equalled the gross amount of British investment abroad in 1815'[110] to justify the choice of such a modest value for the stock.

This starting point was certainly on very slippery terrain for Imlah. Whilst it might be acceptable initially in view of the modest sums involved, it is no longer so when computing also the capital stock of 1913, considering the effects of capitalization on these albeit small elements over a century or so.[111]

The so-called visible trade in the balance on current account estimated by Imlah is therefore the fruit of a combination of two series. The first from 1816 to 1853 resulted from the matching of the declared values for exports and those for imports and re-exports that he calculated himself, whilst the second series, from 1854 to 1913, corresponded to the values of the flows published in the *Annual Statement*.[112]

As far as the import and re-export values in the *Annual Statement* are concerned, these were brought closer to market prices in two different ways; from 1854 to 1870, these movements had been left for valuation by experts, whilst it was only from 1871 onwards that a common criterion was adopted for the declaration of merchants, in the same way as for exports.[113]

Here it is worth noting one of the many peculiarities of Imlah's reconstruction to do with the buying and selling of old and new ships. The *Annual Statement* considered the value of exports from 1899 onwards, and even then only for new ships.[114] This meant that Imlah had to include a separate item among the visible trade containing the value of ships, both old and new, sold in the years between 1855 and 1898. Whilst the purchase of new ships abroad was practically non-existent,[115] Imlah adopted various hypotheses to complete the estimate for old ships. Nevertheless, he did not attribute any value to this item before 1854 as no records on the transactions of either old or new ships were available.[116]

Some differences with respect to more recent approaches to the compilation of the balance of payments can be seen immediately in Imlah's treatment of visible trade. It should be pointed out, however, that these differences do not affect the size of the annual flow available for the purchase of financial or real assets abroad, as illustrated below.

The first problem arose with the inclusion of the movements of gold and silver among the visible items. They were considered as movements of goods, in accordance with the prevailing attitude of scholars at that time when, perhaps, the function of these metals as commodities was of greater importance than their function as money. In fact, over the years the role of silver was reassessed and the Board of Trade's point of view became more generally accepted after it reported, with reference to its own documents (see section 1.5.1), that 'during the past year it became evident that the recorded movements of gold were in large part not connected intimately with trade transactions. It appears desirable, therefore, to regard the movements of gold bullion and specie as more closely related to the movement of capital than to the movement of commodities by way of trade'.[117]

In this way the balance on current account was modified and then corrected by the balance on monetary movements corresponding to the flows of bullion, thus indicating the balance that was considered available for profitable foreign investments. The variations in the stock of bullion concerned an aggregate that was essentially under the control of the monetary authorities for the purpose of coinage and the formation of official reserves.

Equally important for determining foreign investments is the measurement on the basis of the c.i.f. criterion (cost + insurance + freight) of imports adopted by the *Annual Statement* that needed to be corrected on the side of the currency inflows with the estimate for earnings from both shipping and insurance accruing to British operators (see section 1.2). This made the quantification of shipping particularly important, even if a certain percentage of it corresponded to a transfer of funds from importers resident in Great Britain to shipping companies in the same country.[118]

The inflows connected with shipping, although determined separately, were included in a much broader item in the current account called 'Balance on business services', which in turn included other earnings called 'Profits on foreign trade and services' and 'Insurance, brokerage, commissions' respectively.

There is a certain vagueness about the content of this entry which is reflected in the complicated estimate of the values assigned to it. According to Imlah, the economic activity which 'Profits on foreign trade and services' must refer to appears to be strictly linked to the physical circulation of goods and therefore can be distinguished from the other subheading of 'Insurance, brokerage, commissions, etc.'. Imlah also believed that another correction that had to be made to the c.i.f. valuation of imports, other than the one already made through the earnings from shipping, should be entered under the subheading of 'Profits on foreign trade and services'. This broad and miscellaneous subheading also contained currency earnings from banking operations, technical and planning services abroad, British administrative services charged to the Indian government and the savings and pensions of government officials employed in the colonies and in India when they returned home to Britain.[119]

Encouraged by a similar procedure adopted by Jenks, who in turn had drawn on scholars of the time, such as Bourne, Giffen, Newmarch and Seyd (see section 1.5.2), Imlah made his estimate by applying a varying percentage on the total value of British foreign trade: 5.5 per cent for 1816-1818, five per cent for the period between 1819 and 1879, 4.5 per cent between 1880 and 1892, and four per cent from 1893 to the end of the period under consideration.[120]

This criterion, which was reasonable, but arbitrary in the extent and in the choice of the periods of application, was then extended by Imlah to the evaluation of inflows originating from 'Insurance, brokerage, commissions, etc.', once again seconded by the work of other scholars before him, such as Giffen and Jenks. The choice of the rate was made in such a way that it corresponded to half the rate adopted in the estimate of the subheading 'Profits on foreign trade and services', so that the series of currency inflows in question was composed of values that were systematically half those of the previous series.[121]

Imlah's estimate for 'Net credits from shipping' was even more laborious. We have already seen how his predecessors had made a similar effort with their estimates, but Imlah decided to introduce some new significant points in his.

1880 became the base year for the measurement of the earnings of British shipping companies so that he could make use of Giffen's admirable estimate and because it was about half way through the period under consideration. He also introduced the item 'Average earnings per net ton' for steamships and sailing ships separately where the unit of weight referred to the actual amount of goods transported, either entering or clearing, for which there was adequate documentation from as early as 1827. The indicization of the average earnings was made by using a specific price index for imports.[122]

Under the same item of shipping, Imlah tried to reach a plausible estimate for various expenses borne by foreign ships in British ports. He meant to take account of the variation in the proportion of the amount of goods both entering and leaving on foreign ships as compared to the total amount of goods circulating in British ports. This was done in order to determine the amounts to be multiplied by the average earnings, which also differed for sailing ships and steamships, with reference to the base year, that is 1880. These average earnings remained proportionately the same throughout the period for both sailing ships and steamships, though they varied in relation to the dynamics of the import price index mentioned above.[123]

Imlah's empirical analysis later introduced another invisible item that was created for the sake of thoroughness, because its values, all negative for the balance on current account, were the result of estimates which were often highly discretional, although not worryingly so for the simple fact that they had low values. Under the miscellaneous heading 'Balance on other current items', Imlah concentrated on two subheadings 'Emigrant funds', which he estimated to be negative for Great Britain in spite of the strong emigration from the country,[124] and 'Tourists, smuggling and unrecorded imports', which was also negative for the whole period and under which he included other phenomena that affected the currency flows.[125]

Imlah talked in terms of a balance for this item too and therefore did not intend to exclude *a priori* the possibility of positive movements for Great Britain, as for example, in tourism and smuggling. Nevertheless he still believed this balance to be negative on the whole, especially in the last decades of the period when diamonds figured with quite a substantial value amongst the unrecorded imports.[126]

The last item on the current account was the 'Balance on interest and dividends'; it was the last on the list, but it certainly was not the least important at a quantitative level because, as Imlah hinted, this entry 'evergrowing, [...] became, by the mid-seventies, the largest annual net credit item on this balance sheet, and it can be regarded thereafter as the major source of the phenomenally large amounts of capital which Britain continued to place abroad. British foreign investments, then, were a little like a revolving fund'.[127]

Although this last statement by Imlah is debatable because it seems an oversimplification of the mechanisms through which currency movements arising from any operation were redistributed among the various agents before becoming an investment abroad, there can be no doubt about the reference to the quantity of net inflows earned from foreign capital accumulated by British citizens. The use of the term 'net inflows' is not accidental because one piece of empirical evidence, which Imlah himself draws upon, showed currency outflows connected with the payment of the return on foreign capital invested in Great Britain.[128]

Once again, even for such a crucial item as this, scholars like Imlah were able to use and rely on the limited series provided by the *Report of the Commissioners* which provided information only on the so-called identified income[129] from the financial year 1877-1878 onwards.[130] There were even greater difficulties ahead for Imlah who intended to measure the stock of capital invested abroad as well as determine the balance on current account. It was necessary, therefore, to assume an initial stock and an annual rate of return in order to calculate the item 'Balance on interest and dividends' year by year until an estimate could be based on a different criterion. Just as Hobson and Cairncross had done (see sections 1.3 and 1.5.3), Imlah moved forwards but also backwards in time to build his series by using the comparison between identified income and unidentified income in 1907 estimated by Paish.

In his calculations Imlah moved from the bottom to the top and vice versa, so to speak. The first route started from a stock of ten million pounds, which was assumed to exist at the end of 1815, with a rate of return of six per cent that enabled him to measure the 'Balance on interest and dividends' for 1816. For the following years the stock was enriched by the balance on current account and a rate of return was applied that varied over the whole period.

The second route worked around Paish's estimate for 1907, with two adjustments made by Imlah. Firstly, the figures from the *Report of the Commissioners* used in part by Paish (see sections 1.3 and 2.3) referred to the financial year, so Imlah adapted them to the solar year. And secondly, he took into account the increase in income earned by British private investments overseas and the fall in the income paid out to foreign investors in Great Britain.[131]

Table 1.10 Great Britain's balance of payments and export of capital, 1816-1913 (annual values and quinquennial averages, millions of pounds)

	Balance on visible trade			Balance on business services			Balance on other current items					
	A	B	C	D	E	F	G	H	A-H	I	J	K
Year	Merchandise	Gold and silver bullion and specie	Ship sales	Profits on foreign trade and services	Insurance, brokerage, commissions, etc.	Net credits from shipping	Emigrant funds	Tourists, smuggling and unrecorded imports	Net balance on trade and services	Balance on interest and dividends	Balance on current account	Accumulating balance of credit abroad
1815	-	-	-	-	-	-	-	-	-	-	-	circa 10
1816	4.10	-5.00	-	5.70	2.90	9.00	-0.20	-2.50	14.00	0.60	14.60	24.60
1817	-9.10	-2.90	-	6.20	3.10	10.30	-0.30	-2.50	4.80	1.50	6.30	30.90
1818	-21.90	3.90	-	7.70	3.80	12.50	-0.40	-2.80	2.80	1.90	4.70	35.60
1819	-10.60	1.40	-	5.10	2.50	9.40	-0.50	-2.10	5.20	2.10	7.30	42.90
1820	-7.40	-5.40	-	5.10	2.50	8.40	-0.40	-2.20	0.60	2.60	3.20	46.10
Average	-8.98	-1.60	-	5.96	2.96	9.92	-0.36	-2.42	5.48	1.74	7.22	-
1821	0.60	-2.20	-	4.60	2.30	8.20	-0.30	-2.20	11.00	2.80	13.80	59.90
1822	0.20	-2.80	-	4.50	2.20	8.10	-0.30	-2.20	9.70	3.60	13.30	73.20
1823	-9.40	-2.50	-	4.70	2.40	8.60	-0.20	-2.10	1.50	4.40	5.90	79.10
1824	-5.30	3.50	-	4.90	2.40	8.60	-0.20	-2.30	11.60	4.70	16.30	95.40
1825	-26.50	5.40	-	6.00	3.00	11.30	-0.20	-2.30	-3.30	5.70	2.40	97.80
Average	-8.08	0.28	-	4.94	2.46	8.96	-0.24	-2.22	6.10	4.24	10.34	-
1826	-11.60	-4.00	-	4.50	2.20	8.10	-0.30	-1.90	-3.00	5.40	2.40	100.20
1827	-14.80	-3.60	-	5.10	2.60	8.30	-0.40	-2.20	-5.00	5.00	-	100.20

Table 1.10 (continued)

1828	-14.00	0.30	-	5.00	2.50	8.10	-0.40	-2.20	-0.70	4.50	3.80	104.00
1829	-11.70	1.10	-	4.80	2.40	7.90	-0.50	-2.10	1.90	4.20	6.10	110.10
1830	-12.00	-3.50	-	5.00	2.50	7.90	-0.90	-2.30	-3.30	3.90	0.60	110.70
Average	-12.82	-1.94	-	4.88	2.44	8.06	-0.50	-2.14	-2.02	4.60	2.58	-
1831	-18.10	3.50	-	5.30	2.60	8.60	-1.20	-2.20	-1.50	3.90	2.40	113.10
1832	-8.70	-1.20	-	4.80	2.40	8.20	-1.50	-2.20	1.80	4.30	6.10	119.20
1833	-12.30	-2.40	-	5.30	2.60	8.90	-0.90	-2.40	-1.20	4.80	3.60	122.80
1834	-15.10	2.30	-	5.70	2.90	8.80	-1.10	-2.50	1.00	6.10	7.10	129.90
1835	-11.40	0.80	-	6.20	3.10	9.70	-0.70	-2.80	4.90	7.80	12.70	142.60
Average	-13.12	0.60	-	5.46	2.72	8.84	-1.08	-2.42	1.00	5.38	6.38	-
1836	-21.80	1.50	-	7.40	3.70	10.40	-1.10	-3.20	-3.10	8.60	5.50	148.10
1837	-19.00	-2.00	-	6.10	3.00	9.40	-1.10	-2.50	-6.10	8.40	2.30	150.40
1838	-20.80	-	-	7.00	3.50	10.20	-0.50	-3.00	-3.60	8.10	4.50	154.90
1839	-28.40	4.40	-	7.70	3.80	11.90	-0.90	-3.10	-4.60	7.70	3.10	158.00
1840	-29.80	0.90	-	7.60	3.80	12.60	-1.40	-3.10	-9.40	7.10	-2.30	155.70
Average	-23.96	0.96	-	7.16	3.56	10.90	-1.00	-2.98	-5.36	7.98	2.62	-
1841	-22.40	-1.00	-	7.30	3.60	12.30	-1.80	-3.10	-5.10	6.20	1.10	156.80
1842	-20.60	-2.90	-	6.60	3.30	11.40	-1.90	-2.80	-6.90	6.30	-0.60	156.20
1843	-10.90	-3.60	-	6.60	3.30	10.90	-0.90	-3.10	2.30	7.00	9.30	165.50
1844	-12.30	-3.00	-	7.30	3.60	11.10	-1.10	-3.50	2.10	8.30	10.40	175.90
1845	-19.00	-1.00	-	7.90	3.90	12.80	-1.40	-3.60	-0.40	9.70	9.30	185.20
Average	-17.04	-2.30	-	7.14	3.54	11.70	-1.42	-3.22	-1.60	7.50	5.90	-
1846	-20.30	-1.40	-	7.70	3.90	13.30	-1.90	-3.50	-2.20	10.20	8.00	193.20
1847	-41.60	5.30	-	9.10	4.60	16.90	-3.10	-2.90	-11.70	10.60	-1.10	192.10
1848	-26.90	1.00	-	7.50	3.70	13.40	-3.00	-2.60	-6.90	9.00	2.10	194.20
1849	-25.70	1.00	-	8.90	4.40	13.90	-3.60	-3.20	-4.30	8.20	3.90	198.10
1850	-19.60	-1.00	-	9.30	4.70	14.20	-2.80	-3.60	1.20	9.40	10.60	208.70
Average	-26.82	0.98	-	8.50	4.26	14.34	-2.88	-3.16	-4.78	9.48	4.70	-

Table 1.10 (continued)

1851	-22.60	-1.20	-	9.80	4.90	15.00	-3.40	-3.70	-1.20	10.40	9.20	217.90
1852	-18.90	-7.80	-	10.10	5.00	16.00	-3.70	-3.90	-3.20	10.90	7.70	225.60
1853	-32.80	-6.50	-	13.20	6.60	19.20	-3.30	-4.90	-8.50	11.80	3.30	228.90
1854	-36.60	-3.60	-	13.40	6.70	21.40	-3.20	-4.90	-6.80	12.60	5.80	234.70
1855	-26.80	-7.80	0.90	13.00	6.50	21.80	-1.80	-4.80	1.00	12.90	13.90	248.60
Average	-27.54	-5.38	0.18	11.90	5.94	18.68	-3.08	-4.44	-3.74	11.72	7.98	-
1856	-33.00	-1.90	1.20	15.60	7.80	25.10	-1.80	-5.80	6.90	14.90	21.80	270.40
1857	-41.60	6.50	1.20	16.70	8.40	27.70	-1.90	-6.10	10.90	16.20	27.10	297.50
1858	-24.80	-9.90	1.00	15.20	7.60	24.20	-1.00	-5.80	6.50	15.90	22.40	319.90
1859	-23.50	-1.40	0.90	16.70	8.40	25.60	-1.00	-6.50	19.20	16.90	36.10	356.00
1860	-46.00	2.50	0.50	18.80	9.40	27.70	-1.00	-6.90	5.00	18.70	23.70	379.70
Average	-33.84	-0.84	0.96	16.60	8.32	26.06	-1.34	-6.22	9.70	16.52	26.22	-
1861	-57.90	2.10	0.30	18.90	9.40	28.70	-0.70	-6.30	-5.50	19.90	14.40	394.10
1862	-59.50	-2.30	0.70	19.60	9.80	29.70	-1.00	-6.20	-9.20	20.70	11.50	405.60
1863	-52.00	-3.50	0.60	22.30	11.10	34.50	-1.90	-5.90	5.20	21.30	26.50	432.10
1864	-62.40	-4.60	0,90	24.40	12.20	37.70	-1.90	-6.40	-0.10	22.90	22.80	454.90
1865	-52.30	-6.40	1.10	24.50	12.20	40.00	-1.70	-6.60	10.80	24.10	34.90	489.80
Average	-56.82	-2.94	0.72	21.94	10.94	34.12	-1.44	-6.28	0.24	21.78	22.02	-
1866	-56.40	-12.70	1.20	26.70	13.40	43.70	-1.70	-7.60	6.60	26.40	33.00	522.80
1867	-49.70	-9.50	1.10	25.00	12.50	43.40	-1.60	-7.20	14.00	28.20	42.20	565.00
1868	-66.90	-4.60	1.40	26.10	13.10	44.90	-1.40	-7.20	5.40	31.10	36.50	601.50
1869	-58.40	-4.10	0.90	26.60	13.30	44.80	-1.90	-7.60	13.60	33.10	46.70	648.20
1870	-59.20	-10.50	1.70	27.40	13.70	45.70	-2.00	-8.00	8.80	35.30	44.10	692.30
Average	-58.12	-8.28	1.26	26.36	13.20	44.50	-1.72	-7.52	9.68	30.82	40.50	-
1871	-47.40	-4.40	1.40	30.70	15.40	47.10	-1.90	-8.90	32.00	39.50	71.50	763.80
1872	-40.10	0.70	3.30	33.50	16.70	52.00	-2.10	-10.30	53.70	44.30	98.00	861.80
1873	-60.30	-4.70	4.00	34.10	17.00	52.00	-2.30	-10.20	29.60	51.70	81.30	943.10

Table 1.10 (continued)

1874	-72.40	-7.50	3.30	33.40	16.70	52.40	-2.00	-9.60	14.30	56.60	70.90	1,014.00
1875	-92.30	-5.60	1.80	32.80	16.40	50.70	-1.40	-8.90	-6.50	57.80	51.30	1,065.30
Average	-62.50	-4.30	2.76	32.90	16.44	50.84	-1.94	-9.58	24.62	49.98	74.60	-
1876	-118.40	-7.60	0.60	31.60	15.80	52.10	-0.40	-8.00	-34.30	57.50	23.20	1,088.50
1877	-142.10	2.60	0.60	32.30	16.20	56.30	-0.30	-8.00	-42.40	55.50	13.10	1,101.60
1878	-123.30	-5.70	1.50	30.70	15.40	51.30	-0.60	-7.70	-38.40	55.10	16.70	1,118.30
1879	-114.20	4.40	2.40	30.60	15.30	51.10	-1.30	-7.70	-19.40	55.90	36.50	1,154.80
1880	-124.80	2.60	3.70	31.40	15.70	60.00	-1.80	-8.90	-22.10	57.70	35.60	1,190.40
Average	-124.56	-0.74	1.76	31.32	15.68	54.16	-0.88	-8.06	-31.32	56.34	25.02	-
1881	-99.90	5.60	5.40	31.20	15.60	59.60	-1.90	-9.40	6.20	59.50	65.70	1,256.10
1882	-106.40	-2.60	6.40	32.40	16.20	60.80	-2.20	-9.70	-5.10	62.80	57.70	1,313.80
1883	-121.50	-0.80	4.60	33.00	16.50	64.70	-2.50	-9.60	-15.60	64.40	48.80	1,362.60
1884	-94.10	1.60	3.00	30.90	15.40	59.50	-1.50	-9.30	5.50	66.80	72.30	1,434.90
1885	-99.50	-0.20	1.00	28.90	14.50	57.00	-1.20	-8.50	-8.00	70.30	62.30	1,497.20
Average	-104.28	0.72	4.08	31.28	15.64	60.32	-1.86	-9.30	-3.40	64.76	61.36	-
1886	-80.90	0.60	1.40	27.80	13.90	52.10	-1.50	-8.50	4.90	74.00	78.90	1,576.10
1887	-81.00	-0.60	2.50	29.00	14.50	54.70	-2.00	-8.90	8.20	79.50	87.70	1,663.80
1888	-89.10	0.60	3.20	30.90	15.40	57.70	-1.90	-9.40	7.40	84.50	91.90	1,755.70
1889	-112.10	-2.00	7.10	33.40	16.70	60.50	-1.50	-10.00	-7.90	88.80	80.90	1,836.60
1890	-92.40	-8.80	6.10	33.70	16.90	60.60	-1.10	-10.50	4.50	94.00	98.50	1,935.10
Average	-91.10	-2.04	4.06	30.96	15.48	57.12	-1.60	-9.46	3.42	84.16	87.58	-
1891	-126.30	-2.40	4.20	33.50	16.80	60.40	-1.20	-9.90	-24.90	94.30	69.40	2,004.50
1892	-132.20	-3.40	3.30	32.20	16.10	58.60	-1.10	-9.10	-35.60	94.70	59.10	2,063.60
1893	-127.50	-3.70	2.90	27.30	13.60	55.50	-1.10	-8.70	-41.70	94.70	53.00	2,116.60
1894	-134.60	-10.80	3.10	27.30	13.60	56.50	-0.40	-8.60	-53.90	92.60	38.70	2,155.30
1895	-130.90	-14.90	4.40	28.10	14.10	55.40	-0.80	-9.00	-53.60	93.60	40.00	2,195.30
Average	-130.30	-7.04	3.58	29.68	14.84	57.28	-0.92	-9.06	-41.94	93.98	52.04	-
1896	-145.40	6.40	7.50	29.50	14.80	58.20	-0.60	-9.60	-39.20	96.00	56.80	2,252.10

Table 1.10 (continued)

1897	-156.90	0.80	6.00	29.80	14.90	59.90	-0.50	-9.40	-55.40	97.00	41.60	2,293.70
1898	-176.50	-6.20	7.60	30.60	15.30	60.70	-0.50	-9.30	-78.30	101.20	22.90	2,316.60
1899	-155.50	-9.80	1.80	32.60	16.30	64.90	-0.50	-10.60	-60.80	103.20	42.40	2,359.00
1900	-168.70	-7.50	1.70	35.10	17.50	68.50	-0.70	-11.60	-65.70	103.60	37.90	2,396.90
Average	-160.60	-3.26	4.92	31.52	15.76	62.44	-0.56	-10.10	-59.88	100.20	40.32	-
1901	-174.10	-6.20	1.00	34.80	17.40	66.40	-0.70	-11.20	-72.60	106.50	33.90	2,430.80
1902	-179.20	-5.30	0.80	35.10	17.60	67.50	-1.00	-11.30	-75.80	109.10	33.30	2,464.10
1903	-182.20	0.30	0.90	36.10	18.10	72.50	-1.50	-11.60	-67.40	112.20	44.80	2,508.90
1904	-180.00	0.70	0.90	36.90	18.40	73.50	-1.30	-12.00	-62.90	113.40	50.50	2,559.40
1905	-157.40	-6.20	1.50	38.90	19.50	76.30	-1.40	-13.20	-42.00	123.50	81.50	2,640.90
Average	-174.58	-3.34	1.02	36.36	18.20	71.24	-1.18	-11.86	-64.14	112.94	48.80	-
1906	-147.20	-1.80	1.20	42.70	21.40	83.90	-2.00	-15.00	-16.80	134.30	117.50	2,758.40
1907	-127.80	-5.30	1.00	46.60	23.30	91.90	-2.40	-17.00	10.30	143.80	154.10	2,912.50
1908	-136.20	6.80	0.60	42.00	21.00	85.50	-0.90	-15.10	3.70	151.00	154.70	3,067.20
1909	-155.20	-6.50	1.00	43.80	21.90	89.10	-1.40	-15.10	-22.40	158.00	135.60	3,202.80
1910	-144.10	-6.70	1.40	48.50	24.20	93.50	-2.30	-17.20	-2.70	170.00	167.30	3,370.10
Average	-142.10	-2.70	1.04	44.72	22.36	88.78	-1.80	-15.88	-5.58	151.42	145.84	-
1911	-123.30	-6.00	2.10	49.50	24.70	93.40	-2.60	-18.20	19.60	177.30	196.90	3,567.00
1912	-145.70	-4.60	1.90	53.70	26.90	100.20	-2.70	-19.50	10.20	186.90	197.10	3,764.10
1913	-133.90	-11.90	2.30	56.10	28.10	107.40	-2.40	-21.00	24.70	199.60	224.30	3,988.40
Average	-134.30	-7.50	2.10	53.10	26.57	100.33	-2.70	-19.57	18.17	187.93	206.10	-

Source: Imlah (1958), Table 1.4.

Once the new proportion between identified income and unidentified income had been calculated on the basis of these adjustments, it was then applied to the years 1886-1913 with the help of the information on identified income in the annual *Report of the Commissioners*.

At this point, Imlah had all the elements necessary for the presentation of his series of the balance on current account of the balance of payments, that is the yearly flow of new capital accumulated abroad. The total of this flow gives the size of the stock of capital at the end of each year,[132] with some further assumptions.[133]

1.5.5 Feinstein's revision of Imlah's retrospect: 1870-1913

The results obtained by Imlah represented a great improvement in our knowledge of the economic facts of the period leading up to the First World War, especially of Britain's international relations and its citizens' investments abroad. As we have seen, Imlah's research was carried out using the indirect or residual method, which had already been adopted previously by other scholars, but the length of the period under consideration and the quantity of information he provided mean that this research material is absolutely essential for anyone wanting to deal with the subject. Moreover, Imlah's empirical results were given even greater authority by the numerous comparisons made with other authors' estimates[134] which had often been obtained with different methods. It comes as no surprise, therefore, that since its publication the data in Imlah's book has frequently been quoted in the literature and often had quite strong criticisms levelled against it.

There is one scholar in particular who stands out among those who expressed their appreciation for Imlah's work, not just with a quotation or reference, but with a direct testing of his figures. In fact, Feinstein, mainly known as an economist with a particular liking for empirical research, measured himself against Imlah whilst drafting a similar historical work, although it was carried out with rather different scientific objectives.[135]

Feinstein limited his analysis to the period 1870-1913, but he still decided to closely retrace Imlah's complex calculation and came to corroborate the series.

However, a significant difference between the two authors consists in the presentation of their data, which in Feinstein[136] was made by following more closely the procedures that had gradually become well established in international accounting, namely the f.o.b. valuation of imports and exports, complete flows and not only the favourable and unfavourable balances on homogeneous items, a more compact subdivision of invisibles and the placing of gold and silver movements among monetary movements.

On the other hand, with regard to Imlah's work, Feinstein introduced 'some minor adjustments [...] to his estimates for 1900-1913 where it was clearly possible to improve the reliability of the estimates'.[137]

This happened occasionally for the years before 1900 too. For example, diamonds were once again placed amongst the movement of goods, whilst travelling expenses recorded by Prest and Adams for the years 1900-1913 were included among the items both on the credit and the debit side. Furthermore, military expenditure incurred during the Boer War between 1899-1902 was calculated as an outflow under service items, while unilateral transfers and

Table 1.11 Great Britain's balance of payments, 1870-1913 (millions of pounds)

	Credits						Debits						Current balance
Year	Exports and re-exports of goods	Exports of services	Property income from abroad	Exports and property income from abroad	Current transfers: government and personal	Total	Imports of goods	Imports of services	Property income paid abroad	Imports and property income paid abroad	Current transfers: government and personal	Total	Net investment abroad
	1	2	3	4=1+2+3	5	6=4+5	7	8	9	10=7+8+9	11	12=10+11	13
1870	246	80	37	363	1	364	279	25	2	306	3	309	55
1871	285	85	42	412	1	413	304	27	3	334	3	337	76
1872	318	93	47	459	1	459	326	30	3	359	3	362	97
1873	315	93	56	464	1	465	342	30	4	376	3	379	86
1874	301	92	61	454	1	455	341	29	4	374	3	377	78
1875	283	89	62	434	1	435	344	28	4	376	2	378	57
1876	257	89	61	407	1	408	345	27	4	376	1	377	31
1877	253	94	59	406	1	407	363	29	4	396	1	397	10
1878	247	88	59	394	1	395	339	27	4	370	2	372	23
1879	251	86	60	397	1	398	334	27	4	365	2	367	31
1880	290	96	62	448	2	450	378	31	4	413	4	417	33
1881	303	96	63	462	2	464	365	31	4	400	4	404	60
1882	313	99	68	480	2	482	380	32	5	417	4	421	61
1883	310	104	69	483	2	485	393	33	5	431	5	436	49
1884	299	96	72	467	2	469	359	31	5	395	4	399	70
1885	272	91	75	438	2	440	341	29	5	375	3	378	62
1886	270	85	80	435	2	437	322	28	6	356	3	359	78

Table 1.11 (continued)

1887	283	90	85	458	2	460	333	29	6	368	4	372	88
1888	302	94	90	486	2	488	357	30	6	393	4	397	91
1889	323	99	96	518	2	520	393	33	7	433	4	437	83
1890	334	100	101	535	2	537	387	33	7	427	3	430	107
1891	313	98	101	512	2	514	400	32	7	439	3	442	72
1892	295	95	102	492	2	494	390	31	7	428	3	431	63
1893	280	85	102	467	1	468	372	30	7	409	2	411	57
1894	277	86	100	463	1	464	376	30	7	413	1	414	50
1895	290	85	101	476	1	477	383	30	7	420	2	422	55
1896	304	90	103	497	1	498	407	32	7	446	2	448	50
1897	300	92	105	497	1	498	415	32	8	455	2	457	41
1898	302	93	109	504	1	505	433	33	8	474	2	476	29
1899	331	100	111	542	1	543	446	40	8	494	2	496	47
1900	356	111	112	579	1	580	485	50	8	543	3	546	34
1901	349	109	115	573	1	574	485	55	9	549	6	555	19
1902	350	110	119	579	1	580	491	46	10	547	9	556	24
1903	361	118	122	601	1	602	505	38	10	553	6	559	43
1904	372	120	124	616	1	617	512	39	11	562	3	565	52
1905	409	126	135	670	1	671	527	40	12	579	4	583	88
1906	462	139	148	749	2	751	568	43	14	625	5	630	121
1907	519	152	160	831	2	833	603	46	16	665	6	671	162
1908	457	140	168	765	1	766	550	46	17	613	3	616	150
1909	470	145	175	790	1	791	581	47	17	645	4	649	142
1910	536	155	189	880	2	882	632	51	19	702	6	708	174
1911	559	156	197	912	3	915	634	51	20	705	6	711	204
1912	600	168	209	977	3	980	694	54	22	770	7	777	203
1913	637	179	224	1,040	2	1,042	719	58	24	801	6	807	235

Source: Feinstein (1972), Table 5.

additional information about government donations and currency flows connected with migratory movements were taken into account to improve data on both the credit and debit sides.[138]

The final results of this work are given in Table 1.11, which indicates the series of investments overseas which correspond to the annual balances on current account, as required by the method. This series differs from Imlah's, not only for the slight adjustments made to some items, but above all for the way the two scholars treated the movements of bullion.[139]

For Imlah the assimilation of the movements of bullion to the movements of goods, and therefore their inclusion among the items of the current account, led to the calculation of the balance of these items, which immediately indicated the amount available for holding assets abroad. More specifically, as the balances were favourable throughout the period, this amount led to the accumulation of new wealth overseas, in the various forms chosen by its owners and by the monetary authorities in compliance with their institutional duties.

In contrast, Feinstein placed bullion among the items on capital account, thus altering the balances on current account considerably; these balances, therefore, represented a sum of currency resources that could have changed the composition of foreign assets, possibly even with their transformation into bullion.

In the period in question these flows generally occurred in the importation rather than in the exportation of bullion. Therefore the annual values identified by Feinstein as 'Net investment abroad', including this net acquisition of bullion, were on the whole higher than Imlah's, which were called 'Balance on current account' (see Table 1.10).[140]

Feinstein's position, which viewed the reserves of bullion (gold and silver) as a component of foreign assets, 'on the grounds that they represent a potential claim on foreign goods or assets',[141] appears to be rather solitary among the scholars of this subject. Generally they have preferred to concentrate their attention on international wealth as a direct source of income and, consequently, their estimates of the flows and stocks of foreign investments have not taken bullion into account.

Feinstein later gave confirmation of his preference for this approach in another work (see note 141). In his first book, he adjusted the estimate of the stock calculated by Imlah for the end of 1913 and also added the relative value of gold, with the only other specification that he had referred to its 'face value'[142] and thus reached the figure of £4,180 million. Feinstein also proposed a further upward adjustment to £4,300 million to take account of the conclusions reached by Morgan on the balance of short-term assets and liabilities.[143]

In his second work, however, the criterion of incorporating bullion among foreign assets was applied to indicate the growth of British foreign assets by drawing up the two series of values side by side, as can be seen in Table 1.12.[144] The first series resulted from a retrospective extension of Imlah's method and the second referred specifically to bullion, which was of decreasing relevance to the total. Naturally the time frame is the same, going back as far as 1760, so that silver as well as gold had to be taken into consideration since it was widely used over this long period. It is important to note that the measurement concerned not only the reserves of the Central Bank, but also 'the recent estimates [....] of total coin in circulation outside the Bank of England'.[145]

As can be noted, apart from the stock of gold and silver, there was yet another upward adjustment made to Imlah's estimate: £4,165 million for Feinstein as opposed to Imlah's £3,988.4 million (see Table 1.10). This adjustment was brought about by what Morgan had indicated (see note 143) and by other marginal adjustments made by Feinstein when moving between his own personal work and the one in collaboration with Pollard (see bibliography).

Moreover, Feinstein's estimate of £13 million for British foreign assets (excluding bullion) in 1800 also deserves attention. It included the ten million pounds that he had calculated for the same year in another of his studies,[146] but with an appreciable increase of 30 per cent.

Table 1.12   Great Britain's accumulated net holdings of overseas assets, gold and silver, 1760-1913 (millions of pounds)

Year	Accumulated balance on current account (net)	Gold and silver	Total overseas assets (net)
1760	-18	18	0
1800	13	38	51
1830	100	64	164
1850	177	67	244
1860	371	93	464
1870	680	110	790
1880	1,126	115	1,241
1890	1,819	110	1,929
1900	2,400	149	2,549
1910	3,355	167	3,522
1913	4,165	203	4,368

Source: Feinstein (1988), Table 18.3.

With these figures for the first years of the century, Feinstein was moving within a quantitative framework that tended to accept the estimate of ten million pounds for the stock of British foreign investments at the end of 1815, from which Imlah started his reconstruction of the country's current account.

It was within this context that Brezis proposed a laborious construction with the explicit statement that she wanted to adopt Imlah's method in order to measure Britain's balance of payments in the 18th century.[147] She drew on Imlah for more than just the method because, as she herself wrote, 'these estimates are very tentative, but they are derived in a way consistent with that of Imlah, and are also supported by historical evidence'.[148]

Brezis provided a series of data which pointed to a deficit in the British current account that was backed by documentation on Britain's substantial debt towards other countries, especially Holland. In this way she was able to suggest that the industrial revolution had been strongly financed by foreign capital.[149] She believes, however, that the turn of the 18th century marks a crucial phase in British economic events, because 'between 1790 and 1815 the UK passed from being a debtor to being a creditor nation'.[150]

It is exactly this period, which is of great interest to us, that appears to be the least clear in Brezis's construction. She was, in fact, well aware of this, so much so that she suggested an alternative scenario to the one emerging from her main analysis of the international accounts of Great Britain during the 18th century.

The alternative is particularly significant, in so far as it presents a picture of Great Britain as a creditor towards foreign countries even at the end of the century. Brezis considers this to be a consequence of the big differences between the possible estimates for unilateral transfers, an important item in the current account which includes emigrant funds, together with other private and public transfers, that is a series of flows that are particularly difficult to reconstruct.[151] At the same time, however, she maintains it had a potential that could strongly influence the conclusions reached for the foreign financing of Britain's industrial revolution. Consequently, she proposed a very wide range of values that also included a positive stock of credit (£17.54 million) together with a substantial figure for the country's foreign debt at the beginning of the 19th century (£167.5 million).[152]

Also Brezis's work leaves, therefore, sufficient room to allow for the possibility that Great Britain was a creditor towards foreign countries for a sum that was greater than the ten million pounds hypothesized by Imlah for the end of 1815. From this point of view, it is slightly disconcerting that Brezis did not take into consideration the information, admittedly fragmentary, that was offered by the scholars of the time, to which we will return later (see sections 2.2 and 4.2).[153]

Even Imlah had tried to account for his choice on this matter, but, in spite of Feinstein's opinion that it was a 'carefully constructed series',[154] Imlah noted that 'the total value of British holdings abroad in 1815 is quite uncertain'.[155]

In point of fact, doubts are cast on Imlah's evaluation because he failed to give due consideration to those estimates in his main bibliographical references, from Beeke onwards, that supported the view that the stock of British foreign investments in the first decades of the 19th century was in fact more substantial than he himself had actually proposed (see sections 2.2 and 4.2).[156]

1.6 Conclusions

This first chapter has dealt, above all, with the problem of the availability of data required to obtain estimates of the phenomenon being studied that are as accurate as possible. Naturally the need for data depends essentially on the objectives of the research. In our case, the aim was to give, on the basis of the works written on this topic, a reliable quantification of the evolution of Great Britain's foreign investments for more than a century before the First World War. It has been shown that three main methods have been adopted by scholars to estimate this evolution and each one of them requires a large amount of empirical data.

The first method, called the indirect or residual, is based on the measurement of the balance on current account of the balance of payments, which is then accumulated, usually year by year, to reach an estimate of the stock of capital invested abroad.

The second method starts from the identification of the flows of various types of income (profits, dividends, interest and rent) that can accrue from capital invested overseas. The choice of a years' purchase for the components of this wealth, which are considered to be homogeneous, means that the flows of income can be transformed into stock and the aggregation corresponds to an estimate of the total value of the capital invested abroad at a certain date.

The third method, called the direct method, rests on the collection of information on all foreign assets, both financial and real, owned by residents in a country.

This chapter has focussed on a review of the literature that has chosen the first method, though quite a few authors have often adopted more than one method in their works. Firstly, it has to be said that the main objective of this kind of research has, at times, been the compilation of the balance on current account through estimates made in the absence of official data for some items. In fact, estimates of the trend of the current account of Great Britain were, in themselves, an important source of knowledge about the economic affairs of a country that had managed to penetrate the world market not only very early on and also very successfully, as the data on both visible and invisible items clearly shows.

The estimates on the evolution of Britain's foreign investments calculated with the aggregation of the annual balances of these items also involved a crucial choice. The problem was how to project the reconstruction of the balance on current account back as far as the beginning of transactions with other countries producing currency inflows and outflows. This meant hypothesizing a net stock of capital, either in surplus or in deficit, at a certain date, on which the income could be calculated and included as either a credit or debit item in the current account of the country in the following year.

In fact, those applying this method, both scholars who were contemporaries of the period under consideration and scholars working on a historical reconstruction, have at times avoided this problem and concentrated on the measurement of Britain's balance on current account. This is what Shaw-Lefevre (Table 1.2) and the Board of Trade (Table 1.6) did when they worked on estimates covering short periods of time, and also Schooling who made a rather singular estimate of the balance for only thirty of the years leading up to the First World War (Table 1.5).

Other scholars discussed in the course of the chapter have been more interested in the evolution of the flows and stocks. We have considered, in chronological order, Seyd, who perhaps provided the first information on the size of British foreign wealth in the second half of the 19th century and an estimate of a noteworthy series of the country's balances on current account. This estimate has also been compared with the one Shaw-Lefevre proposed in the same period (Table 1.3).

We then considered Hobson's research, which obtained results that were all the more significant in view of the length of the period he examined that went up to the eve of the First World War and the items he included in the balance on current account (Table 1.4). He should also be remembered for having tried to compare his estimates of the annual flows of British foreign investments obtained by the indirect method with those obtained by the direct method, which will be discussed later (Table 2.11). It is a pity that he did not consolidate his results by proposing an explicit estimate of the stock of British foreign investments at the various points in time marked out in his empirical analysis. This is, in fact, what Cairncross was to do later. At the same time he estimated the stock of foreign investments by making a number of revisions to the two biggest credit items in the current account estimated by Hobson, namely 'Shipping earnings' and 'Interest on foreign investments' (Table 1.8 and 1.9).

Jenks also adopted both the direct (Table 1.7) and the indirect method (Table 2.12) and added important elements to our knowledge of the evolution of Britain's foreign accounts, as well as making useful suggestions about how to approach this phenomenon. Unfortunately, the time limits he set to his research make the results obtained inadequate for the purposes of the present book which has a much broader perspective.

However, the most significant contribution of a scholar applying the indirect method came from Imlah, who prepared a series of the flows and stocks of Britain's foreign investments for the whole century before the First World War (Table 1.10). It has been seen how he tackled the extraordinary difficulties caused by the lack of both official and unofficial data for quite a significant part of the period under consideration, but also how the solutions he adopted have often been met with some misgiving. Particular attention has been given (and again in section 3.3) to the question of the value of the initial stock of net capital invested abroad by British residents at a set date which was to be used to calculate the items in the country's balance on current account, including the flows produced by this capital. In the case of Imlah this date was the end of 1815 and from then onwards the flows were always positive. Obviously, given the length of his series, the measurement of the initial size of the stock of foreign investments was to have an appreciable influence on the total stock reached at the end of the period of his research, that is on the eve of the First World War.

At the same time, Imlah's observations suggested two crucial hypotheses on which the indirect method rests: the neutral effects of the gains and losses on capital account for the various components of the stock of foreign investments, as well as the empirical irrelevance of the repayments of wealth owned abroad by British residents during the long historical series. Whilst Imlah's pertinent observations are appropriate for Great Britain, they cannot necessarily be extended to all cases in which the indirect method is applied.

Imlah also provided valuable information about Great Britain's balance on current account in the 19th century which pointed out, on the one hand, the structural nature of the unfavourable visible trade and, on the other, how it was more than balanced out by the invisible items, thus enabling the country to accumulate assets towards the rest of the world. As for the size of the stock of this wealth, we will just note that the estimate for 1913, the last year in Imlah's series, stood at £3,989.6 million; in fact, it is the value of this stock, as we will see in the following chapters, that stimulated a heated debate among scholars.

At the end of the chapter the discussion of Feinstein's work has helped to introduce both an authoritative confirmation of the basic value of Imlah's series and also some marginal, but valuable revisions to the series. These revisions often concerned the presentation of the data, which is more in line with the accounting methods used nowadays in the preparation of the foreign accounts of various countries, especially for gold and silver movements, whereas the revision of the data centred on the flows for diamonds, military expenditure and unilateral transfers (Tables 1.11 and 1.12).

The next chapter will assess the results obtained by scholars using the other two methods already mentioned here, or a mix of them, in order to determine Great Britain's foreign investments. At times, these scholars, as in the case of Hobson (see section 1.3), have also used the estimates obtained with the indirect or residual methods dealt with in this chapter.

Notes

[1] See Hobson (1963), p. x.

[2] It should be noted that the methods of estimate for the various items are not completely independent. For example, the earnings from investments overseas could be estimated with the residual method and the stock of these investments with the direct method. See Butlin (1962), p. 405. For the methods of estimate, see Cottrell (1975), pp. 11 ff.

[3] See Platt (1986), pp. 17-20.

[4] *Ibid.*, pp. 5 ff.

[5] Among these, Hobson, in particular, should be remembered because he applied both the indirect and the direct method in his main work on this subject; see Hobson (1963), chapter VII.

[6] See Tiberi (1988), chapter 1.

[7] The term 'residual' is also used in Thomas (1967), p. 8 and others.

[8] See Imlah (1958), p. 67. In fact, the portfolios of British residents, as far as financial assets were concerned, were generally re-invested abroad, sometimes with a change in their geographical destination, until the First World War when foreign assets had to be liquidated to finance the war.

[9] The data on Britain's trade balance was published in the *Annual Statement of the Trade of the United Kingdom with Foreign Countries and British Possessions* from 1853 onwards. See Tiberi (1984) chapters 1 and 2 about sources for the years before the publication of the *Annual Statement*. In line with the author's earlier work, the term (Great) Britain has been preferred to United Kingdom, as happens in most of the literature on the subject.

[10] On the question of Britain's balance of trade until the First World War, see Tiberi (1984).

[11] On the accuracy of the data in the *Annual Statement* it is worth remembering the authoritative opinion of the Trade Figures Committee, which stated that 'in the absence of any general system of *ad valorem* duties on either imports or exports, there is no reason to assume that under the system of declared values there is any bias towards either under or over valuation'. See Trade Figures Committee (1926), p. 3. There is an earlier statement made by the Inspector General of Imports and Exports on the soundness of the British trade balance; see *Messenger* (1865).

[12] See Schlote (1938).

[13] See Imlah (1948).

[14] See Imlah (1958).

[15] For a more extensive examination of this topic, see Tiberi (1984), section 2.2. An interesting point that emerged from Schlote's and Imlah's estimates is the presence of recurring trade deficits between 1801-1853 (according to Schlote) and 1796-1853

(according to Imlah). Furthermore, these figures were considerably greater for the years from 1840 onwards than for those already indicated in the mixed measurement. In fact, data published in the *Annual Statement* shows that these deficits in the British trade balance became a structural characteristic of the economy until the First World War.

[16] These deficits had reached such an abnormal level in the 1870s that they prompted a moderate but attentive magazine to send out a warning with the editorial, 'Are we consuming our capital?'; see *The Economist* (1877c). This leader provoked a very animated debate; see Tiberi (1988), section 2.1.

[17] See, among others, Bourne (1875, etc.), McKay (1877), Newmarch (1878), Giffen (1882). The first doubt about this criterion, which applied a percentage to the total value of exports and imports, arises from the fact that this last item, that is the imports calculated with the c.i.f. criterion, already contained a part of the commissions; on this point, see below, sections 1.5.4 and 3.3.

[18] See, among others, Bourne (1875, etc.), Giffen (1882), Hobson (1963), Board of Trade (1920a, etc.), North and Heston (1960). With regard to the relationship between the valuation of freight and the estimate of imported goods (the c.i.f. valuation) or exported goods (the f.o.b. valuation) for the composition of the current account, see Tiberi (1984), chapter 3.

[19] The *Report of the Commissioners* was presented annually and published regularly in the Parliamentary Papers (see bibliography).

[20] For example, in the anonymous article which was later identified as Newmarch's, the dynamics of British capital in the mid 19th century did not include a specific item for foreign investments, which were in fact incorporated in a miscellaneous aggregate. See *The Economist* (1863), p. 1413.

[21] 'And certainly there has seldom been a period when it was more important than at the present, to understand the leading phenomena of the commercial position of this country', stated the President of the Statistical Society in his *Opening Address*. See Shaw-Lefevre (1878), pp. 574-575.

[22] See Bourne (1875, 1877), McKay (1877), Rathbone (1877), *The Times* (1877), Newmarch (1878), Seyd (1878), Shaw-Lefevre (1878).

[23] See McKay (1877), pp. 1458-1459.

[24] These questions were raised by the editor of the magazine who felt obliged to note at the foot of the letter that 'Calculations of the above description, however ingenious, are always open to some objections from a pratical point of view, and our correspondent's observations come within the range of this remark'. *Ibid.*, p. 1459.

[25] See Bourne (1877), *The Economist* (1877a, 1877b, 1877c, 1877d), Newmarch (1878), Seyd (1878), Shaw-Lefevre (1878). For a close examination of these works that appeared in the 1870s, see Madden (1985) and section 3.2 below.

[26] On this point, see Tiberi (1988), sections 2.2.1 and 2.2.2.

[27] See Seyd (1878), Tables I and II. The starting date of 1854 was obviously chosen because the values for the trade balance published by the *Annual Statement* were more reliable (see pp. 5-6).

[28] By synthesizing the analytical corrections suggested by McKay (see note 23) into one percentage, Newmarch modified the values of trade balances by deducting five per cent from imports and adding ten per cent to exports. It should be noted, however, that these percentages differed from those that could be derived from McKay's corrections, which actually corresponded to 8.5 per cent of imports and 13.5 per cent of exports. But, as Newmarch informs us, 'I feel great confidence in saying that these percentages, when applied to the whole of the two categories, are beyond the truth, and while I do not pretend to be able to give percentages which are exact, I have a strong opinion that [...] we shall be not far from the actual state of things'. See Newmarch (1878), p. 220.

[29] It is evident that, from the accounting point of view, one correction on the export side alone can be the same as different corrections to both imports and exports. However, it should be noted how the accounting estimates were made without too many qualms, especially in the absence of data or time to search for at least some more information.

[30] See Seyd (1878), p. 1.

[31] Although most authors do not agree with it, the choice made by Seyd is not unfounded, given the characteristics of the service provided by British ships. *Ibid.*, p. 6.

[32] In fact, it was only from the end of the 1870s that the *Report of the Commissioners* gradually provided more satisfactory documentation on income from capital invested overseas by British residents (see pp. 6-7).

[33] He himself said, 'It has taken me some months of labour' and 'I have taken great pains' in order to follow year by year the evolution of income which was determined by underlying changes in the qualitative and quantitative structure of Britain's 'international wealth'. See Seyd (1878), pp. 8-9.

[34] Seyd gave very few details about the 'careful estimate' he made moving from one figure to another in his reference years 1816 and 1854; *ibid.*, p. 8. On Seyd, see below, section 4.2.

[35] Seyd also mentioned some changes in the composition of this stock; in particular, he stated that the total value of ships was no more than £75 million and therefore would account for less than ten per cent of the stock. See Seyd (1878), p. 6. Moreover, apart from the figures in the table, Seyd also talked about a stock of £1,100 million for 1872 in the same article; *ibid.*, p. 6. This very same figure had been indicated by Seyd himself in a previous work, but for the beginning of 1876; see Seyd (1876), p. 310. For Seyd's most useful estimates, see Table 4.1.

[36] Here only one of Seyd's tables, that is Table II, is shown with some variations in the headings, because it is the most pertinent to the subject of this book. For more complete information on Seyd's contribution, see Tiberi (1988), section 2.1. On the other hand, when talking to members of the Society of Arts, Seyd himself admitted that, even though he had made a great effort to limit the work of pure conjecture, 'I want you to understand that I may have made great mistakes, and that other people might proceed in a more effective way'; see Seyd (1878), p. 8. It should also be pointed out that Seyd's paper contains some rather minor discrepancies between the statements in the text and the data in his tables (see note 35).

[37] See Shaw-Lefevre (1878), p. 575.

[38] *Ibid.*, p. 586. Naturally this series was also partially estimated, even though it contained currency flows, such as the remittances from India that were well-documented.

[39] The total of about £467 million can be easily calculated *ex post* by taking account of the flow of interest estimated at £28 million for 1865 and a rate of return hypothesized at six per cent.

[40] See Giffen (1878), p. 4. Another work that directly influenced Shaw-Lefevre's contributions was Clarke's (1878) which contained useful data on British investments in foreign government securities. See Shaw-Lefevre (1878), p. 586. In comparison with Shaw-Lefevre's original table, the headings are much shorter and some errors have been corrected.

[41] A similar table can be found in Tiberi (1988), Table 9.

[42] See Giffen (1882).

[43] See Palgrave (1894), p. 340. The entry 'Commerce' was compiled by the editor of the work.

[44] *Ibid.*

[45] Positive flows, on average £56 million a year, were also recorded by *The Economist* for 1892-1896. This fact was remembered in a report published in *The Times* on a conference held by Ritchie, the President of the Board of Trade, who had in turn proposed a broadly similar estimate for 1898. See *The Times* (1898), p. 9.

[46] Further reference will be made to the *Report of the Commissioners* later to show how limited this progress was; see, for example, section 2.1.

[47] See Bastable (1887). The forerunners of Bastable include Foster (1804), Steuart (1805), Goschen (1861), Cairnes (1873, 1874).

[48] Chamberlain was an advocate of the strongest protectionist positions that aimed to establish the 'imperial preference'. This consisted in the creation of an economic area through bilateral or multilateral agreements, especially with the colonies where British exports were to be favoured over exports from countries like Germany, the United States and others that by this time were capable of threatening the commercial position of Great Britain. See, among others, Kirby (1981).

[49] This was not in contradiction with the ever growing ability of other countries to penetrate foreign markets with their exports. For an outline of the political confrontation of the period, see *The Times* (1905), p. 8 and (1909), pp. 7-8.

[50] For the comments made at the time, see, among others, Tiberi (1988), section 2.2.2 and the final bibliography.

[51] See Hobson (1963), although the first edition was published in 1914. As the author noted in the preface, 'Foreign investment has hitherto received but scant and cursory attention on the part of economists, but the importance of the subject has grown by leaps and bounds in the last few years. It has appeared to me desirable that the question should be examined in a more thorough and detailed way than has hitherto been the case. Information has, therefore, been brought together, and as far as possible systematised'. *Ibid.*, p. v.

[52] The title of the chapter was, in fact, *Capital exports and the balance of trade;* see Hobson (1963), chapter VIII.

[53] The term 'balance of trade' had been included under a separate heading prepared by Nicholson in *Palgrave's Dictionary* (1963, pp. 84-85). On the development from the balance of trade, made up of just the current account, to a complete balance of payments, see Tiberi (1988), chapter 3.

[54] In his book Hobson examined the phenomenon of the export of capital from a theoretical and historical point of view in the belief that 'Economics is at the present time by far the most exact of the social sciences, and as such can rightly claim precedence in the actual discussion of social problems'; see Hobson (1963), p. XI. The estimate of the balance on current account for 1913 was briefly elaborated by Hobson in a later article; see Hobson (1921). The present author has tried to make this estimate homogeneous with Hobson's series for the years 1870-1912; see Tiberi (1992), section 2.1.

[55] See Hobson (1963), p. 166.

[56] It should be noted that a different place in the balance sheet would change the size of the balance measuring the performance in the current account, but not the balance indicating the amount of new overseas assets, which were normally calculated net of the value of bullion.

[57] See Hobson (1963), p. 168.

[58] As, for example, the number of different fares according to the type of ship, good or route that could be taken into consideration.

[59] Hobson himself was very guarded about the quality of his valuations. See Hobson (1963), *passim.*

[60] Among these, the freight index estimated by the Board of Trade for 1884-1903 was very useful.

[61] It is true, however, that Hobson's estimate of shipping for the 1870s was significantly higher overall than Giffen's estimate. See Giffen (1882), Table on p. 222; Hobson (1963), Table on p. 187.

[62] *Ibid.*, pp. 188-190.

[63] On the other hand, in a long-term perspective the amount of bias caused by the lapse of time between the year in which the earnings were produced and the year of their tax assessment does not seem particularly relevant.

[64] See Paish (1909). In fact, Paish's research also helped to collect useful information on the sectoral and geographical distribution of British overseas investments.

[65] The total for identified income in the *Fifty-first Report of the Commissioners* was about £80 million for the year in question, that is the financial year 1906-1907. Paish added that the total sum was not inclusive of earnings from capital invested privately and bank deposits abroad (an added source of currency inflows) on the one hand, and of earnings on foreign capital in Great Britain (a source of currency outflows) on the other hand. See Paish (1909), pp. 472-473 and section 2.3 below.

[66] In fairness to Hobson it has to be said that he did look for some kind of agreement amongst the different measurements of the flows of British investments abroad, both in the estimates of other scholars and in his own research. See Hobson, especially chapter VII; on this aspect of Hobson's contribution, see section 2.4.

[67] See Hobson (1963), chapter VII and, in particular, the table on p. 204.

[68] See Schooling (1911). Similar works on Britain's overseas relations had already been published by Schooling in 1905 and 1908.

[69] As far as the visible items are concerned, however, it should be noted how Schooling, with greater precision than other authors, proceeded to include the currency movements resulting from the trading of ships, which were favourable to Great Britain, or the trading of diamonds, which were unfavourable to Britain, with the appropriate estimates for the years provided by the *Annual Statement. Ibid.*, pp. 170 ff.

[70] For these services there existed numerous estimates, such as Bourne's, Giffen's and others' (see section 1.2) which may well be challenged, but certainly should not be ignored by scholars, as Schooling did.

[71] See Giffen (1882) and Parliamentary Papers (1903). These two estimates should not be considered as entirely independent, because Giffen had held responsible positions at the Board of Trade for many years.

[72] For a broad description of the various methods adopted to evaluate currency movements originating from shipping, see Giffen (1882), pp. 206-217.

[73] See Tiberi (1988), pp. 80-86.

[74] On the other hand, Schooling should have been embarrassed by the figures he used, which were published in the *Report of the Commissioners* and showed a growing flow of identified income that could not be easily justified without taking into account the progressive accumulation of investments abroad.

[75] See Schooling (1911), Table 101. The elaborate headings of the table arise from the desire to follow Schooling's headings, which reflected the style that was still widely used at a time when there was as yet no well-established tradition in international accounting.

[76] See Stamp (1916), p. 234. However, Schooling's contribution to the more analytical information on Britain's foreign trade, with his books and also the original presentation of the numerous historical series he prepared, is worth remembering. He made use, for instance, of a moving average for ten-year periods to illustrate more clearly the tendencies, rather than the cyclical fluctuations, in the phenomena analysed.

[77] See League of Nations (1922), p. 318.

[78] See Board of Trade (1920a), p. 71. The motivations indicated in the text can be found with similar formulations in this article in the *Board of Trade Journal*. As for the evolution of the British official sources from the balance on current account of the time up to the more recent balance of payments, both in their use of terms and in their contributions, see Gregory (1928), pp. 120-126 and Tiberi (1988), chapter 1.

[79] Understandably, all this required a careful evaluation of fares and tonnage to take into account the heterogeneity of the ships in the fleet. Incidentally, the information contained in the articles in the *Board of Trade Journal* was very succinct. See Board of Trade (1920a, 1920b, 1921, 1923), *passim*.

[80] This table is a partial reproduction of the table published in the *Board of Trade Journal* (1923), p. 386. The figures contained in the table, apart from those concerning the movement of goods and bullion that were taken directly from the *Annual Statement*, were extracted and corrected with small common-sense adjustments from the work of Giffen and Paish, as mentioned in the articles quoted in note 79. The data on security issues was taken from *The Economist* and from the *Monthly Review of the London Joint City and Midland Bank*. The heading of the table did not appear directly in the articles of the *Board of Trade Journal*. It could, however, in a certain sense, be deduced from the title of the articles. On the changes in terminology and in the contents of the Board of Trade's tables, including the question of bullion, over the years, see Tiberi (1988), pp. 7-12.

[81] See *Trade Figures Committee* (1926), p. 1.

[82] Among these it seems opportune to remember what is perhaps the most complete list of sources of currency earnings for business services, which, at the suggestion of the Committee, were to be included in the newly coined item 'Short interest and commissions': 'Acceptance credits commission, Discount on foreign bills, Bank interest (i.e., short interest), Commissions, stamp duty and expenses on new issues paid by overseas borrowers, Merchanting commissions on overseas produce, Brokers' commissions, Insurance remittances from abroad and Earnings on exchange transactions'. *Ibid.*, pp. 5-6. Furthermore, the remark made about the estimates on the earnings from shipping by the Board of Trade should not be overlooked. 'But in view of the many elements which have to be estimated in the calculation it would seem desirable to give round figures only. Any other course gives an unjustified impression of accuracy'. *Ibid.*, p. 3.

[83] The surplus on current account could be used to finance both private and public foreign investments in the short- and long-term, whilst the market of new issues in London, which was a very important market, but not the only one, could be affected, for instance, by the decisions of many operators, residents and non-residents, who wanted to modify the composition of their wealth; *ibid.*, p. 2. On this point see, *The Economist* (1931a, 1931b) and below, section 2.4.

[84] See *Board of Trade Journal*, from January 27, 1927 onwards at yearly intervals.

[85] See Jenks (1971), p. 1.

[86] *Ibid.*, note 5 on pp. 411 ff.

[87] More precisely, the percentage is applied only to the total of the exports and imports of goods, excluding therefore re-exports, perhaps to avoid double-counting. *Ibid.*, p. 412.

[88] *Ibid.*, p. 414. Obvious printing errors have been eliminated from the table. The data in Column 1 indicates unfavourable balances.

[89] The crucial hypothesis proposed by Hobson was the parity between the opposite flows of capital entering and income leaving. This is certainly a convenient hypothesis, but not a particularly strong one, given the modest size of these flows at least until the early years of the 20th century. See Hobson (1963), chapter 8. This modest size of flows would have been more likely for the years examined by Jenks, when the movements could easily have been ignored without invalidating the whole estimate, at least for this reason.

[90] The lack of any reference to Shaw-Lefevre and Hobson suggests that Jenks was not aware of these works.

[91] See section 1.2. Among other things, Jenks's valuation was significantly lower than the estimates of stock proposed by Bowley, Seyd, Giffen and Nash which Jenks himself mentioned in a note. See Jenks (1971), pp. 412-413 and section 2.4.

[92] On Jenks, see also Tiberi (1992), section 2.3, as well as a second contribution by the author himself; see Jenks (1944).

[93] See Cairncross (1975), p. XIII.

[94] *Ibid.*, p. 170. In Hobson's table the column was headed as 'Income from investment abroad'.

[95] *Ibid.*, pp. 171-172. Cairncross explained this choice by saying that 1907 had been a good year for shipping, as proved by other data which was not, however, clearly indicated. This statement raises some doubts about the choice of a particularly favourable year as the base year for the calculation of the indices that Cairncross was to use later for the construction of the whole series. Moreover, Cairncross applied the chosen rate of profit to the capital value of the British fleet estimated at £150 million, as compared with Hobson's £160 million. As Cairncross himself noted, there were a number of differing estimates. *Ibid.*, p. 171.

[96] The final estimate for 'Earnings from shipping' was fixed at £72.5 million by Cairncross; *ibid.* It is useful to remember that Hobson reached his estimate for the same year, 1907, by choosing an intermediate value amongst those obtained with three different methods; see section 1.3 and, in particular, Table 1.4.

[97] See Cairncross (1975), pp. 171-173.

[98] *Ibid.*, Table 39.

[99] Hobson's fundamental work included, in fact, the estimate of the balances on current account until 1912, with the further specification by the author that the values attributed to the earnings on foreign capital for 1911 and 1912 were provisional, probably because of the time lags in the tax assessments recorded in the *Report of the Commissioners;* see Hobson (1963), Table on p. 204. The estimate of the same item for 1913 was actually not made known by Hobson until 1921; on this point, see Tiberi (1992), section 2.1, as well as note 54 above.

[100] Cairncross's table, Table 40, is on p.180 of his book quoted in the notes above. For reasons of homogeneity, the table has been presented in a different way from Cairncross's: furthermore, some printing errors have been eliminated. On Cairncross's contribution, see Tiberi (1992), chapter 3.

[101] The balance on current account for 1870 has not been included in the total to avoid double-counting. The estimate of the stock in 1870 can be found in Cairncross (1975), pp. 183-184.

[102] See Imlah (1948, 1950, 1958).

[103] See Imlah (1958), pp. 1-2. Imlah made it clear that, by emphasizing the characteristics of British hegemony, he wanted to propose a very different interpretation, naturally to be verified, of the world order established after the First World War, when 'a similar opportunity was open to the United States'; *ibid.*, p. VII.

[104] On this subject, see Tiberi (1999). This work, moreover, contains many remarks on the importance of Britain's foreign investments for the rest of the world, as well as for the country itself.

[105] The 'economic elements' were also highlighted in the title of his book; see Imlah (1958).

[106] In any case Imlah gave due consideration to the works of his predecessors in his research, even when they had followed different valuation criteria.

[107] It has already been remembered that Schlote, with a similar procedure, had gone back as far as 1801; see section 1.2. On Schlote's and Imlah's works, see Tiberi (1984), section 2.2.

[108] See Imlah (1958), pp. 20-24.

[109] *Ibid.*, p. 43.

[110] *Ibid.*, p. 66.

[111] On this point, see, apart from note 24 in chapter 2, sections 1.5.5 and 4.2.

[112] See Tiberi (1984), chapter 3.

[113] *Ibid.*, note 50.

[114] From 1855 onwards, data on the number and tonnage of steam vessels and sailing vessels was available in official sources. It was rather disaggregated in the *Annual Statement of the Navigation and Shipping of the United Kingdom* and aggregated in the *Statistical Abstract*. From 1886 this information was extended to old ships.

[115] The *Annual Statement* introduced a specific item for this from 1903 onwards for what were effectively irrelevant amounts. See Tiberi (1988), note 244 and p. 116.

[116] See Imlah (1958), pp. 46-47.

[117] See Board of Trade (1832), p. 216. On this question, see Gnesutta (1983), Statistical Office of the European Communities (1983), Gandolfo (1994).

[118] To avoid this artificial swelling of currency movements, the criterion of f.o.b. (free on board) registration is generally adopted nowadays and therefore the value of imported goods is calculated at the time of their loading in the country of departure.

[119] See Imlah (1958), p. 47. Here Imlah mentioned the existence of currency outflows for services of the same type paid by British citizens to foreign operators. He did not attempt any estimate, convinced as he was, with some reason, of the modest size of the figures involved.

[120] See Imlah (1958), pp. 47-48 for the reasons for these variations in the applied rate and also for the inclusion of the value of re-exports in the aggregate to which the rate was applied, an issue which has often been ignored by other scholars.

[121] *Ibid.*, p. 48.

[122] See Imlah (1958), pp. 47-53. The use of the size of 'the tonnage entered and cleared from and to all foreign and colonial ports' overlooked the earnings from carrying trade on British ships between third countries which were not recorded in Britain's official statistics.

[123] *Ibid.*, pp. 53-56.

[124] The documentation is very limited. Imlah tried to take into account the currency outflows from emigrants' savings, which were admittedly modest but deserved to be mentioned amongst the statistics because of the large number of people leaving Great Britain. At the same time he did not attach particular importance to their remittances, given the permanent nature of emigration in most cases. *Ibid.*, pp. 56-57.

[125] Naturally Imlah was fully aware of the fact that smuggling into Great Britain had become less important after the successful repeal of import duties by Britain in the 19th century.

[126] These values, like those rather limited ones for the export of diamonds, were in fact published in the *Annual Statement* from 1901 onwards, but were not included in the tables showing the flows of all other goods.

[127] See Imlah (1958), p. 60. On this point, see Devons (1950), p. 4; Ford (1958-1959), pp. 302-303.

[128] See, among others, the numerous contributions of Crammond and Paish, whom we will discuss below (see section 2.3).

[129] To be more exact, the *Report of the Commissioners* specified 'income from abroad so far as it can be identified'; see section 2.3.

[130] It has already been remembered how this identification, at first purely marginal, improved in the course of the years; see section 1.3.

[131] The estimate of these outflows emerged from the debate following the presentation of Paish's paper in 1909. Imlah clarified this point in note 37 on p. 63 after a long explanation of the criteria adopted in the estimate of the item 'Balance on interest and dividends'. See Imlah (1958), pp. 59-64.

[132] The table is presented here after some minor errors have been eliminated from Imlah's original table. The calculation and the presentation of the five-year averages for the various components of the series, except for capital stock, had been intended to level out the 'inaccuracies of particular years'. *Ibid.*, p. 44.

[133] Neither gains and losses on capital account nor the repayments of investments overseas were taken into consideration; *ibid.*, p. 67 (see above, p. 4). We will return to this and other questions as well as the immanent risk of double-counting in Imlah's analysis; see chapter 3 and especially section 3.3.

[134] See Imlah (1958), pp. 64-81. Some of these estimates have already been examined; we will discuss the others later.

[135] See Feinstein (1972).

[136] *Ibid.*, chapter 6.

[137] *Ibid.*, p. 113.

[138] *Ibid.*, chapter 6. In this chapter Feinstein explained all his adjustments to Imlah's estimates. A table that compares the two series of the current account can be found in Tiberi (1992), Table 8. For travelling expenditure, see Prest and Adams (1954), pp. 173 ff.

[139] See Feinstein (1972), Table 15. In the table Feinstein used the heading 'International transactions' in line with the normal practice in national accounting today, which he followed throughout his research. The basic content of his table, however, is that of a balance of payments, even if it did refer in an analytical way to the current account only. Moreover, the heading 'Balance of payments' was used by Feinstein in another table for 1900-1965, in which the balances on current account for the years 1900-1913 corresponded to the ones in Table 15. *Ibid.*, Table 37.

[140] In point of fact Feinstein's table contained a double heading for the column indicating the final balance of the so-called 'International transactions': 'Current balance' and 'Net investment abroad'. *Ibid.*, Table 15.

[141] See Feinstein (1988), p. 395.

[142] See Feinstein (1972), p. 205.

[143] *Ibid.*, Table 9.8. In fact, Morgan had maintained in one of his research works that 'in 1913 there was a large credit balance in favour of London, and that balance was wiped out during the war'. See Morgan (1952), p. 332. On the creditor position of Great Britain, and for the short-term assets too, on the eve of the First World War, see, among others, Sykes (1932), p. 255 and Bloomfield (1963), pp. 71-72.

[144] See Feinstein (1988), Table 18.3. Data for 1920 has been omitted from the table.

[145] *Ibid.*, p. 397.

[146] See Feinstein (1978), Table 15.

[147] See Brezis (1995).

[148] *Ibid.*, p. 59.

[149] *Ibid.*, pp. 53-55. See also Oppers (1993), pp. 25 ff.

[150] See Brezis (1995), p. 55.

[151] 'This series is not stable from one decade to the next, rendering extrapolation extremely hazardous' (*ibid.*, p. 62). In fact, Nash also raised objections against other parts of the accounting picture outlined by Brezis, who later replied to these criticisms. See Nash (1997) and Brezis (1997).

[152] *Ibid.*, Table 2.

[153] Moreover, important traces of flows of British foreign investments at that time are occasionally found in Parliamentary Papers; see, for example, (1854a), Vol. 39, pp. 469 ff.

[154] See Feinstein (1978), p. 71.

[155] See Imlah (1958), p. 66.

[156] By contrast, Feinstein at least took account of Beeke's contribution, although he considered it, in an unconvincing way, to be less reliable than Imlah's. See Feinstein (1978), note 176.

Chapter 2

The Application of Other Methods

2.1 Introduction

In the previous chapter it was mentioned that scholars have used two other methods to hypothetically measure Britain's stock of investments in the absence of data, official or otherwise.

The direct method is the name accorded[1] to those estimates based on the calculation of the wealth owned overseas by British residents obtained by making a record of the stock at a certain point in time or of the movements of the assets forming this wealth over the years. In the first case, the problem arises of how to collect information about the ownership of financial and real assets belonging to both individuals and institutions of various kinds. In the second case, success in reaching an acceptable estimate of the stock owned at a certain time depends on the possibility of reconstructing the annual evolution of these flows right from the very first year.

It will be seen later that even the most ambitious researcher has had to fix a starting point that inevitably left a substantial part of that wealth unexplained. In fact, as in the case of the indirect method (see chapter 1), the limited amount of information available has made it impossible to calculate the earlier flows with the chosen method. The very nature of the method has meant it has been necessary to draw on all the existing sources capable of providing information, above all on the financial history of securities, shares or bonds of both old and new issues representative of the foreign investments made by private investors and enterprises.

Apart from the basic difficulty of calculating for years in the distant past, there is another crucial point that has to be made clear before proceeding to more specific questions. Even with a satisfactory amount of information available, it was no simple task to determine the flows of assets that corresponded to the genuinely new flows of investments traceable to individuals resident in Great Britain. This is because the market operations reported in numerous financial journals and publications[2] referred in many cases to a transformation of wealth that already existed or did not involve an immediate transfer of British funds abroad. Furthermore, these market operations were frequently made by individuals or institutions of foreign nationality, as is to be expected in international financial centres like the British Stock Exchanges, and especially the London market.

Therefore there can be no suggestion of a very close quantitative connection between the net balance on current account and the financial investments resulting from documentary sources for a particular year (see sections 1.5.1 and 2.4). Moreover, this method could not deal with the part of foreign investments that were made without passing through the financial markets.[3]

The real value of the research carried out by applying this method lies not so much in the estimation of the flows and stocks of British investments abroad as in the amount of information provided on significant aspects of this phenomenon. These aspects are largely ignored by the indirect method, which focuses more successfully on the temporal evolution of the quantitative dimension of the phenomenon.

The other method that has been widely used is the capitalization of the flows of income produced in any one year by the wealth owned abroad by residents in Britain. This kind of estimate is almost always part of a much broader estimate of the total wealth of the country, both domestic and international.[4] The indisputable advantage of this method is its rapid application, especially if the aim is just to find the approximate total of the stock of capital invested abroad at a certain point in time.

The obvious premise for the use of this method is the availability of information, even as an aggregate, on the income produced from the total amount of foreign investments. As has already been pointed out (see, for example, section 1.3), this premise did not always exist throughout the period before the First World War when the best source of information was the *Report of the Commissioners*. As its compilers freely admitted, even the increasing amount of data provided by this publication over the years could never give a satisfactory coverage of the whole range of British foreign investments because of tax evasion and the possession of wealth concealed from the attention of the Inland Revenue in a completely legal way (see section 1.2).

It should also be noted that the estimate of the income from these investments per solar year remained a fairly rough calculation. To begin with, the financial year ran from April 1st to March 31st. Secondly, for some types of income tax was calculated on the basis of the values of the last three years, whilst other types of income were subject to taxation for that particular financial year.[5] Furthermore, the information available was the total resulting from the aggregation of income from a variety of financial sources, though they were generally well-identified.

Consequently, as has happened in the case of more elaborate research work, capitalization has to be done by resorting to years' purchases[6] selected according to the prevailing market conditions at least for fairly broad, but homogeneous aggregations of assets. Hence, many cyclical factors inevitably prevail. The skill of the scholar using this method can avoid obvious inconsistencies in the estimates, but, at the same time, the very nature of the method does not favour an accurate measurement of the annual flows of investments abroad.[7]

Once again, it is worth noting the difference between the invisible item of investment income estimated and included in the balance on current account by those adopting the indirect method (see chapter 1) and the value of this income used as a reference base for capitalization. In the first case, for some years where part of this documentation is missing in the *Report of the Commissioners* the item can be estimated by adopting an average annual rate of return, which is revised periodically by the scholar to account for changing market conditions and then applied to the initial capital stock which grows year by year with the annual balance on current account.[8]

In the second case the direction is inverted, because the currency flows act as the starting point for the determination of the stock of capital and its variations over the years; some of the components of these flows will, in any case, have already been partly estimated when all the sources of foreign income were being considered.

The capitalization method, like the direct method, has in turn provided a very strong stimulus to research in a number of directions, namely in the disaggregation of data on foreign income published in the *Report of the Commissioners* for many years,[9] the search for hidden income, occasional comparisons of estimates of the capital stock obtained with other methods and our knowledge of the composition of Britain's international wealth.

And lastly, it is worth remembering that in some cases an estimate of the stock of capital is obtained by applying the direct method for one part of the assets and the capitalization method for the remaining part, whilst in other cases the same author may apply both the direct method and the indirect method to obtain separate evaluations of the dynamics of foreign flows of capital.[10]

2.2 The results of the capitalization of the annual flows of income

The flexibility of this method has naturally appealed to many experts in the field, though unfortunately they have not always taken care to reflect on its reliability. In fact, if the scholar is too bold in his approach, a single piece of information, such as the income produced in any one year, may be considered sufficient to hazard a guess at an estimate of the capital stock generating that income simply with the help of a discretionally chosen capitalization coefficient and with an eye on the market rates of return.[11] Nevertheless, although there had always been clear evidence of Britain's investments abroad, as in the case of the East India Company from the 17th century onwards,[12] it was only when a tax was levied on the productive activities of private business that the prerequisites for information on overseas income were created.

In other words, we have to wait until the introduction of Income Tax in 1798[13] to have some data, albeit sporadic and aggregate, on taxable income from financial and real assets owned abroad by residents in Great Britain. This new form of taxation encouraged forecasts and reports on the expected revenue from Income Tax, but these documents did not delve so far as to systematically identify the income from foreign investment. In any case, the uncertain progress made with the application of the tax certainly did not help the accuracy of the accounting system. The tax underwent a number of modifications in the first years of its implementation which was, in any case, rather short-lived as it was abolished in 1816. It was later reintroduced in 1842 to compensate for the progressive elimination of customs duties, which had basically guaranteed the fiscal equilibrium of what had been 'protectionist Britain'.

One of the measures adopted in the early years of Income Tax was the presentation of five schedules[14] listing all income subject to taxation with a concise description of its various sources. Foreign income appeared in Schedules C and D. Schedule C contained income, similar to that earned inside the country, which was the result of financing to foreign public bodies, mainly governments, in the form of the subscription of fixed interest securities. In the other schedule, domestic and foreign income were grouped together in a rather miscellaneous way. Over the years this foreign income included the profits, interest and dividends that financial assets in the private sector generated for their owners at either a fixed or variable return, the large profits earned by railway companies and also income earned from other assets, specially real assets, owned abroad by British investors.[15]

However, in the years immediately after the introduction of Income Tax, there was a definite shortage of analytical data, as mentioned above.[16] Nevertheless, some income from abroad did appear. For example, Beeke mentioned this income in the book which, as the title suggested, re-examined the figures provided by William Pitt, the minister responsible for economic matters, when he informed Parliament and the public about the expected revenue from the tax he was proposing.[17] When discussing the potential assessments made for 1799, Pitt included a figure of five million pounds under the item 'Income from possessions beyond sea', which, even in the absence of further details,[18] can perhaps be considered the first explicit official documentation on the amount of currency inflows that Great Britain was able to earn thanks to its wealth owned abroad.

In point of fact, Beeke discussed this figure in his critical revision of Pitt's set of figures. He explained that this income came from the East and West Indies and expressed his doubts about it being exclusively income, since it could be the result of a mixture of both income and capital flows.[19] The fact remains that Beeke considered Pitt's overall forecast to be somewhat optimistic and reduced it to four million pounds in his table.[20]

Rather more interesting than this first official piece of information on income from foreign investments is the reference made by Beeke to the total value of wealth owned abroad by Great Britain at the end of the 18th century. In fact, after having recalled the results of his detailed research on the amount of wealth present inside the national borders, Beeke attributed a value of at least £100 million to capital owned abroad by British citizens.[21] This estimate of the stock of British wealth abroad must be dated about the end of 1799 for it to be relevant to the above-mentioned flow of income that could have been produced from that wealth over the year.

He did not write anything else about his estimate of the stock. It is reasonable to suppose, however, that this estimate was reached by an implicit capitalization of the four million pounds cautiously calculated by Beeke himself as the foreign income earned in the year under consideration and calculated with a years' purchase of 25. At this point, we cannot help but express possible doubts about such an unsophisticated evaluation procedure which was not even clearly explained. It grouped together a set of assets which, even then, differed greatly from each other in their use and potential income-generating capacity. The four per cent chosen implicitly as the average rate of return could, in fact, appear to be sufficiently cautious, but no mention was made of the existence of foreign-owned wealth located in Great Britain, which has already been seen to have had a certain importance (see section 1.5.5).

The important point to emphasize, however, is the comparison that can be made between the figure that emerged for the stock of foreign investments attributed to Great Britain at that time and, for example, the figure Imlah adopted for his estimate of the same entity at the beginning of his series. Imlah, in fact (see section 1.5.4), calculated the stock of foreign investments at the end of 1815 at ten million pounds. This figure produced a net currency inflow of £600,000 under 'Total interest and dividends' for the following year, which marks the beginning of his estimate of the British current account, using a hypothetical average return of six per cent for the first years of his long series. Imlah also mentioned foreign capital invested in Great Britain, without actually attempting to estimate its value, though he did note that some indication of the amount of this capital could be found in the Parliamentary Papers of the time which reported on the estimates of the taxation the capital should have been subject to.[22]

The importance of Beeke's evaluation should not be underestimated as this initial sum serves as the basis on which the calculations of the final figure accumulated at the end of a very long period lasting about a century have to be made.[23] It could, in fact, lead to a substantial increase in all the annual stocks in Imlah's series including the final one, net of the foreign capital in Great Britain.[24]

On the other hand, there are no obvious reasons for discarding Beeke's estimate (see section 4.2). Indeed, there is another proposal made by another highly reputable scholar, Colquhoun, who suggested the sum of five million pounds for repatriated foreign income for 1812 in his estimate of an item he called 'Property created in Great Britain and Ireland'.[25]

It is also true, however, that Colquhoun's information is rather disorienting for anybody looking for reliable data on capital invested overseas by Great Britain and on the income it produced. In fact, after having suggested the estimate of five million pounds, Colquhoun stated that, on the one hand, there was good reason to believe that foreign income could be in excess of that sum and that, on the other, the item he suggested could include flows that did not concern capital income in the strict sense of the term.[26]

Not even Lowe's *Estimate of the taxable income of Great Britain* can provide any real help. This estimate included an item of £20 million explicitly covering sources of foreign income, such as the East India Company's and other general foreign securities, but mixed with all other domestic securities, except for 'those of our government'. Consequently, in the absence of any further explanation it is impossible to identify how much of the £20 million can be attributed to earnings coming from British residents' investments abroad.[27]

The abolition of Income Tax between 1816 and 1842 probably meant that the only potential and official source of documentation on income produced by foreign investments was lost. The word 'potential' is used here intentionally because, as mentioned above (see section 1.2 and *passim*), many years were to pass before the *Report of the Commissioners* began to publish more reliable data on this income, even after Income Tax had been reintroduced.[28]

For many decades, therefore, only fragments of information can be found about both the evolution of the stock of capital invested abroad and the income earned annually. Among the official sources[29] it is worth mentioning a parliamentary document that indicated an estimate of about £100 million for Britain's foreign investments in the period 1816-1832.[30] However, there are a number of reasons why this information cannot be considered immediately credible as the net stock of Britain's foreign capital at that time. Firstly, it is not absolutely clear which years this data refers to, because Marshall, the expert who prepared the presentation and explanation of the numerous tables, gave a very concise picture of Britain's international accounts for the years 1814-1830 accompanied by an introduction in which he spoke only of funds 'transferred from England since 1816' in the form of 'Foreign Loan Transactions [which] have aided those of Commerce during the last Sixteen Years'.[31]

Secondly, Marshall mentioned, with reference to the same period, movements of foreign-owned financial assets whose flows and stock cannot be clearly quantified. These movements, allegedly going to the financing of excess exports, could be completely virtual.[32] In fact, it has already been pointed out that only repeated errors of undervaluation in the accounting of imports resulted in trade surpluses, which Schlote's and Imlah's later revisions have convincingly proved to be non-existent (see section 1.5.4).

This does not detract from the value of Marshall's statement as a testimony to the existence of foreign capital invested in Great Britain. It is consistent with the various Parliamentary Papers that provide concrete evidence of the presence of foreign capital invested in British assets at levels that were not totally insignificant for the time.[33] Furthermore, there is a very interesting table in the documents attached to an important report showing a notable difference between the nominal values and the issue prices in the case of numerous foreign loans issued in England between 1818 and 1829.[34]

As far as the stock of capital itself is concerned, the only sources of information available were still fragmentary, even at the beginning of the 1860s when *The Economist* once again tried from its usual position of anonymity to estimate the wealth accumulated by residents in Great Britain, including financial assets held abroad.[35] This estimate, however, referred only to the total amount of wealth accumulated over the years under examination without actually identifying for each year the wealth owned at home and abroad by residents in the country. The methodology followed was to capitalize the income subject to Income Tax that could be credited to the various components of wealth in the *Report of the Commissioners* and to choose for each type a certain number of years' purchase, that is the coefficient of capitalization applied to calculate the relevant income. At least this was the principal criterion of reference, even if the lack or partial lack of data available persuaded the author to integrate it with the identified annual flows on the one hand and by using his own common sense on the other.[36]

One of the various items chosen was 'Foreign and colonial investments'; however, the author did not propose a specific estimate for it. One part, devoted to investments abroad (ships, stocks of goods, trading advances), was included in a sum which covers the so-called trading capital and the other part explicitly represented foreign and colonial investments (loans, railways, public works, etc.). Both parts were included in a very miscellaneous aggregate of £60 million per year which also included the capital accumulated at home (drainage of soil, machines, workshops, hospitals, works of art, etc.).[37]

A few years later the method of capitalizing identified annual income underwent an enormous improvement thanks to the work of Giffen,[38] who explicitly drew on the article published in *The Economist* in 1863 that has been mentioned above. However, unlike Newmarch, the author of the article, Giffen was also able to take advantage of the greater amount of documentation made available in the *Report of the Commissioners* by that time.

The method applied was clearly illustrated by Giffen in the following terms:

> to discriminate as far as possible in these returns the different sources of income, capitalise these at a suitable number of years' purchase, and then make an allowance or conjecture for the capital of the income not liable to Income Tax or which otherwise escapes assessment, and for capital which is not treated in the Income Tax returns as income yielding.[39]

In fact Giffen estimated all the capital owned by residents in his country by referring to two different years, 1865 and 1875, because one of the objectives of his work was to trace the trend of the accumulation of capital in Great Britain over that decade. This coincided with the period when there was much debate about whether the country was consuming its own capital, especially because of the peak in the negative balances on current account around the mid 1870s.[40]

Whilst determining the national wealth, Giffen also tried to propose an estimate of the wealth owned overseas. He chose to start from 1875 rather than 1865 because there was more data available, though still incomplete, despite the fact his source of information in both cases was the *Report of the Commissioners*.

Three types of income from capital invested abroad were identified in the *Report of the Commissioners*[41] for the financial year 1874-1875 (Schedules C and D), namely interest due on loans made to public institutions (£20.767 million),[42] mixed income from property and securities owned abroad and in the colonies (£6.836 million) and profits from railway companies (£1.330 million).[43]

Giffen, an expert of long-standing experience, was aware of the existence of flows of income from investments made by private individuals abroad that had not been identified by the fiscal authorities.[44] He himself identified, for example, three sectors that could, on the whole, be considered visible (trading companies, insurance companies, banks) for which he proposed an estimate of £40 million, pointing out, however, that this evaluation did not allow for a slice of capital invested abroad by private individuals.[45]

Giffen, therefore, considered four sources of foreign income and allocated to each one a different years' purchase: 25 for public securities, 15 for other securities, 20 for financial securities and 10 for trading companies, insurance companies and banks.

The final result deserves careful attention because it was the first estimate of British foreign investments to be reached by a competent use of the capitalization method (see Table 2.1).[46]

Table 2.1 Great Britain's stock of foreign investments, 1875 (thousands of pounds)

	Annual income	Years' purchase	Stock
Public funds (Schedule C)	20,767	25	519,175
Foreign and Colonial securities (Schedule D)	6,836	15	102,540
Railways out of United Kingdom (Schedule D)	1,330	20	26,600
Foreign investments not in Schedules C or D	40,000	10	400,000
Total	68,933		1,048,315

Source: Giffen (1889), Table B.

Once the methodological paradigm was defined,[47] Giffen extended its application retrospectively to 1865, a year that was poorly documented. In fact, Giffen managed to identify only two items for the income from foreign investments: the first stood at £8.426 million for interest on public funds (Schedule C) and the second at £10 million for income from investments not included in Schedules C and D.[48]

It is of greater interest to see how Giffen extended the method to the year 1885, when he practically maintained the same composition of total income from foreign investments: about 41 per cent for identified income, because it was included in Schedules C and D of Income Tax and 59 per cent for unidentified income, in so far as it was not openly included in these Schedules in the *Report of the Commissioners*.[49]

The set of data referring to the financial year 1884-1885, following Giffen's estimate, can be summarised as in Table 2.2.[50]

Table 2.2 Great Britain's stock of foreign investments, 1885 (thousands of pounds)

	Annual income	Years' purchase	Stock
Public funds (Schedule C)	21,096	25	527,400
Foreign and Colonial securities (Schedule D)	9,859	20	197,180
Railways out of United Kingdom (Schedule D)	3,808	20	76,160
Foreign investments not in Schedules C or D	50,000	10	500,000
Total	84,763		1,300,740

Source: Giffen (1889), Table A.

In this work Giffen tried to give a more solid foundation to his estimate with various comments. First of all, he insisted on the presence of a large amount of foreign income that was not declared, even if this was completely within the law in some cases.[51] With an estimate based on reliable sources, he also documented the presence of much higher levels of income accruing from securities of various types, both public and private, in foreign countries and colonies than those actually present in Schedules C and D.[52] And lastly, he dwelt on the annual dynamics of British foreign investments with their relative estimates.

He was greatly reassured by the fact that the increase in income between 1875 and 1885 arising from the combination of data from the *Report of the Commissioners* and his estimates, equal to about £16 million,[53] would have resulted in an estimate of about £320 million for the capital accumulated over the same ten years. This is the same result that would have been obtained by applying an average years' purchase of 20, which would not have been particularly eccentric with respect to those used for capitalizing different types of income.[54]

For Giffen the size and reliability of the estimate are the result of a comparison with two other significant pieces of data he himself had constructed. On the one hand, the amount of securities issued in Great Britain in the decade under consideration, 1876-1885, was much higher than £320 million, even though it should be remembered that these issues, amounting to £361.8 million, did not lead to an equivalent investment of British capital (see section 2.5.1).[55] On the other hand, the sum of accumulated capital that resulted from the balance on current account had already reached the figure of £300 million, though it did not refer to the whole decade.[56]

It is worth recalling a passage from another of Giffen's works that has already been cited (see note 71 in chapter 1), because it illustrates once again how important it is to move cautiously when faced with so many alternative estimates. In fact, Giffen wrote, for example, that 'Our investments of capital abroad at the present time are not less than 1,500 million pounds sterling'.[57] This estimate of the stock in an intermediate year between 1875 and 1885 was then quietly put to one side when in a later contribution Giffen attributed a lower value of about £1,300 million to the stock for 1885, the last year in the chosen period (see Table 2.2).[58]

The call to move cautiously is even more justified, if we consider how Giffen's obviously disproportionate estimate was later used by Bowley, another authoritative scholar of the British economy, without taking into account the work done later by Giffen to correct it. In fact, Bowley started from Giffen's estimate, which he considered to be reliable because of the excellent reputation of the expert who had made it, and then worked both forwards and backwards in time, attributing the following values to the stock of British foreign investments: £550 million in 1854 and £750 million in 1860, a little less than £1,400 million in 1875, about £1,500 million in 1880 and £2,000 million in 1890.[59] The explanation he gave for the evolution of the stock was very brief. For the 1854 estimate Bowley probably drew on Seyd's figure, though he made no specific reference to it.[60] For the others Bowley moved according to the canons of the indirect method (see chapter 1), because he automatically took account of the balance on current account without providing any documentation.[61]

Money, another reputable scholar of applied economics, also had occasion to follow in this methodological tradition with one of his works on fiscal questions in Great Britain.[62] Almost inevitably he started from the identified income for the financial year 1901-1902 in the *Forty-sixth Report of the Commissioners* with a figure of about £62.5 million. He pointed out, however, that this did not take into account the income produced by 'British capital invested in every quarter of the globe, in every foreign country, and in every British possession'. As a consequence, he proposed a total estimate that, in his opinion, 'may be safely taken at not less than £ 90,000,000 per annum', without bothering to give any hint of why he had fixed the total of unidentified income at about £27.5 million.[63]

Money was even more elusive, so to speak, about the following capitalization, for which he suggested a value of £2,000 million invested abroad that corresponded to an average return of 4.5 per cent. Although this figure is not extravagant, no explanation of it is given at all.[64] It should be noted how the ratio between identified and unidentified income is inverted, as can be seen from a comparison of Giffen's and Money's work. In fact, Giffen had proposed percentages of about 41 per cent for identified income and 59 per cent for unidentified income. Money, on the other hand, was probably more optimistic about the Inland Revenue's improved ability to ascertain income and proposed percentages that were 69 per cent and 31 per cent respectively.

In a later work, Money gave another estimate of the stock of Britain's foreign investments, updated to 1908, based once again on the capitalization of annual income flows. The identified income in the *Report of the Commissioners* amounted to £88.8 million and the unidentified income to £51.2 million.[65]

The total of £140 million, in this case, was made up of identified income for 63 per cent and of unidentified income for 37 per cent.[66] The years' purchase applied for the capitalization of identified income was clearly indicated as 25 for public securities (foreign and colonial) and 20 for all the others, including railways, which set the figure for the value of the stock at £1,937 million. However, Money offered no explanation for the capitalization of unidentified income, simply proposing a figure of £700 million which gave an overall total of £2,637 million.[67]

As he moved from one estimate to another, Money clearly changed both the composition of the annual flow of income from foreign investments and the years' purchase, without giving any explanations.[68] He said that his evaluations were generally cautious but, at the same time, he did not bother to measure the net stock of British international wealth that would have required an estimate of foreign-owned wealth in Great Britain.

On the whole Money's inadequate clarifications do not enhance the value of his estimates which, nevertheless, testify to the effort made by scholars to calculate the volume of British foreign investments.

One work that did stay more in line with the capitalization method so systematically applied by Giffen was first published anonymously in *The Economist*[69] and later republished in the up-date of Porter's classic work of statistics with an explicit reference to the author.[70]

The British weekly magazine had in fact been serving a double function as both informer and commentator on the theme of capital invested abroad.[71] For example, two years before Hirst's research, an article in the magazine containing estimates based on the direct method had attracted a lot of criticism.[72]

The method used by Giffen may be questionable, as we have said, but it is easily applied. It involves obtaining data on various types of income, knowing in advance that it could be inaccurate either because of the limits of fiscal controls or because of cyclical effects on securities with variable returns that could swell or diminish the inflows.[73] There is also the other delicate stage of choosing the years' purchase for the flows to be converted into stock values which can influence the partial and final estimates in a decisive way and are in any case rather discretional.

Hirst's work was particularly ambitious because he first made a brief, but competent, review of the many works that had assessed quantitatively the growth of wealth in Great Britain from the distant past up to his own times, before going on to make his own calculations for the years between 1895 and 1905 to maintain the ten-year interval used by Giffen and for the year with the latest data available, that is 1909. Within this broad topic the part actually focussing on the specific question of foreign investments was naturally limited, but it did reveal the growing importance of Britain's international wealth in relation to its total domestic wealth, as shown by the percentages in Table 2.3, taken from Hirst's paper.

Table 2.3 International wealth as a percentage of the total wealth of Great Britain: 1885, 1895, 1905, 1909

Year	1885	1895	1905	1909
Percentage	13	15	15.5	16.7

Source: calculation made from data in *The Economist* (1911e).

As far as the data is concerned, Hirst undoubtedly used information on Income Tax included in the *Report of the Commissioners* for the years covered by the study, but he stated only that he had been very cautious in evaluating the component of unidentified income. He gave no more specific information. He mentioned that in this sector there could be 'successful and unsuccessful ventures' and that 'in this class of investment there is, in fact, a certain amount of wastage'. He also added, and this is very important for his total estimate, 'The figure [.....] is a minimum rather than a maximum'.[74]

At this point Hirst's three new estimates have brought us up to the eve of the First World War with the capitalization method (see Table 2.4).[75]

At the same time it is appropriate to remember the closing sentences of Hirst's work, bearing in mind he was dealing with the question of Great Britain's wealth:

Sir Robert Giffen's method must therefore be applied with caution, and it must not be assumed that a very accurate result can be obtained by its means. But it has the merit of continuity, and from the historical point of view gives the only available indication of the growth of the nation's wealth.[76]

This statement obviously deserves to be given due consideration and also to be placed in its proper historical context, because numerous other contributions following different methods have been proposed since then.[77]

Table 2.4   Stock of Great Britain's foreign investments: 1895, 1905, 1909
(millions of pounds)

Year	1895	1905	1909
Stock	1,600	2,025	2,332

Source: *The Economist* (1911e).

2.3 The original experiences of Crammond and Paish

There are various reasons for turning our attention to Crammond and Paish together. Both placed the question of British foreign investments at the centre of their scientific interests and wrote a number of papers on the question[78] and both focussed not only on the quantitative, but also on the qualitative aspects of these investments. Furthermore, both came from non-academic professional backgrounds and were working at a time when the extraordinary imperial adventure of Great Britain was at its zenith, before its power began to wane during the First World War and its aftermath. And lastly, both worked on their estimates without completely clarifying the method or methods followed.

In contrast, there are differences between them at a political-cultural level, in so far as the two authors adopted divergent, if not exactly opposing, positions in the debate between free traders, who had influenced the British political ruling classes especially in the second half of the 19th century, and advocates of a protectionist policy.

To be honest, this debate had never died down completely, even though the protectionists had managed only occasionally to hold their own against free traders.[79] The debate began to heat up again at the beginning of the century when moderately protectionist ideas gained ground within the Liberal party. The most authoritative spokesman of this approach was Joseph Chamberlain, an advocate of a fiscal reform that would lead to the creation of the 'Imperial preference', that is an area made up of countries highly dependent on Great Britain where British industrial products and the raw materials of British possessions would be able to circulate relatively free from foreign competition.

For Great Britain this would have meant protection from the growing penetration of goods coming especially from the US and Germany, but also from France, Italy, Russia, etc., that is, countries that had re-introduced fairly high tariff barriers to encourage the development of their infant industries, in accordance also with the canons of free trade economists like John Stuart Mill.[80]

Certainly the discussion between the different points of view had been stimulated in the 1870s by the worry of having to draw on national wealth to manage the large deficits in the balance of trade (see section 1.2), whereas at the beginning of the 20th century the most controversial point was whether Britain should continue to invest large sums abroad rather than allocating larger amounts of resources to domestic investment to boost employment at home.[81]

In this context, a knowledge of the facts, including the volume and types of Britain's foreign investments,[82] served, if not as a premise, at least as a fundamental ingredient in the intellectual debate. Crammond and Paish worked precisely in this direction. Crammond proved to be more responsive to the worries of Chamberlain's followers, whilst Paish sided with those in favour of maintaining free trade.

Of the two Crammond was the first to take up the question and immediately pointed out that the official information in the *Report of the Commissioners* was important, but 'limited and unsatisfactory'.[83] This persuaded him to follow a different route from Giffen's and to utilise other sources of information that were private, but nevertheless had a certain amount of publicity and transparency. Among these were the lists of all the Stock Exchanges in Great Britain because, as Crammond himself noted, even though the London Stock Exchange was by far the most important financial centre in the world, the exchanges in other British towns had to be considered in order to identify as many securities representative of foreign assets as possible. Even then it was still not possible to have a complete list and therefore yet another publication, *Burdett's Official Intelligence*, had to be consulted.

Obviously Crammond wanted to start off with a complete inventory of foreign and colonial securities, though he was well aware, as he later stated, that there were many reasons why a list of these securities did not correspond to the total amount of foreign investments by residents in Britain.

The difficulty facing Crammond was very similar to the one facing scholars researching British annual income from abroad. These scholars could make use of the data about Income Tax provided by the *Report of the Commissioners,* even though the very authors of the annual document openly admitted it was incomplete. The margin of divergence between the official situation and the real situation was compensated for by adopting different procedures (see chapter 1), though they were all imbued with some degree of arbitrariness. Part of this statistical mystery was complicated by private capital being invested abroad without passing through the financial markets.

The route undertaken by Crammond did not produce any real advantages, at least as far as this component of Britain's international wealth is concerned. Nevertheless, it did potentially bring the researcher into contact with a part of the wealth held in securities whose income was not present in official records owing to tax evasion.

But the crux of the matter remained how to estimate the total amount of this financial wealth belonging to people resident in Great Britain and present in the lists of Stock Exchanges and in the lists of *Burdett's Official Intelligence*. In some quite significant cases, such as the securities issued by foreign and colonial governments, the crosscheck made by examining Schedule C of Income Tax, which was published analytically in the *Report of the Commissioners* in Crammond's day, was on the whole[84] adequate. In other cases, however, Crammond's statement that he had fixed the quota of the American railroad bond and share capital held in Britain 'after consulting many persons who are in a position to form an opinion upon this matter' does not help to dismiss any doubts about the validity of the method followed.[85]

It may be useful to remember the main sources of this unidentified income from overseas which the *Report of the Commissioners* included under the general heading of 'Businesses, Professions, &c., not otherwise detailed (including salaries of employés)' in Schedule D.[86] In this way it is possible to have a more precise idea of the economic importance of this area which was almost totally unexplored from a fiscal point of view:

> Case (f). – Concerns (other than railways) situated abroad but having their seat of direction and management in this country, *e.g.*, mines, gasworks, waterworks, tramways, breweries, tea and coffee plantations, nitrate grounds, oil fields, land and financial companies, &c.
> Case (g). – Concerns jointly worked abroad and in this country, such as electric telegraph cables, and shipping.
> Case (h). – Foreign and Colonial branches of banks, insurance companies, and mercantile houses in the United Kingdom.
> Case (i). – Mortgages of property and other loans and deposits abroad belonging to banks, insurance companies, land, mortgage and financial companies, &c., in this country.
> Case (j). – Profits of all kinds arising from business done abroad by manufacturers, merchants, and commission agents resident in the United Kingdom.[87]

Crammond, nevertheless, set about the arduous task of estimating the volume of British foreign investments by following the items one by one and indicating the destination of these investments in securities at either a fixed or a variable return. All things considered, it is exactly the same route that had previously been followed by Nash to measure the value not only of foreign investments, but also of domestic investments.[88] He checked all the items, that is securities issued by the government or other public bodies, financial companies, utilities such as water, gas or electricity and companies in any sector, against the lists of the Stock Exchanges in London and other British cities for securities quoted in the market and against the lists in *Burdett's Official Intelligence* for those not quoted.

The results were skilfully presented according to the broad geographical areas of America, Asia, Australia and Europe with other data broken down for each area as follows: firstly, according to the individual countries in each area,[89] both at a nominal value and at the market value, and secondly, according to a general classification by sector.[90]

A similar presentation was made by Crammond for data referring to 1897, though the information he provided was very concise and in the form of tables only. The choice of the year seems to have been influenced by the author's intention to give an idea of the trend of the phenomenon over the decade,[91] in which, as we have seen above, new worries began to emerge about the well-being of Britain's international accounts.

Before showing the table synthesizing Crammond's results, it should be noted that the type of presentation adopted by Crammond enabled him to cover most of Britain's investments. At the same time, however, it prevented him from including some important financial assets representing quotas of investments abroad[92] because of the difficulty of first separating the home country from the rest of the world and then of subdividing the latter into its various component countries. The discretionary estimate of the residual set of hidden assets (see note 86) completes Crammond's estimates that are given in Table 2.5.[93]

Table 2.5 Total estimated value of British investments abroad: 1897, 1906 (millions of pounds)

Year	Nominal amount	Approximate market value
1897	2,400	2,550
1906	3,150	3,220
Estimated increase during the decade	750	670

Source: Crammond (1907), Table on p. 260.

Crammond explained the juxtaposition of the two series of values by his decision to highlight the variations in the capital account of the assets held abroad by British investors who benefited from various types of annual currency inflows, whether profits, dividends, interest or rent.

In fact, Crammond himself warned that the difference between the market and nominal values of the assets should be taken as a general tendency rather than as a completely reliable figure, because the market values were taken from quotations on the Stock Exchange on any day. Furthermore, the nominal values did not necessarily correspond to the capital paid up by investors resident in Great Britain; for example, there was often a quite significant difference between the nominal figure of the securities underwritten and the figure actually paid up, or at times some shares were assigned at no cost to favour the capitalization of the profits realised. It could also be that operating losses led to a reduction in capital, though this did not happen very often.[94]

Special attention needs to be given to Crammond's use of the flows of the annual issues of securities as reference variables to evaluate the evolution of the stock of Britain's foreign investments. Although he stressed the basic limitations of the data on the subscriptions of securities issued, he did not rely on the balance on current account in order to track the dynamics of the stock of foreign investments, as the indirect method would. Therefore, when he was constructing Britain's accounts with foreign countries for 1906, he did not aim to estimate the balance of payments, but rather to quantify some aggregate items in the balance, including the outflow of British capital. He introduced the deliberately low figure of £70 million for the 'Estimated amount of capital invested abroad during 1906', because:

from various sources of information it is possible to state that the total amount subscribed in the United Kingdom last year for investment abroad was upwards of 70,000,000*l*.[95]

In point of fact, the dynamics of security issues cannot be traced back to the dynamics of the balances on current account, as was explained at a conceptual level, for example, by the 1926 document of the Trade Figures Committee and also at an empirical level by a number of scholars, including Hobson, who prepared the estimate of the two series for the years 1870-1913.[96]

In order to complete the description of the approach in Crammond's empirical work we have to mention the criterion he applied to estimate the item in the 1906 balance of payments indicating the sum of income accruing annually from the foreign holdings of residents in Great Britain. Naturally Crammond consulted the information published in the *Report of the Commissioners*, but after exploring the very wide range of data on securities owned by British investors that was filtered by the authority, he could not help but consider the figure of £66,062,109 for the financial year 1904-1905 given in the official publication to be completely inadequate.[97]

Crammond made a very aggregated estimate of £3,150 million (see Table 2.6), which was based first of all on the nominal value of British investments at the end of 1906 that he had estimated himself. By applying what he called the 'average rate of interest' of 4.5 per cent per year to the nominal value of foreign assets, Crammond reached the sum of £141,750,000.[98] This figure corresponded to about twice the figure for identified income, whose official volume amounted to £73,899,625, even if it were moved forward to the following financial year 1905-1906, the reference date Crammond chose for this income.[99]

Table 2.6 Estimated value of the stock of British foreign investments, 1906
(millions of pounds)

	Outward stock	Inward stock	Net stock
Nominal values	3,150	325.00	2,825.00
Market price values	3,220	332.15	2,887.85

Source: calculation made from Crammond's data (1911).

Another of Crammond's estimates worth noting is the one he proposed for income from capital invested in Great Britain by foreign residents, which he fixed at £13 million for 1906 and included among the items of the incomplete balance of payments he calculated.[100] He also added some information about the nature and amount of the capital which produced this currency outflow. He spoke specifically of investments in British securities and companies, as well as profits from foreign firms engaged in business in Great Britain.[101] On the basis of the details provided by Crammond, the capitalization of this outflow would lead, with a years' purchase of 25, to a figure of about £325 million in nominal value that has to be subtracted from the gross stock of £3,150 million (see Table 2.6) to reach the net total of wealth owned abroad by British residents.[102] If the same adjustments are made for the estimate at market prices and, for the sake of simplicity, the same proportional difference between nominal values and market prices used for British investments abroad is applied to foreign assets in Great Britain, this will result in an estimate of about £332 million (see Table 2.6).[103]

In his many papers that followed Crammond did not add anything new and significant to the criteria adopted to determine the fundamental variables of the international accounts of Great Britain. They did, however, provide a useful update of information on these variables.

The first of these papers, which appeared in the same journal and with the same title as the previous work,[104] presented the same empirical procedure, though with a few differences in the content and structure of the explanation. He placed the focus above all on the estimate of the stock of capital accumulated overseas and substituted the years 1897 and 1906 from the first article with the years 1896 and 1910 in the second. The procedure did not present explicit changes. As Crammond wrote, the earlier estimates for the decade 1897-1906 had been 'revised and brought up to date'[105] in order to compare the years 1896 and 1910.

The work of revision and updating done by Crammond showed some incongruities which the author passed over.[106] First of all, he did not re-propose the double series of British investments with nominal values and market prices as in the first article and he also failed to specify clearly whether the estimates were calculated at nominal values or at market prices. Moreover, he presented a table with the heading '1896' without specifying whether the estimate for 1896 was completely independent of the one that had appeared in the previous article for 1897; and yet the disaggregation of the stock according to countries and geographical areas[107] often indicated figures for 1896 that were identical to those already presented for 1897 at nominal values and in some cases (India, Ceylon, Europe) the figures were almost exactly the same as those presented for 1897 at market prices. Furthermore, he reached an estimate of £2,442 million at nominal values for the 1896 stock, which was actually higher than the one fixed at £2,400 million at nominal values for 1897 without making any comment, as might have been expected in this situation.

In fact, as Crammond's analysis shows, the generally favourable trend of Britain's balance on current account gave good reason to believe that the amount of subscriptions of new capital for investment abroad by the country's investors would be equally favourable. This would have led then to an increase in the stock of capital invested abroad measured at its nominal value between 1896 and 1897. The different and contradictory result which emerges from Crammond's papers should therefore have been explained, not passed over.

In the course of his second paper Crammond proposed two different estimates for the stock of foreign investments for 1909 and 1910. The first was obtained by applying the method of capitalization of the annual income that could be attributed to this type of investment; the second, with no clear explanation offered by Crammond, would appear to have been calculated at nominal values.

As for the first estimate, it should be pointed out immediately that it was done in a completely cursory manner, therefore far from the tradition of Giffen which concentrated on a certain disaggregation of the international wealth of Great Britain (see section 2.2). Crammond took the figure of about £89 million that the *Fifty-third Report of the Commissioners* recorded as the flow of identified income from capital abroad for the financial year 1908-1909[108] and added to it a flow of exactly the same size (50 per cent of the total), which was roughly assigned to the unidentified income, thus reaching a total of £178 million. This figure was then capitalized by applying a years' purchase of 20, thus producing what Crammond called 'the aggregate capital sum' of £3,560 million, which could be placed between the end of 1908 and the beginning of 1909.[109]

As for the second estimate, a total capital value of £3,722 million was reached from the estimate of £3,272 million for all those investments that Crammond believed could be subdivided amongst the countries of destination, to which the sum of £450 million was added for residual investments that could not be divided geographically. Together they gave the total value of £3,722 million indicated above for the end of 1910.[110]

This was, nevertheless, still gross accumulated capital because there were also currency outflows for 1910 corresponding to income owing to foreign investors in Great Britain, which Crammond included among the items in the balance of payments for a total of £15 million.[111] It is relatively easy then to arrive at the capital value of foreign investments at their nominal value by following the same procedure as for 1906.[112]

At this point the net wealth owned abroad by British residents at the end of 1910, measured at its nominal value on the basis of the elements provided by Crammond, can be said to be equal to £3,347 million.[113]

Further information on the quantitative dynamics of British foreign investments in the years shortly before the outbreak of the First World War appeared in Crammond's later works, which were, however, on more general topics and therefore dealt only marginally with the question of the wealth accumulated overseas by British citizens.[114]

In the first of these works, Crammond's ideas were contained in his usual incomplete presentation of the balance of payments which he prepared for 1911.[115] He included an estimate of three significant items, namely the sum of capital invested abroad (£175 million),[116] the interest paid on foreign investments in Great Britain (£20 million) and interest on British foreign investments (£180 million).[117]

As for the stock of capital invested abroad, Crammond presented precise information only on the property of those resident in England and Wales, who certainly represented the largest part of the population, but cannot be considered the whole country. In proposing this estimate for 1910 Crammond explicitly used the method of the capitalization of the income flows developed by Giffen. He thus tested the procedure he was to follow in a later work in which he estimated the stock of foreign investments for the whole of Great Britain.[118]

In fact in his 1911 paper Crammond focussed on the measurement of the total wealth of England and Wales. He relied on the figures published in the Report of the Commissioners for the financial year ending March 31, 1910[119] and worked out the capitalization of the income accruing from government bonds (£24.260 million), other foreign securities (£32.889 million), railway companies (£24.376 million) and from all other unidentified assets,[120] amounting to about £2,937 million.[121]

However, Crammond did not extend his estimate to the whole of Great Britain, giving a general indication in a later statement that the capital value of British investments abroad amounted to 'no less than 3,800,000,000l.'.[122] He neither clarified the year to which this figure referred nor the method adopted to obtain it.

With this lack of information there seems to be no point in updating the evaluation of the gross and net stock of British foreign investments for 1910 with Crammond's figures (see p. 74). Nor can we consider as correct, as Crammond's paper seems to imply, the procedure by which the total value of the securities underwritten in 1911 (see note 116) is added to the stock of capital invested abroad valued in nominal terms at the end of 1910, because in general it only represented an approximate net direct addition to the previous stock (see pp. 20-21).[123]

Crammond proposed the same approach to the estimate of the main items in Britain's balance of payments for 1912 in his 1914 paper.[124] The three items most directly connected with foreign investments were firstly, the sum of capital invested abroad that could be considered to coincide more or less with the sum of issues subscribed in the country (£185 million), secondly, the currency outflow to remunerate foreign capital (£20 million) and lastly, the inflow of income from investments abroad (£185 million).[125]

Using the method developed by Giffen, Crammond extended to the whole of Great Britain his estimate of the wealth owned on March 31, 1912, the last day of the financial year recorded in the *Report of the Commissioners* which provided the data on the various types of income to capitalize.[126]

An extract from Crammond's table showing only the items relevant to Britain's international wealth is given here in Table 2.7.[127]

Table 2.7 Stock of British foreign investments, 1912 (millions of pounds)

	Annual income	Years' purchase	Stock
Public funds	35.050	20	701.000
Foreign and colonial securities	40.829	20	816.580
Railway companies	28.016	20	560.320
Income not repatriated from investments abroad or from shipping, banking and business services	60.000	15	900.000
Total	163.895		2,977.900

Source: Crammond (1914), Table on p. 803.

This estimate of foreign investment, which should have been net like the rest of the table containing the estimate of the national wealth of the country, was then unexpectedly followed by Crammond's statement that:

> in the case of the United Kingdom, 3,800,000,000*l*., or 23 per cent. of the national wealth, consists of capital investments in the Overseas Dominions and Possessions and in foreign countries.[128]

This unexplained figure coincided with a figure Crammond had let slip in his previous work. This coincidence is particularly disconcerting because it is hard to understand on what grounds he could re-propose the same figure two years later when in the meantime there had been a well-documented expansion in capital invested abroad by British citizens.[129]

The last of his works to be considered here was published in the *Quarterly Review*, which marked a return to the journal that had hosted his first two articles on Britain's foreign investments. Crammond abandoned Giffen's method and once again adopted the approach he had followed in his estimate of the overall value of these investments.[130] The article in question was clearly conditioned by the prevailing wartime mood, so that it is not surprising that Crammond dedicated a short passage of his work to the creditor position of his country towards the rest of the world. As he rightly said, 'our ability to bear the financial strain of the war is greatly increased by the resources placed at our disposal by our investments abroad'.[131]

According to Crammond's approach, the estimate of the 'aggregate capital value' of these investments was the synthesis of their distribution in various countries, grouped into two large areas: British dominions, colonies and possessions (India, Australia, Egypt, etc.) on the one hand and foreign countries (the United States, Argentina, Brazil, etc.) on the other. The first area received £1,845 million in British investments, whilst the second area £1,709 million, for a total of £3,554 million.

Crammond wrote that it was necessary to add 'the very considerable amounts of British capital invested abroad privately', which was estimated at about £350 million. When added to the previous value, it gave a total value of £3,904 million for the stock of British foreign investments placed in a period of time defined only as 'on the eve of the outbreak of war'.[132]

Crammond did not say very much more[133] and therefore the figure he provided, which is very important for our purposes, should be considered with great caution. To begin with, as mentioned above, the date of reference was not clearly defined.[134] He did not specify whether these figures were at nominal values, or as is more likely, at market prices and he did not explain why, in this case, the residual total only referred to 'capital invested abroad privately' and not to other investments (shipping, banks, etc.) that had been included in this residual in his previous articles. Furthermore, he did not take into account, as would seem relevant to the purpose of his article, the foreign investments in Great Britain in order to determine the total net wealth of British holdings abroad.

At this point our discussion of Crammond's numerous contributions draws to a close. Crammond, a scholar who devoted a lot of time and energy to the problem of Britain's foreign investments, stands out for the eclecticism of his approach to the quantitative evaluation of this question. He pursued his objective of measuring the stock of these investments by resorting to both the method of the capitalization of the flows of annual income applied by Giffen and the direct method, that is the identification of all assets, financial and otherwise, owned abroad by British residents in a particular year. And he did all this at the same time as keeping an eye on the general picture of the international accounts of Great Britain, even though he did not adopt the canons of the residual (or indirect) method fully for the calculation of the flows and stocks.

In the application of this eclectic method, he should be given credit for having taken into consideration the assets of British residents that were not transacted on financial markets, the stock of foreign-owned British wealth and the various methods used for the estimate of the different assets. But, at the same time, it has to be said that other aspects of his work are not satisfactory; for example, the criterion adopted sometimes for the identification of existing British financial assets, his discussion of the problems connected with the existence of different evaluation criteria for financial assets and the documentation in support of his estimates.[135]

Although Paish wrote only three works on capital investments made overseas by British residents (see note 78), and therefore fewer than Crammond, all three received much more attention from scholars of the subject.

The starting point for Paish's first contribution, which was presented to the Royal Statistical Society,[136] was the data in the *Fifty-first Report of the Commissioners* (see note 99) referring to the financial year 1906-1907, a source of information that, in a certain sense, had always been *de rigueur* for experts in this field. It included, first of all, a detailed list of the income earned from loans made to governments and other public institutions of numerous countries which amounted to more than £31 million.[137]

The other flows of identified income concerned, as is well-known, the earnings from non-government securities at a fixed or variable rate of return and those from railway companies operating abroad but managed in Great Britain. Their total was more than £48.5 million, so that the overall sum of all identified income amounted to £79.6 million.

However, it is also well-known that Paish concentrated his innovative research on a wide range of assets whose income was not identified in the *Report of the Commissioners*.

Although he did not present an extensive documentation on the results obtained, he did give useful indications about his sources of information. They were 'statements of their capital and of their profits' prepared by 'companies operating abroad that have raised capital publicly in this country'. Furthermore, as Paish specified, these declarations 'are compiled from reports covering the year 1907, and in some cases the early portion of 1908'.

Paish's paper initially dealt with investment income, including the income identified in the *Report of the Commissioners*. Paish's estimate for this identified income amounted to £82.8 million, which was slightly higher than the one in the *Report*. In the absence of any explanation from the author, this divergence may be considered to depend on the different nature of their sources; in the case of the *Report* tax records were used and therefore a public source, as opposed to company reports or Stock Exchange records, and therefore private, in the case of Paish. Furthermore, a certain distortion arose from the different time references of the data, 1906-1907 for the *Report*, 1907 and part of 1908 for Paish's survey.

The amount assessed for the stock of capital, especially the portion producing unidentified income, is of much more interest. When measuring this stock, Paish included figures taken from the reports of companies (2,172 according to Paish) that produced unidentified income, according to the list presented in the *Report of the Commissioners* (see p. 70).[138] As we are interested here in the quantitative aspect of the stock,[139] Table 2.8 presents a synthesis of Paish's estimate based on the disaggregated analysis of the various components in which the financial resources of British residents were employed (loans to foreign and colonial governments, railways, mines, banks, etc.).[140]

Table 2.8 British capital invested abroad and the income derived therefrom, 1907-1908 (millions of pounds)

Capital	Income	Rate of interest (%)
2,693.748	139.791	5.2

Source: Paish (1909), Table on p. 475.

What Paish vaguely called the interest rate was actually an average rate, whereas he indicated the interest rates for each type of foreign investment in his table. These rates appeared to have been obtained as a result of a systematic, item by item, comparison of capital and income. Paish did not provide clarifications on this passage so that it may well have been that of the three values, capital, income and interest rate, the interest rate was the unknown that had had to be calculated. It should also be pointed out that Paish estimated the proportion between identified and unidentified income to be 59 per cent and 41 per cent respectively, as opposed to Crammond's 50 per cent each.[141]

Paish did not propose a precise measurement of the stock, either of its gross and net volume or its place in time. As far as the first point is concerned, Paish had to admit that, on the credit side, his research did not include bank deposits and capital invested abroad privately, that is invested without going through financial markets or being subject to the obligation of a public notice required by companies (see note 141), whereas on the debit side, foreign investments in Great Britain were noted, but not measured analytically. In the course of his discussion Paish maintained they could account for ten per cent of all the stock previously indicated, that is about £270 million. This was more than compensated on the credit side by the £500 million that he believed could be attributed to 'capital privately placed abroad', thus giving a net stock of the value of about £2,925 million.[142]

Paish added that he had not taken into account the income from capital (and therefore the capital itself) invested in shipping. It is worth remembering that Crammond, in line with the *Report of the Commissioners*, included this, or at least part of this income, under the miscellaneous heading of unidentified income, whereas scholars of British international accounts tended to estimate earnings from shipping as a separate invisible item, and therefore included the income obtained from capital employed in this sector in the same item.[143]

As far as the time reference is concerned, a small discordance can be found in Paish's documentation which presents two different tables with exactly the same figure for identified capital invested abroad, in one case for 1907-1908 and in the other for the end of 1907. At the same time he added data on capital subscribed in Great Britain in the years 1906-1907, 1907-1908 and 1908-1909,[144] measuring it at its issue price and not at its nominal value, but excluded subscriptions of loans made to renew loans that were about to mature or any kind of subscription to convert assets already existing (grouped together as the so-called *conversions*) in order to give a more accurate picture of the capital that was actually added and transferred abroad by British citizens.[145]

About one and a half years later Paish presented a second report to the Royal Statistical Society, which contained some very interesting information.[146]

What was new and significant about this work was the more explicit indication of an estimate for the total stock of capital invested abroad by British residents at the end of 1910 that, as Paish wrote, 'would be not much short of 3,500,000,000*l*.'.[147]

The many extra details Paish gave in this paper in comparison with his previous one help to show how he actually arrived at this estimate.

First of all, he started from his estimate made for capital invested at the end of 1907, which overstepped marginally into 1908 as shown in Table 2.8. According to Paish this estimate was obtained by elaborating the official data of the *Fifty-first Report of the Commissioners*[148] and the data in documents he had collected from 2,172 companies. In responding to comments on his report, he specified the criteria adopted in his estimate: market prices for central or local government securities at a fixed return, except for non-interest bearing loans; the nominal amount of capital for all other assets, except for the types of financing mentioned above; the values of a company's shares resulting from its balance sheet, where possible, which coincided more or less with the capital raised by the firm, without taking into account its gains or losses in the capital account, even though the gains are usually expected to be larger than the losses; and lastly, for private capital invested abroad the only comment was that 'it was very difficult to make any estimate of the amount'.[149]

Starting from this amount of stock for the end of 1907, Paish then used the estimates for the flows of securities issued in the years 1908, 1909 and 1910 to calculate the updated amount of the stock of British foreign investments. This criterion, which was first proposed by Paish (see above) as documentation rather than as a real estimate of the capital invested abroad, seems questionable.

As these figures were £130 million, £160 million and £165 million respectively for a total of £455 million, the stock of capital at the end of 1910 should have been £3,148.738 million (that is £2,693.738 million at the end of 1907 + £455 million in new issues), whilst the figure indicated by Paish was £3,192 million. The difference of more than £43 million is not relevant, given the overall total of the estimate proposed, but it still remains a mystery.[150]

The final positive item for the stock, however, should also include one further component, that is capital invested abroad privately in all its various forms, except for those handled in foreign financial markets. Paish gave the purchase of land, mortgages, bank deposits, entrepreneurial ventures in manufacturing, merchant and trading businesses, etc., as examples of these forms.[151] This amount, as already mentioned, was an unknown quantity, which counterbalanced the sum of foreign capital participating in various ways in the wealth of Great Britain. It was a partial counterbalance, at least according to the impressionistic evaluation of Paish, who decided to increase the estimate of British international wealth to a figure 'not much short of 3,500,000,000*l*.'[152] in view of the different sizes of the two sums.

The similarity between Paish's and Crammond's results from a quantitative point of view confirms the value of their work, though Crammond's estimates were less valid from a qualitative point of view. The appreciation shown to Paish's innovative effort cannot obscure, however, the doubts that have been expressed about these estimates ever since their presentation to the Royal Statistical Society and that have been raised once again here in the course of the discussion of his investigations.

Paish pursued the objective of identifying the stock of Britain's foreign investments in a logical way, but the lack of data obliged him at times to move in a not entirely coherent manner in his calculations.

First of all, the evaluation criteria included a number of values: the market value, the nominal value, the issue value, the accounting value and the value of the capitalization of returns. Secondly, the information on new issues was taken apparently from all the British Stock Exchanges in his first work, but only from London in the second. For these new issues he eliminated investments due to the renewal of matured loans and therefore not really new investments, but avoided the question of delays in the actual payment of the capital subscribed.[153] Similarly he tried to identify the actual amount of the subscriptions of British citizens at the moment of the issues,[154] but ignored possible transfers of assets already subscribed and sold to foreign residents by British citizens, even if they were considered to be not entirely marginal in their amount by some experts of the time. He also opened up a new unknown area of unidentified income, but still left a part of both British capital abroad and non-British capital in the home country unexplored.

Paish seems to have cast aside the need to proceed with inventiveness, but also with precision in his last work too, which dealt with the export of British capital before the First World War.[155] Since foreign investments probably were not the only, indeed not even the main theme of the article, Paish in fact presented just a few tables summarising the phenomenon with the addition of a brief comment.

Table 2.9 Stock of British foreign investments, 1913 (pounds)

Estimated stock at the end of 1907	2,693,738,000
Amount subscribed in 1908*	145,878,300
.... 1909*	182,408,050
.... 1910*	189,053,705
.... 1911*	163,972,455
.... 1912*	160,042,544
.... 1913*	196,668,606
Amount of capital invested privately	300,000,000
Total stock	4,031,761,660

* Calculated at prices of issues, and excluding all conversion loans and shares issued to vendors.

Source: calculation made from Paish's data (1909, 1914).

He based his estimates for the evolution of the stock of British foreign investments until the end of 1913, firstly, on the value he had previously calculated with reference more or less to the end of 1907, secondly, on the sum of the subscriptions of capital in the following years and thirdly, on a purely subjective estimate of the capital invested abroad through private channels. A synthesis of this aggregation of heterogeneous data is given in Table 2.9.[156]

The new value of the stock of securities in circulation, which was obtained in this way and integrated with the capital invested abroad privately, gave the overall sum of 'not less than £4,000,000,000'.[157]

Apart from any observations of a general or specific nature that can be made about Paish's fundamental contribution,[158] it should be noted that the quality of his last article was definitely inferior to his two previous papers. He did not explain that the sum obtained in this way was to be considered gross wealth, because it did not take into account the foreign capital present in Great Britain. Nor did he specify that the capital invested privately had been valued at £500 million at the end of 1907 (see p. 78). He spoke about subscriptions made in the country in the years between 1907 and 1913, whereas in the preceding article he had referred to the subscriptions on the London market with practically exactly the same values, as can be seen for the years 1907-1910 common to both works. And furthermore, he did not attempt to eliminate the quotas of capital issued to foreign investors from the figures indicated, as he had done correctly in the preceding paper.

These elements are on the whole sufficient to undermine the rigour, but certainly not the reliability of this estimate proposed by Paish, whose unquestionable scientific contribution ensues from the two valuable papers he had previously presented to the Royal Statistical Society that provided the basic premises of his last paper.[159]

2.4 The estimates obtained with the direct method

We have already discussed the characteristics of the so-called direct method (see section 1.1) and it has also been said that the use of this method in estimating the size of both the flows and the stocks of British foreign investments has been taken into consideration in some of the works examined. Furthermore, it has just been shown that both Crammond and Paish proposed measurements in which they had tried to incorporate, at least in part, the stock of directly identified British assets abroad, thus referring, for example, to the value of the securities at a fixed or variable return which were believed to be owned by residents in Great Britain.[160]

As we shall see later, those applying the direct method have had to deal with difficulties arising, on the one hand, from the lack or shortage of data and, on the other, from the incongruence of the method itself. Over the many decades in which the expansion of British capital abroad took place, economic literature occasionally provided fragments of information about the stock at particular historical moments, with particular attention being given to the size of the portfolio of foreign securities owned by Britons.[161] Gradually more analytical data on the movements of financial assets was made available, thus providing a basis for a concise estimate of Britain's international wealth, or at least the most important part of it, that is securities.

One early, but significant breakthrough (see note 30) came with the presentation of a table in a publication edited by the London Statistical Society.[162] It dealt with only one component of British foreign investments, namely loans made to foreign governments, though, as some indications suggest for this period, they accounted for almost all these investments. They were said to be loans made by England, and in actual fact we do know that most foreign investments made by British residents came from that part of Britain.

The estimate of this aggregate of securities at a fixed return was meant to indicate the stock accumulated over the decade 1816-1825, which amounted to £96 million and was measured at issue prices net of sinking funds.[163]

Then at the beginning of the 1870s a brief, but illuminating article appeared in *The Economist* dealing with the international wealth of Great Britain at the end of 1869.[164] However, the information only concerned securities, which were classified according to individually named foreign countries and colonies. Admittedly most of the wealth owned abroad by British residents was held in the form of securities, but we have already seen with Giffen (see section 2.2) that there was a certain part of foreign investments not held in securities.

The author of the article did not indicate clearly which evaluation criterion had been adopted, though it is reasonable to presume on the basis of a partial check that nominal values had been used. He did, however, give a detailed description of the downward revisions made to the figures taken from the so-called *Fenn on the Funds* (see bibliography) to allow for the existence of quotas of amortisation or for the foreign securities quoted on the Stock Exchange that could be attributed to foreigners.

Obviously the author of the article was not interested in measuring the stock of the net international wealth of the country, as that would have required some reference to the possible existence of foreign-owned wealth in Great Britain which was nevertheless difficult to identify.

The total estimate presented by the anonymous journalist was £570 million for about the end of 1869, which was divided between £500 million for foreign securities and £70 million for colonial securities.[165]

About a decade later, at the beginning of the 1880s, Nash presented the first documented estimate of Britain's foreign investments made with the direct method.[166]

There is no question about Nash's familiarity with the data, which he had acquired during his twenty-year experience at the Stock Exchange in London, as he himself declared at the beginning of the first edition of his work.[167] In fact, his research was intended, at least initially, to provide experts with a comparative examination of the returns on the various financial assets from both dividends and variations on capital account. Only in the last edition did Nash present a table with these domestic and foreign assets, together with some precious observations that had already been published elsewhere (see note 166).[168]

The five items that represented the foreign assets of Great Britain are shown in Table 2.10.[169]

Table 2.10 Estimate of British investments in foreign securities, 1880 (millions of pounds)

Indian government and railway stock	180
Colonial government debentures, City loans, etc.	145
Foreign government and corporation bonds	700
Colonial and foreign railway securities	200
Colonial and foreign bank shares	25
Total	1,250

Source: Nash (1881), Table on p. 133.

Nash did not provide detailed information about the sources of his data.[170] As suggested by some of his remarks scattered here and there in his works, his prime source would seem to be the *Stock Exchange Daily Official List* of the London Stock Exchange, which was later re-elaborated in the *Investors' Monthly Manual*, a supplement of *The Economist*. It can also be presumed that his estimate generally referred to the nominal values of the securities under consideration. On this last point, in fact, Nash added that at market prices a certain number of securities had been found above par, but more had been below par. Nevertheless, 'I am inclined to think that I have rather underestimated our total holdings'.[171]

It follows, therefore, that important components of Britain's international wealth other than securities quoted on the Stock Exchange in London remained outside the scenario proposed by Nash. These included securities from other domestic and foreign Stock Exchanges, wealth held in forms other than financial assets and short-term bank deposits. It has to be said, however, that at the time when Nash was writing, there were very few Stock Exchanges in Britain outside London and only Liverpool, Glasgow and Manchester had reached a reasonable, but in no way comparable size, especially in dealings with foreign assets.[172] Nash made two points, the general relevance of which needs to be borne in mind when examining research work conducted with the direct method. He noted that there existed, on the one hand, packets of British securities owned abroad and, on the other, substantial portfolios of foreign government securities handled in all their various phases on the Stock Exchanges of Great Britain, but owned also by non-residents in the country.[173]

Another fragment of information, which was well prepared, though very succinct, appeared in *Palgrave's Dictionary*, where Harris presented an estimate of the stock of Britain's foreign investments.[174]

Whilst the various items were classified according to a mixed criterion of geographical area and sector, the estimate of the stock of securities was made at nominal values and great care was taken to include only the securities belonging to residents in Great Britain at the end of 1892.

The estimated volume of the stock was £1,698 million, a figure that Harris himself believed could 'be considered moderate' in so far as it included an estimate of only £250 million for so-called private investments, that is not in the form of securities. Harris pointed out that an authoritative expert like Giffen had recently proposed an estimate of £500 million for a similar item for the end of 1885 (see Table 2.2).[175]

Even less information was provided by two very similar estimates published in *The Economist*, which the anonymous writer claimed had been obtained with the method that is nowadays normally defined as 'direct', that is by 'studying the actual capital issues made in this country on behalf of foreign or colonial borrowers'.[176]

The writer of the article was well aware of the existence of sources of income that were difficult to identify, as he revealed in his discussion of Money's estimate that had been obtained by the capitalization of income from abroad (see pp. 65-66). The observations he made about the two estimates referred, however, to the inconsistencies typical of the direct method, such as the identification of the sum actually paid up by subscribers, the possible return of quotas of loans to Great Britain in the form of bank deposits, the use of funds collected in the conversion of existing assets into other forms or other expiry dates, or the difficulty of estimating the parts of the debt already paid back.[177]

Although some observations can be made about the total amount proposed as the estimate of the wealth accumulated abroad by Great Britain, it should be remembered that 'the capital issues form a fairly clear guide to the direction and extent of our foreign investments'.[178] In this specific case, in fact, apart from the closeness of the total figures proposed, the common element shared by the two estimates is the classification of the capital invested according to its geographical area.

The first estimate signed *A correspondent*, whose identity was never revealed, indicated a total of £3,050 million. The second estimate was attributed to Beaumont, 'a prominent member of the London Stock Exchange', who fixed the figure of £2,750 million for total assets, except for those involving European countries (see note 145). On the basis of the *correspondent's* estimates these European assets could be valued at between £100 million and £200 million, thus bringing the estimates very close to each other. Actually, this is not very surprising considering the fact that both authors referred to the data in the Stock Exchange lists.[179] Even though great uncertainty still surrounded the quantification of the British stock at that time, the journalist of *The Economist* went so far as to state, 'We may conclude that our total capital invested abroad amounts to a sum between 2,150 and 3,000 millions sterling', and then significantly specified that 'we are inclined to think that the latter sum is nearer the truth than the former'.[180]

It is perhaps superfluous to give details of the geographical classification of the identified stock, but in both estimates the size of investments in India stands out in particular (£470 million in the first one, £500 million in the second) and it also attracted the attention of a sceptical Keynes.[181] At the same time it can be added that the estimates given in *The Economist* can be considered to be in agreement with the figure of £2,500 million indicated by Speyer the previous year at a lecture given at the Institute of Bankers. This estimate was not actually accompanied by convincing documentation, but it was defined as 'conservative' by the speaker.[182]

Hobson's most significant contribution at an empirical level has already been examined in the chapter on the indirect method (see section 1.3), where it was mentioned that we would meet him again when discussing the direct method (see note 66 in chapter 1). In fact, Hobson also tried to construct the time series of Britain's foreign investments on the basis of the annual movements of financial assets in order to make a concomitant comparison of the two estimates obtained with different methods and to pursue the question of the relationship between domestic investment and foreign investment in that historical period.[183]

The first important innovation that Hobson introduced concerned the length of the period observed, 1870-1913, with the data about security issues presented at annual intervals. Another innovation was that securities issued both in London and on foreign markets, the so-called *partials*, appeared separately. Hobson solved the difficulty of identifying what part of these securities was actually owned by British investors, but issued in financial markets abroad, in a rather controversial manner by simply attributing half of these issues to subscribers resident in Britain.[184]

As for the data itself, even Hobson could not help but draw on *The Economist* and its supplement *Investor's Monthly Manual*, as he himself stated. Whilst doing this, however, Hobson made a rather surprising mistake that was quite out of character with his usual precision in empirical work. In fact, it was probably because of Hobson's meticulousness, which inspired so much confidence in his research, that the presence of this error was spotted only by Edelstein, out of all the experts in this field.

Among the various criteria on which a series of aggregate values for financial flows could be constructed, there was one based on the *created* values corresponding to the nominal value of issued securities and another based on the *called* values, that is the sum of the values actually paid up by subscribers. *The Economist* with its supplements[185] also provided information on the issue prices and market prices of the securities under consideration. However, the monthly and annual surveys, apart from occasional inconsistencies,[186] adopted the two criteria mentioned above.[187]

These surveys also contained the total value of *created* or *called* securities together with just one big subdivision of this total between securities issued only in Great Britain on the one hand, and those issued in Great Britain and elsewhere on the other. A further subdivision between domestic and foreign securities could be obtained only by a patient and careful perusal, followed by the re-aggregation, of all the items of securities listed analytically in the publications mentioned above.

Hobson took the annual evaluation of *called* capital for the years 1870-1902 from these sources, whilst he unexpectedly used the aggregation of the nominal values of *created* securities for the years 1903-1913. The following table (see Table 2.11) given in his book was the result of the operations mentioned above:

1. the identification of the capital sent abroad through securities issued only in Great Britain[188] and believed to be subscribed by residents in the country;
2. the allocation to residents of half the securities which were also issued at the same time on foreign markets;

The Accounts of the British Empire

Table 2.11 British foreign investments, calculated with the direct method and the indirect method, 1870-1913 (thousands of pounds)

Year	Direct method			Indirect method
	For investment abroad	Subscribed partly on the Continent	Column 1 plus half of column 2	Capital exports
	1	2	3	4
1870	22,375	45,643	45,196	31,700
1871	23,678	121,224	84,290	63,500
1872	35,153	163,363	116,834	83,500
1873	33,468	42,799	54,867	72,300
1874	42,371	44,071	64,406	53,000
1875	25,316	19,773	35,202	26,500
1876	25,944	0,770	26,329	-3,400
1877	9,948	7,545	13,720	-15,400
1878	17,902	14,227	25,015	-1,300
1879	22,411	9,276	27,049	12,100
1880	22,994	35,384	40,686	4,100
1881	34,120	51,857	60,048	33,200
1882	33,519	32,519	49,778	25,300
1883	38,822	13,303	45,473	17,900
1884	48,790	16,348	56,964	41,000
1885	48,369	15,051	55,894	33,900
1886	47,680	17,134	56,247	61,800
1887	60,921	9,507	65,674	67,800
1888	95,534	11,389	101,228	74,500
1889	99,236	15,792	107,132	68,800
1890	91,119	20,290	101,264	82,600
1891	46,616	9,234	51,233	48,500
1892	26,323	12,050	32,348	35,300
1893	21,121	8,202	25,222	40,100
1894	43,112	11,556	48,890	21,300
1895	47,695	19,855	57,622	22,700
1896	28,141	18,281	37,281	39,300
1897	32,817	7,747	36,690	27,100
1898	40,299	21,412	51,005	17,200
1899	41,788	8,144	45,860	27,900
1900	19,841	12,456	26,069	31,200
1901	26,050	1,857	26,978	13,900
1902	57,282	9,844	62,204	11,200
1903	56,436	7,155	60,013	23,000
1904	56,308	16,617	64,616	27,200
1905	100,737	19,760	110,617	62,800
1906	64,085	17,821	72,995	104,400
1907	68,108	22,452	79,334	140,200
1908	93,591	48,561	117,871	129,900
1909	137,262	26,413	150,468	110,100
1910	152,522	54,620	179,832	150,800
1911	119,868	45,745	142,740	192,300
1912	123,605	41,910	144,560	226,000
1913	138,884	21,702	149,735	189,200

Source: Hobson (1963), Table on p. 219.

3. the juxtaposition of the series resulting from the sum of values obtained in this way and the series of values determined with the application of the indirect method (see section 1.3).[189]

The heterogeneous nature of the criteria adopted during the compilation of the series of issued securities was passed over by Hobson, who was more concerned about explaining the problems that may arise in these series when measuring the quantity of capital actually exported in the course of each year.[190] There could be issues that represented asset *conversions*, such as the transformation of family companies into joint stock companies or loans that were simply renewed. There could also be issues that in some cases gave rise to the duplication of subscriptions of trust companies' securities and subsidiary companies' securities,[191] capital could have been invested by British residents outside financial markets or securities could have been purchased on foreign markets or subscribed by non-residents.[192]

Naturally, the quantification of currency flows that were not identified in the available documents could be carried out by using estimates based on reasonable hypotheses about the trend in the unknown quantities. Hobson had done this when applying the residual method, but he probably had some doubts about whether to venture into this area to fill the basic gaps in the data on capital movements. There is no doubt, however, that the data available on the issues of securities did not help Hobson to obtain a reliable estimate of the annual flows and of the final stock of British foreign investments. The export of capital, as indicated in column 4 of Table 2.11, was identified with the results that were obtained by applying the indirect method and were noticeably different from the ones in the previous column. It is interesting to discover, as Hobson himself did, the existence of a similar evolution in time in both series.[193]

Another author who deserves to be mentioned among the appliers of the direct method is Jenks. Like Hobson, he has already been remembered amongst those who played an important part in advancing the indirect method towards the end of the 1920s (see section 1.5.2). From a strictly quantitative point of view, Jenks did not make any remarkable contribution to the measurement of British foreign investments before the First World War. However, he should be given credit for being the first scholar, even if only implicitly, to have shown how the direct method can be applied more effectively if the various phases in the life of the foreign financial assets of a country are followed item by item, that is: issue, payment, conversion, repayment, repudiation, etc. Nevertheless, at least two important problems remained unsolved in the actual execution of this enormous empirical work, namely the identification of the presence of non-residents as investors in Great Britain and the choice of the evaluation criteria of securities (nominal value, issue price, value actually *called*, market price).

For Jenks, in fact, it must be said that the objectives of his research were more of a qualitative than a quantitative nature. He was interested in the phenomenon of the strong expansion of British capital abroad around the mid nineteenth century in order to further his understanding of the socio-economic context from which it arose. He wrote:

Our story is not so much of where the money went as of how it got there. Our quest is less for what happened than for the mechanisms, the habitudes, the animating spirit which arose in the migration of British capital.[194]

The fact remains, however, that within the framework of the reconstruction of this phase of the British economy the quantitative aspects of the question have always attracted a lot of attention.

At this point it is worth marking out some passages in Jenks's work in which he traced the evolution of the stock of Britain's foreign investments with different levels of empirical elaboration and also using calculations made with the indirect method (see section 1.5.2).

The first reference point in Jenks's reconstruction falls at the end of the 1830s with his own estimate, which, though with some reservations, drew on a contemporary work of accounting by Marshall (see section 2.2), where there was talk of £100 million as the sum of funds accumulated for foreign loans 'transferred from England since 1816'.[195]

The lack of adequate analytical support does not detract from the value of this information, which was taken from a reliable source. Nevertheless, Jenks revised the figures downwards and advanced his own very concise estimate that had been made on both a geographical basis, in which investments in Europe dominate, and on a sectoral basis, in which investments in mines prevail. As a result this estimate amounts to about £90 million of net investments, above all in public securities issued throughout the world for the years around 1830. The vagueness of this indication does not depend only on the limitations of the data available to Jenks, but also on a certain approximation in the values that he used, together with Marshall's, on this occasion.[196]

The second reference used by Jenks was a little more precise than the previous one. The year was 1854 and the financial assets were listed as aggregates with values taken between a minimum and a maximum and once again partly according to their geographical area, where the presence of the United States (between £50-60 million) is predominant, and partly according to their sector, where the French and Belgian railways (between £30-35 million) are preponderant.

The overall estimate, fluctuating between £195-230 million, referred to the nominal value of the securities in question, as far as can be understood from the context, and was not adjusted either upwards or downwards with items such as non-financial investments and British wealth, financial or otherwise, owned by non-residents.[197]

Jenks also made a third estimate which moved in a parallel way to the important one he proposed within the framework of the indirect method (see section 1.5.2).

In fact, a close look at the terminology used by Jenks in the titles of his tables will show that he talked about 'Net movements of capital' when he constructed the balance on current account of the balance of payments with the indirect method in the years 1854-1880 (see Table 1.7), whilst he referred to 'Foreign security issues' when he presented the series of the flows of this financial aggregate in the years 1860-1876 (see Table 2.12).

From this second calculation no attempt was made to reach an estimate of the stock of British capital in those years. Thus, when Jenks claimed in a fleeting passage in his book that 'the nominal value of Britain's foreign wealth had swelled by 1875 to about £1,200,000,000', it is clear that it was a reasonable indication made by an expert on the subject who did not want to present the result of a rigorous estimate of the phenomenon.[198]

No matter how creditable Jenks's effort was to construct a coherent table on the trend of the issues of foreign securities (excluding *conversions* and *vendors' shares,* reference to the *called* price of securities, etc), some pieces of the mosaic that could help to correctly represent the net stock of British foreign investments were still missing.[199] Nevertheless, on the whole Jenks produced one of the most important works of the period[200] and it is therefore interesting to present one of his main tables (see Table 2.12).[201]

Table 2.12 Summary of foreign security issues made in London, 1860-1876 (millions of pounds)

Year	Foreign Government loans	Colonial and Indian loans (including Railway guarantees)	Foreign and Colonial Railways and other companies	Total
1860	5.8	13.2	6.7	25.7
1861	0.6	12.7	4.8	18.1
1862	22.5	12.4	7.4	42.3
1863	8.9	7.9	12.9	29.7
1864	13.5	5.4	14.2	33.1
1865	22.0	9.6	20.9	52.5
1866	8.0	11.6	11.0	30.6
1867	11.4	9.4	6.5	27.3
1868	22.1	11.9	9.7	43.7
1869	20.1	10.8	8.8	39.7
1870	35.0	6.4	9.8	51.2
1871	40.1	4.9	15.3	60.3
1872	43.3	2.6	31.2	77.1
1873	16.5	4.8	29.8	51.1
1874	27.0	17.7	26.0	70.7
1875	20.4	13.0	10.6	44.0
1876	3.5	7.6	6.4	17.5
Total	320.7	161.9	232.0	714.6

Source: Jenks (1971), Table on p. 425.

The research carried out by Ayres was of a very different kind to Jenks's. It was more deeply rooted in the empirical context of British foreign movements and it also focussed on another historical period, that is 1899-1903.[202] Furthermore, his analysis of financial flows was not made with the intention of proposing either an annual or overall estimate of capital accumulated abroad by residents in Great Britain. However, our interest in his work lies in the innovative elements he brought to the approach which aimed to identify the operations of financial markets in order to study the various aspects of Britain's foreign investments.

The time horizon chosen by Ayres partially coincided with Hobson's, but Ayres's work differed on the following points: firstly, the constant, though questionable use of estimates expressed at nominal values; secondly, the various disaggregations highlighting the characteristics of creditors, sectors, etc., and lastly, the attempt to overcome some of the limitations of the documentation proposed by *The Economist* by drawing on numerous sources with a consequent, though limited, divergence of the data from that documentation.[203] This divergence can be seen in Table 2.13, where the information from the two sources is presented for the years covered by Ayres's research.[204]

The period after the Second World War saw the publication of numerous contributions by economists using the direct method in the analysis of the quantitative problems originating from the expansion of British investments overseas, even though, as we have already seen with other authors, they did not set themselves the specific objective of computing the overall volume of these investments at a certain point in time.

From this point of view, Cairncross can be seen as an exception, because he included some references to the size of the stock of capital invested abroad by residents in Great Britain when revising Hobson's estimate (see section 1.5.3). The link between his estimates based on the indirect and direct method was not made explicitly, but it emerges almost by chance from the estimates proposed by Cairncross according to the geographical distribution of this stock in certain years.

These direct estimates concerned investments in securities calculated at market prices for the end of 1870 and 1885, but they did not take into consideration the possible existence of British securities owned by non-residents, even if limited to that period.

The value indicated by Cairncross for 1870 was £785 million distributed between two aggregates: £459 million for government securities and £326 million for various kinds of securities, though predominantly railway securities. For 1885 the total estimate was £1,300 million divided into £675 million and £625 million for the two aggregates.[205]

In contrast, Hall actually focussed on the movements of British capital in a number of works,[206] of which the first is certainly the most pertinent here. In this article, in fact, the series of nominal values of the issues of securities, which are taken in an aggregate form for the years 1885-1889 from *The Economist* and in a disaggregate form for 1899-1913 from Ayres (see Table 2.13),[207] provide Hall with his initial data. However, he did make some corrections that were accompanied by very brief explanations.

Firstly, he made a distinction between domestic and foreign investments by substituting the classification according to geographical destination with the one adopted by *The Economist* according to the location of the financial markets. He then corrected the flat rate of 50 per cent that Hobson had applied when attributing to British residents their part of foreign issues made in various markets (see Table 2.11). Furthermore, Hall also noted the inadequacy of this type of measurement to

Table 2.13 Total amount of issues on British financial markets, 1899-1913 (millions of pounds)

	Ayres's estimates							The Economist's estimates		
	Issued only on London		Issued on London and some other centres for investment		Total		General total	Created and issued		Total
Year	at home	abroad	at home	abroad	at home	abroad		only in Great Britain	in Great Britain and elsewhere	
	1	2	3	4	5=1+3	6=2+4	7=5+6	8	9	10=8+9
1899	67.438	56.295		8.977	67.438	65.272	132.710	124.192	8.978	133.170
1900	132.322	29.716		3.382	132.322	33.098	165.420	160.953	4.546	165.499
1901	118.439	36.284		3.945	118.439	40.229	158.668	155.618	3.720	159.338
1902	85.505	53.388		13.762	85.505	67.150	152.655	140.050	13.762	153.812
1903	39.529	61.171	2.000	5.155	41.529	66.326	107.855	101.308	7.155	108.463
1904	48.410	57.681		16.617	48.410	74.298	122.708	106.403	16.617	123.020
1905	46.218	101.317		19.330	46.218	120.647	166.865	147.427	19.760	167.187
1906	36.669	66.157	0.207	17.296	36.876	83.453	120.329	102.352	17.821	120.173
1907	29.962	70.591	0.207	22.245	30.169	92.836	123.005	101.178	22.452	123.630
1908	46.589	94.140	1.975	49.036	48.564	143.176	191.740	143.643	48.561	192.204
1909	17.491	136.763		27.392	17.491	164.155	181.646	155.944	26.413	182.357
1910	53.697	157.836		48.334	53.697	206.170	259.867	212.819	54.620	267.439
1911	26.181	119.833	0.165	46.180	26.346	166.013	192.359	146.014	45.745	191.759
1912	38.022	129.236		41.910	38.022	171.146	209.168	168.940	41.910	210.850
1913	31.628	142.490		22.579	31.628	165.069	196.697	174.835	21.702	196.537

Sources: Ayres (1934), Table 7; *The Economist* (from the supplement *Commercial History and Review*, various years).

represent the real use of new British capital abroad, because it could not account for the repatriation of funds in all their various forms, nor the '*called* capital' as opposed to the capital merely underwritten, nor the presence of transfers of funds abroad which were only apparent as they were actually made between British residents (particularly in the case of mining companies) or were *conversions* of foreign assets that already existed.[208]

However, it seems obvious that Hall did not intend to use his work for an estimate of the international wealth of Great Britain. In fact, he worked to identify the relative strength of British financial markets in providing support to domestic companies for their investments inside the country.[209] When, as happened in other works, Hall found himself faced with the quantification of this wealth, he too cautiously made use of the results obtained by his predecessors, such as Hobson, Paish, Feis and Jenks.[210] Nevertheless Hall's estimate in the following Table 2.14 is worth reporting.[211]

Table 2.14 English new capital issues, 1895-1913 (millions of pounds)

Year	New capital issues for investment		
	at home 1	abroad 2	Total 3=1+2
1895	39.7	58.5	98.2
1896	77.5	61.8	139.3
1897	86.9	64.6	152.5
1898	75.1	57.0	132.1
1899	69.2	59.5	128.7
1899	67.4	60.8	128.2
1900	132.3	30.9	163.2
1901	118.4	38.3	156.7
1902	85.5	60.3	145.8
1903	40.5	63.7	104.2
1904	48.4	66.1	114.5
1905	46.2	111.0	157.2
1906	36.7	74.8	111.5
1907	30.1	81.7	111.8
1908	47.6	118.7	166.3
1909	17.5	150.5	168.0
1910	53.7	182.0	235.7
1911	26.2	142.9	169.1
1912	38.0	150.2	188.2
1913	31.6	153.8	185.4

Sources: 1895-1899: various years of *Commercial History and Review*, supplement of *The Economist*; 1899-1913: Ayres (1934), Table 7.

Another careful scholar to be recruited by the direct method was Simon, who, either together with Segal[212] or alone,[213] studied the movements of British capital in the decades before the First World War and drew directly on Jenks's work. The paper written in collaboration with Segal is important for an understanding of the objectives and approach of the research which initially was limited to the years

1865-1894.[214] The authors intended to provide a very broad empirical picture of Britain's foreign investments, including their aggregate size, together with some important disaggregations (geographical, sectoral, etc.). However, the disaggregation into portfolio investments and direct investments was not taken into consideration, even though it had become a focus of attention in the literature in recent years.

In point of fact, this is a consequence of the definition Segal and Simon gave to these investments. For them, direct investments were those made by companies or individuals without creating securities. Therefore, they did not acknowledge the important question of the control of companies acquired with the purchase of shares, which has become a fundamental aspect of the definition of direct investments by international organizations, even if it has undergone a number of revisions over the years.[215]

This position became evident with the publication of two individual papers presented by Simon in 1967, in which the term portfolio investments was used even in the title. He identified them as those made with the purchase of both shares and bonds on financial markets, as emerged in the course of the two works.[216]

As far as Simon's approach is concerned, it is obvious that the adoption of the direct method meant that the main source of information had to be publications on the trends in the markets. Pride of place went to the monthly supplement of *The Economist*, the *Investor's Monthly Manual*, which has already been cited a number of times, integrated with the *Stock Exchange Year Book*, *Burdett's Official Intelligence* and all the other sources of information available.[217] Nevertheless, there still remained the problem of how to reach a reliable estimate of the net wealth accumulated abroad by residents in Great Britain.

Edelstein expressed in fairly clear terms the type of national accounting appropriate to this purpose, even though he shared the same definition of portfolio investments and direct investments that this group of scholars favoured. According to Edelstein, any research on the flows and then on the stock of foreign investments, with a specific interest in British foreign investments, should be based on the following accounting identity:

> annual purchases of foreign securities by individuals and companies resident in Great Britain – annual sales of foreign securities previously owned by individuals and companies resident in Great Britain to overseas residents
> + annual direct investments abroad by individuals and companies resident in Great Britain – annual direct investments and portfolio investments in Great Britain by residents in foreign countries
> + annual short-term loans to residents in foreign countries by individuals and companies resident in Great Britain – annual short-term loans to residents in Great Britain by individuals and companies resident in foreign countries
> = net total annual flow of British savings in foreign assets.[218]

It is clear from a close scrutiny of this identity that the estimate of annual flows included in the first item is the only one that could be reasonably attempted using the empirical documentation available, especially if the estimate was meant to cover a certain number of years. It was Simon himself who had to acknowledge, after reasoning in accounting terms, though in a less punctilious way than Edelstein, that 'it has been impossible to develop annual measures of short-term capital movements or of long-term direct overseas investments'.[219]

Within this limited framework Simon's contribution was really of great significance, because the series of British portfolio investments he constructed marked a considerable improvement in the knowledge of 'one segment – although a highly significant one – of the capital account'.[220] This includes both the so-called *created* capital, that is what, according to the *Investor's Monthly Manual*, 'includes only that part of the registered capital offered for immediate subscription by the public',[221] and *called up* capital, that was actually paid up to the seller of securities by residents in Great Britain.[222]

Simon decided to concentrate on this last series of estimates, because it served better his purpose of measuring the real flows of British exported capital. Thanks to his work, the values of *called up* capital were brought closer to the values of *created* capital, though they still remained some way off, in his first paper published together with Segal.[223]

To obtain this result, Simon examined rather fragmentary information collected here and there from the numerous sources consulted, from which it would have been much easier to draw just the one piece of information available about the issue of foreign assets. Inevitably, in view of the value of these assets engaged in investments in big public works (railways, canals, ports, aqueducts, etc.), the requests for payments to subscribers of capital were spread over a long period.[224] Given these time lapses, it was normal for the sum of *called up* capital to exceed the *created* capital in some years. However, as a result of Simon's careful work the ratio between the total amount of *called up* capital and *created* capital moved from about 80 per cent for the period 1865-1894 (Segal-Simon's article of 1960) to about 98 per cent for the period 1865-1914 (Simon's article of 1967).[225]

Simon also attempted to remove the so-called *vendors' shares*, that is the shares retained by their sellers that did not give rise, at least initially, to payments of British capital (see note 208), from the calculation of *called up* capital. At the same time he avoided double-counting in the calculations of the financial assets as far as possible by trying to identify supplies of securities corresponding to simple *conversions* of capital that was already held in a different form. And, lastly, he went on to identify British capital involved in securities that were floated on markets in Britain and other countries (*partials*), as Hobson had started to do (see p. 85). We cannot help but note that, even in Simon's sophisticated research, subscriptions of British securities with their subsequent payments by non-residents in Great Britain were ignored.[226]

It is true to say, therefore, that some very important requisites were still missing in order to qualify Simon's research as a valid estimate of the net stock of British foreign investments on the eve of the First World War. The failure to determine items that would have corrected the gross stock downwards, such as the underwriting from foreign capital, the repayment of financial debts,[227] the buy-back on the market, the defaults of debtors, made this impossible. Nor can we hope to seriously compensate in a rough way for the absence of these negative items with positive items, which would certainly have been the net so-called direct investments and short-term investments in Edelstein's terms.

As far as direct investments are concerned, there are no doubts in the literature about the fact that the penetration abroad of individual or company investments by British residents in a non-share form preponderated over the insignificant level of investments in the opposite direction by non-residents in Britain.[228] As for short-term investments, sterling was beginning to make itself felt as an important reserve currency, which led to the formation of considerable deposits of British currency, especially in London. Nevertheless, the limited amount of empirical evidence available shows that even for short-term assets Great Britain was creditor towards the rest of the world.[229]

And lastly, Simon's work also lacks any precise indication of the situation of the stock of Britain's foreign wealth up to the end of 1864, that is before the great work of reconstructing the historical series from 1865 onwards started, even though many sources have led us to believe that British foreign investments had already reached a significant level by the mid-19th century (see sections 1.5.4 and 2.2).

On the other hand, Simon himself did not pretend to provide an estimate of the net stock referring to the pre-war years and considered his works as a contribution to our knowledge not only of the actual quantitative aspect, but also of other aspects of British financial investments overseas.

On this last point Simon rightly insisted on emphasizing the similarities as well as the differences in the absolute values[230] between the trend in Imlah's series of annual flows of investments abroad made with the indirect method (see Table 1.10) and his own series of portfolio investments.

This comparison is illustrated in Table 2.15 for those years where this is possible. It should be noted that Simon's series refers to *called up* capital. This seemed more appropriate in a context where the measurement of the real annual flows of net capital invested abroad by residents in Great Britain is being discussed.[231]

The particular relevance of the work of these two authors within the framework of their respective methods justifies the graphic presentation of the two series in Figure 2.1 that provides a picture, at least an intuitive one, of the plausible link between the results of the balance on current account (indirect method) and the flows of the so-called portfolio investments (direct method). As mentioned in note 230, this link was not so strong for the annual values of the two series, which at times diverge substantially because of the trends of their underlying phenomena, whereas it is reasonable to suppose that this link could be particularly significant when referring to the long-term trend for these annual values and the stock originating from their accumulation.

Table 2.15 Estimates of the flows of British foreign investments, calculated with different methods, 1865-1913* (millions of pounds)

Year	Imlah (indirect method)	Simon (direct method)
1865	34.9	42.5
1866	33.0	25.2
1867	42.2	18.4
1868	36.5	29.1
1869	46.7	21.9
1870	44.1	44.7
1871	71.5	70.2
1872	98.0	93.9
1873	81.3	69.3
1874	70.9	74.5
1875	51.3	46.1
1876	23.2	30.4
1877	13.1	19.4
1878	16.7	31.7
1879	36.5	30.5
1880	35.6	41.7
1881	65.7	74.2
1882	57.7	67.5
1883	48.8	61.2
1884	72.3	63.0
1885	62.3	55.3
1886	78.9	69.8
1887	87.7	84.4
1888	91.9	119.1
1889	80.9	122.9
1890	98.5	116.6
1891	69.4	57.6
1892	59.1	39.8
1893	53.0	32.1
1894	38.7	48.3
1895	40.0	77.7
1896	56.8	68.5
1897	41.6	78.4
1898	22.9	76.6
1899	42.4	78.2
1900	37.9	49.6
1901	33.9	49.5
1902	33.3	89.3
1903	44.8	82.9
1904	50.5	88.0
1905	81.5	128.9
1906	117.5	85.0
1907	154.1	116.3
1908	154.7	147.4
1909	135.6	175.7
1910	167.3	198.0
1911	196.9	169.2
1912	197.1	200.7
1913	224.3	217.4
Total	3,533.5	3,878.6

*Imlah's data for the years 1816-1864 can be found in Table 1.10; Simon's data for *called up* capital in 1914 was £203.2 million.

Sources: Imlah (1958), Table 4; Simon (1967a), Table 2.

In order to judge the validity of the information provided by Imlah and Simon, certain econometric instruments have been used.[232] The first result obtained was that the dynamics of the short-term period of the two series was certainly correlated, but in a rather weak way. This result is in line with the notable conceptual differences between the two methods of calculation used for the two series.[233]

The second result is also quite interesting and consists in accepting the hypothesis that the two series in the long run share the same stochastic trend.[234]

Fig. 2.1 Estimates of the flows of British foreign investments, calculated with different methods, 1865-1913 (millions of pounds)

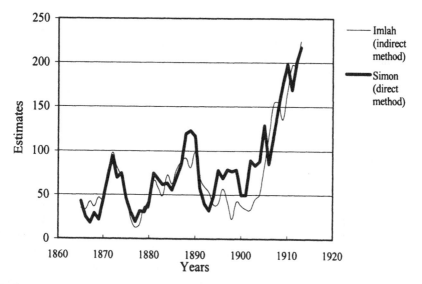

* The data is taken from Table 2.15.

Bearing in mind what has been said, it is misleading to represent the estimates linked to Simon's name as 'British capital exports', as Stone did in the title of a recent book. However, to avoid misunderstandings he specified that:

It is recognized that not all capital raised in Britain found its way overseas nor was it subscribed entirely by British nationals. It was financial investment.[235]

Nevertheless Stone took almost the whole series from Simon, making a correction of £2.5 million only as far as the final amount of the stock of these financial investments was concerned. Therefore, with Stone we have a total of £4,079.3 million as opposed to Simon's total of £4,081.8 million of *called up* capital for the years 1865-1914.[236]

Stone introduced some new features to the characteristics of British foreign investments that can be illustrated through appropriate disaggregations of the overall data, such as the division into percentages by sectors or geographical areas that can generally be considered useful, even if there remain the usual reservations about the absolute values of the series.[237]

Davis and Huttenback, the most recent of the important contributors using the direct method, adopted a much more careful approach to these questions. It should be pointed out immediately, however, that their research, which was carried out just as laboriously as other scholars', especially Segal and Simon's, explicitly expresses the intention not to determine the flows and stocks of Britain's foreign investments through the series of issues of securities on financial markets. In a certain sense their position can appear too drastic when they write that:

> Since there is no straightforward relationship between financial issues and capital transfers, any approach presuming such a relationship has been severely criticized.[238]

In fact it is wrong to consider the issues of securities and the actual transfer of capital as two separate worlds. Firstly, because there is clear evidence of the predominant position of long-term securities as the typical form of foreign investment for British residents; and then, as Edelstein's identity showed (see p. 93), there is a connection between issues and net investments, only that it is also shown by the behaviour of other flows that cannot be easily identified in the period under discussion.[239] Therefore, there is no preconception about applying the direct method, except that it involves verifying in concrete terms the degree of approximation that it is capable of achieving with its measurements.

Davis and Huttenback's contribution can be considered an attempt to define the most appropriate size of the British financial market in terms of the estimated absolute values[240] by proposing three different estimates for financial issues. All refer to investments inside Great Britain and all refer to *called up* capital. These three series can be referred to as the minimum, intermediate and maximum estimates and are divided into quinquennial periods to attenuate the effects of the cyclical movements and to simplify their exposition. The first series refers to the *called up* capital for the issues made in Great Britain which are directly documented. The second series repeats the geographical limitations of the issues, but, unlike the minimum estimate, it takes into account the requests for capital that can be found indirectly in the sources consulted. And lastly, the third series adds the *called up* capital for the issues of securities made in collaboration between British and non-British markets (*partials*), without quantifying, as Hobson, Hall, Segal and Simon had done, the amount of issues that were actually underwritten by British residents.[241]

Table 2.16 collects the data presented in Davis and Huttenback's original table with a few marginal adjustments, but only for the sums going abroad.[242]

As noted above, a close examination of the aggregate sums of *called up* capital obtained with the intermediate and the maximum estimates shows that they differ from Simon's estimate: the first result is lower and the second higher. This is absolutely plausible since the basic data for the estimate of *called up* capital is fundamentally the same.[243] Davis and Huttenback actually do not have much to say about it, but the few remarks they did make refer to the numerous financial publications consulted by Simon, though with a few extra items.

Table 2.16 Three alternative estimates for *called up* capital in Great Britain, 1865-1914 (quinquennial averages, thousands of pounds)

Quinquennial period	Minimum estimate	Intermediate estimate	Maximum estimate
1860 (2)	105,441	140,364	241,924
1870 (1)	172,555	177,545	541,985
1870 (2)	142,558	150,780	394,735
1880 (1)	304,003	346,552	384,858
1880 (2)	373,940	438,901	455,710
1890 (1)	235,951	332,325	346,821
1890 (2)	224,996	297,998	323,267
1900 (1)	321,997	395,212	398,006
1900 (2)	582,770	754,494	775,178
1910 (1)*	700,533	911,164	916,091
Total	3,164,744	3,945,335	4,778,575

* The data goes up to 1914.

Source: Davis and Huttenback (1985), Table 1.

Having said this, the difference arises from the different treatment given to the issues of securities involving more than one market, the so-called *partials*. They were absent in Davis and Huttenback's intermediate estimate, but present in Simon's series in his attempt to measure the part that could be attributed to British residents. They were once again present in Davis and Huttenback's maximum estimate, but without Simon's due caution. And so, in this way it is possible to explain the gap, which is larger even than with Simon's, between Imlah's and Paish's estimates for the stock of Britain's foreign investments on the eve of the 1914-1918 war on the one hand, and Davis and Huttenback's estimates for the large aggregate of financial investments referring to the same period and obtained as described above on the other hand.[244]

It is opportune to remember, however, that irrespective of the particular research programme the application of the direct method can be encumbered by a basic lack of information and for no other reason. Every method of evaluation of the flows and stock of foreign investments needs both reliable data and plausible assumptions in order to obtain empirical results that are sufficiently representative of the real facts.

2.5 Conclusions

As suggested by the title, this chapter has examined the estimates of British foreign investments made with methods other than the indirect method, which was discussed in the previous chapter.

The first of these other methods entails the capitalization of income produced in a certain year by overseas investments, which is obtained by applying a years' purchase. This is done, of course, by aggregating income from fairly homogeneous groups of assets, which have to be identified first in some way, and then discretionally choosing the years' purchase which depends on the average rates of return that can be attributed to each group of assets. A prerequisite for the successful application of this method is the availability of reliable data on income. This explains why research in Great Britain has normally been oriented towards calculating the total wealth owned by residents in the country and, within this context, to identify the part representing foreign investments.

It has also been seen how the reliability of the method depends on the degree of discretion needed, which may be limited in the case of long-term securities with fixed returns, but becomes particularly significant in the case of securities with variable returns or other types of assets.

This characteristic of the method makes it unsuitable for tracing the dynamics of the annual flows of foreign investments in a country. The difference between the stock calculated on the basis of the income produced and its capitalization may not correspond very closely to the actual amount of capital accumulated by residents in Great Britain over that one year. Probably this can explain why those who have preferred to adopt this method, namely Giffen and later Hirst (see Tables 2.1, 2.2 and 2.4), presented their estimates at ten-year intervals. Giffen also took the added precaution of keeping an eye on all the possible information on the flows of foreign investments made on financial markets and the trend of the current account in the period under consideration.

The flexibility of the capitalization method seems to have appealed to Crammond and Paish too, who both relied on the basic elements used by those applying the direct method in their research and, in particular, used the documentation on the movements of financial assets. The coexistence of the two methods in their numerous papers means that these authors are considered eclectic, although the different quality of their work has been noted. Both aimed at the measurement of the net wealth owned abroad by British residents and, in fact, there was unequivocal evidence of the presence of various types of investments made by non-residents in Great Britain affecting the total amount of the country's wealth abroad.

The good convergence of the estimates of the stocks of British foreign investments proposed by these two scholars (see Table 4.1), especially for the years before the outbreak of the First World War, cannot hide the fact, however, that Paish paid greater attention to the coherence and transparency of the estimates.

He skilfully dealt with problems such as the various prices (nominal, issue, called and current) that could be used to estimate financial assets, the issues of securities which were not accompanied by real payments of capital, as in the case of *conversions* and *vendors' shares*, the underwriting of securities by non-residents, especially *partials*, the movement on secondary markets, etc. This accounts for the widespread recognition Paish's estimates have always won, especially the 'not less than £4,000,000,000' for the end of 1913 (see section 2.3), which coincides more or less with Imlah's estimate obtained with the indirect method (see sections 1.5.4 and 1.6).

Nevertheless, the problem of how to quantify accurately the volume of foreign wealth producing tax-evading income or what, in the terminology of the *Report of the Commissioners*, is called 'unidentified income' still remained unsolved. Statistically this item was certainly of a significant size, as research from Hobson onwards has always maintained (see Chapter 1 and *passim*).

The last section of the chapter has considered the works that have used the direct method when dealing with the phenomenon of British foreign investments. As recalled in the Introduction and elsewhere, this method consists in identifying in all available sources the flows of financial assets purchased by residents in Great Britain as investments abroad.

In actual fact, the direct method has often been used to provide a snapshot picture of the wealth accumulated abroad by Great Britain in the form of financial assets. This was done mainly in works written in the 19th century, such as the more or less detailed studies made by the London Statistical Society (1827), *The Economist* (1869), Nash (1881) and Harris (1896) (see section 2.4). However, it did happen occasionally in the last century too, with *The Economist* again (1909a), Speyer (1905), Jenks (1971) and Cairncross (1975) (see section 2.4).

The other contributions considered here have tried to follow the evolution of British foreign investments, or rather their main part made up of financial assets, over different lengths of time.

It has been pointed out that these investments were defined as 'portfolio investments' in the terminology generally used in these works, even when they actually involved financial investments made to gain the control of companies. Nowadays these investments would be referred to as 'direct investments', a term which has, instead, been used by the literature discussed in this book to denote investments made without moving through the financial market, which in any case are very difficult to quantify.

It has also been seen that this type of research has often provided information that went beyond the overall quantitative dimension, thus enabling an interesting classification of British foreign investments according to various types of disaggregation, such as geographical area, final destination, sector. These aspects have not been dealt with in this book, which has been concerned with the trend of the flows and stocks of foreign investments as aggregates.

It has to be said immediately, however, that even the most attentive researches carried out with the direct method on the trend of these flows have, on the whole, taken very little interest in the related calculation of the stock of British foreign investments. It is not surprising, therefore, that Hobson was no exception. In fact, the quality of his series of the country's flows of foreign investments estimated with the direct method has already been noted (see section 1.3), as indeed his indifference towards the calculation of the stock of these investments.

Hobson has, nevertheless, been rightly credited with identifying some of the inevitable problems that arise when the direct method is used to estimate the flows of foreign investments. In some cases these problems have simply been reported, such as the issues of securities that represented simple *conversions*, investments of capital abroad made without passing through financial markets, subscriptions of capital made by non-residents, etc. In other cases, as for example the issues floated on British and foreign markets (*partials*), Hobson suggested a solution such as a certain percentage of the issues be attributed to British residents.

Another scholar who, like Hobson, has been remembered for his work adopting the indirect method is Jenks (see section 1.5.2). He also adopted the direct method to propose not only the estimates of the stocks on certain dates as mentioned above, but also the estimates of the flows for the years, 1860-1876, which is not a particularly significant period. Although this research on the flows was carried out satisfactorily by Jenks, it was never intended to measure the stocks at the same time.

A similar approach characterised Ayres's work on the crucial phase of the years between 1899 and the eve of the First World War (see Table 2.13). Some of the qualitative characteristics of the flows of overseas investments were well-documented here and new sources of information were introduced, but there were no important elements to help determine the stocks of overseas investments. Furthermore, the estimates based on the nominal values applied by Ayres also raise some questions about the purpose of measuring real payments of capital in terms of flows.

Of particular interest within the framework of the direct method are the estimates made after the Second World War, because they contributed to the refinement of the method, enabling it to reach more accurate estimates of the real flows of capital transferred abroad by British residents who wanted to take advantage of favourable moments on the financial market.

Hall highlighted some of the critical aspects of the method which is not able to distinguish easily between *created* and *called* capital, the repatriation of funds, *conversions* and the transfer of ownership from one resident to another. As far as his estimates are concerned (see Table 2.14), credit must be given to Hall for the effort he made to improve the reliability of the percentage for the underwriting of *partials* that can be attributed to British residents.

Simon continued the work along this line of research, at first with Segal and then on his own, and produced estimates of British foreign flows representing just the so-called portfolio investments which successfully accounted for the problems inherent in the method that had been identified, but not solved satisfactorily by other scholars.

In fact, Simon broadened the range of securities under consideration, refined the procedure used to distinguish between *partials* belonging to residents and non residents and tried to identify the *conversions* which generated new capital; in other words, he worked to avoid any risk of omission or double-counting in the wide context under consideration.

At the same time Simon did not aim to measure either the gross or net stock of these investments because both foreign investments in Britain and investments made by residents in assets other than securities, that is direct investments, remained outside the limits of his estimates. Consequently, there is a wide gap between Simon's series calculated with the direct method and Imlah's calculated with the indirect method (see Table 2.15 and Figure 2.1). In view of the analytical quality of the two works, it has been hypothesized that, even though the two series evolved very differently year by year, they nevertheless could share the same long-term stochastic tendency. This hypothesis was tested with Engle and Granger's co-integration analysis and was basically accepted.

Whilst Simon's estimates were, by and large, just re-launched by Stone and integrated with a few disaggregations, Davis and Huttenback's important work was conducted along the lines suggested by Simon (see Table 2.16) and led to an indisputable improvement in our knowledge of the behaviour of British portfolio investments, but without any relevant progress in the specific calculation of the gross and net foreign wealth owned abroad by residents in the country.

These authors bring to a close this review of the estimates of the stocks of British foreign investments up to the outbreak of the First World War, or at least the most important, converging estimates. It is only right, however, that the next chapter should be given over to the few, but distinguished, voices of dissent among the scholars of this phenomenon.

Notes

[1] See, for example, Butlin (1962), p. 405 and Platt (1986), chapter 1.

[2] For example, *The Economist*, with its supplements *Investor's Monthly Manual* and *Commercial History and Review*, *Fenn's Compendium*, *Stock Exchange Daily Official List*, *Burdett's Official Intelligence*, *Investors' Review*, and so on.

[3] On this point, see what has been written, for example, by Phelps Brown and Handfield-Jones (1952), pp. 300-301; Platt (1986), p. 26 and section 2.4 below.

[4] Theoretically the amount of the two types of wealth, international and total, could be determined as the sum of the wealth owned individually, but it is easy to imagine the kind of problems that need, or needed at least at that time, to be overcome with this procedure.

[5] See Spicer and Pegler (1916), chapter II.

[6] In the work of all the authors who applied this method, and Giffen in particular, the flows of the annual income are multiplied by a number which differs according to the various components of domestic and international wealth. This number is called years' purchase. None of these authors offered an explanation of any kind for the origin of this number. My own research on this question has led me to the plausible conclusion that it is the expression used originally to calculate the selling price of estates starting from the value of their yearly income. In our case, however, it is a pure number corresponding to the reciprocal of the rates of return hypothesized at a particular point in time, but for an infinite horizon and for any type of British foreign asset. On this point, see de Finetti (1955), pp. 177-183.

[7] A quick glimpse through the series published in the *Report of the Commissioners* is sufficient to observe the overall instability of capital income over the years. In fact, in a number of years the annual currency flow can be seen to actually fall even in the presence of a positive accumulation of foreign capital in the previous year, as can be verified easily with different criteria.

[8] This was the method adopted, for example, for most of his series by Imlah (see section 1.5.4), who nevertheless specified that 'the annual adjustments made are necessarily only roughly determined. It is scarcely possible with the limited data available to distinguish one year from another with confidence until the Inland Revenue returns begin to supply more precise guidance on annual fluctuations'; see Imlah (1958), p. 63. This statement suggests

the main reason why Imlah included the quinquennial averages alongside the series of yearly estimates. *Ibid.*, Table 4 and *passim*.

[9] In fact, from the last decades of the 19th century onwards the *Report of the Commissioners* contained a limited disaggregation of the annual currency flows, based on the so-called Schedules C and D that were part of Income Tax regulations.

[10] An example of the first type was Paish (see section 2.3) and of the second type Hobson (see section 1.3). There were also a few scholars, like Crammond, who made estimates following extremely pragmatic methods (see section 2.3).

[11] See below, Tables 2.1 and 2.2.

[12] On this point, see Colquhoun (1815), Appendix.

[13] There are numerous official and unofficial bibliographical sources on Income Tax. Here it will be sufficient to mention the *First Report of the Commissioners....*, Parliamentary Papers (1857), Vol. 4, pp. 30-34 and *passim*, as well as Parliamentary Papers (1920) among the official sources, and Spicer and Pegler (1916) among the unofficial sources.

[14] See *First Report of the Commissioners.....* (1857), pp. 30-31. The so-called Schedules A, B, C, D and E remained basically unchanged in the period we are interested in. However, the difficulties arising from legislative and administrative changes, no matter how small they were, should not be underestimated, because they affect the homogeneity of the data presented in long historical series. An important case in point has been dealt with in the previous sections where Hobson's, Paish's and Imlah's estimates of capital income have been compared on the basis of the distinction between identified and unidentified income as suggested by the *Report of the Commissioners* in the years leading up to the First World War; see sections 1.3 and 1.5.4.

[15] This last aggregate included a series of economic assets (mines, plantations, banks, etc.) located both in Great Britain and abroad and with either a centralised or decentralised management. In this case there were a number of quite important problems to do, firstly, with the identification of earned income and, secondly, with the allocation of the part of this income due to the countries involved. These problems are still very familiar to those who are interested nowadays in economic questions concerning the activity of multinational companies.

[16] See Imlah (1958), pp. 59-64.

[17] See Beeke (1800).

[18] In fact, Pitt's sources were the statistical surveys carried out for a number of years by Rose who, at a certain point, introduced a table containing the item 'Income from possessions beyond sea' with a sum of £5 million. See Rose (1799), Appendix, note 7. The connection between Rose and Pitt is explicitly mentioned in Beeke (1800), p. 4.

[19] When Beeke mentions the mixture of income and capital in connection with the East India Company, this brings to mind currency movements associated with the repatriation of capital that had previously been given as a loan or with the inflow of foreign capital. On the other hand, Beeke believed that the currency inflow from the West Indies was very limited as the income earned there was almost entirely re-invested in the area. It should be noted that, from an accounting, if not a fiscal point of view, any income belonging to British residents used in this way should nevertheless be taken into consideration in any research on capital stock invested abroad by Great Britain. See Beeke (1800), pp. 41-43.

[20] *Ibid.*, p. 128. The reason for this correction is in the mixture, mentioned in note 19, that in Beeke's opinion could lead the beneficiaries of these currency inflows to claim they were only partially taxable income; *ibid.*, p. 42.

[21] As Beeke himself specified, this is the international property 'which belongs to settled inhabitants of this country; and which, therefore, if sold, and if the produce of their sale were remitted to Great Britain, would obviously be considered as a part of the national capital', *ibid.*, p. 185. Beeke's statement about the amount of international wealth was

surprisingly ignored by Giffen in his presentation of Beeke's overall estimate of Britain's wealth. See Giffen (1889), p. 95 and Appendix IV.
[22] See Imlah (1958), p. 66. The figures in the Parliamentary Papers varied in their amounts and reached a maximum of more than £20 million in nominal value for 1812. See also note 33 below.
[23] This capitalization should be done with a variable rate which increases slowly over the century, as suggested by Imlah (see section 1.5.4).
[24] In order to appreciate the financial effect of an initial stock that could be considerably higher than the one suggested by Imlah, suffice it to say that just one pound capitalized at four per cent for a century would result in a final total of more than fifty pounds.
[25] See Colquhoun (1814), p. 88. Colquhoun's estimate was in a certain sense confirmed by Lowe, who used it to develop his own research on Britain's economy at the beginning of the 1820s. See Lowe (1822), pp. 248-249.
[26] 'The fortunes of individuals residing in India and transmitted yearly to the United Kingdom are all that can be considered as falling under the denomination of foreign income'. See Colquhoun (1814), p. 88.
[27] See Lowe (1822), p. 249. The value of these assets owned abroad by British residents was still ignored by Lowe in this estimate of 'national property'; *ibid.*, pp. 82 ff.
[28] The disaggregation of income in Schedule D, which helps to identify two of the basic components of income from capital abroad, that is 'Foreign and Colonial Securities and Possessions and other Profits' on the one hand and 'Railways out of the United Kingdom', on the other, appeared for the first time in the *Nineteenth Report of the Commissioners....*, Parliamentary Papers (1876), Vol. 20, p. 503. It was only with the *Twenty-first Report of the Commissioners....*, which published the disaggregation of the table for the financial year 1876, that income from abroad in Schedule C 'Dividends from India, Colonial and Foreign Stocks' could be identified for the first time. The *Twenty-eighth Report of the Commissioners* published yearly data for income from non-public securities starting from the financial year 1868-1869 and for 'Income from railways out of the United Kingdom' from the financial year 1873-1874. See Parliamentary Papers (1885), Vol. 22, pp. 331-332.
[29] For non-official sources providing useful information, see Jenks (1971), p. 400.
[30] See Marshall (1834), p. 120*b* and the table following p. 120*d*; this is a collection of statistical data, which was made official by a decision in the House of Commons. For a quite respectable private source providing interesting information in the same period, see London Statistical Society (1827), Table on p. 112. For this information see section 2.4.
[31] See Marshall (1834), p. 120*b*.
[32] *Ibid.*
[33] In fact, various official documents (see note 22) provided information about tax concessions granted to foreigners owning assets worth about £20 million in 1812 and about £17 million in 1815. See Parliamentary Papers (1808), pp. 97 ff and (1814-1815), Vol. 10, pp. 113 ff.
[34] See Parliamentary Papers (1831-1832), Vol. 6, p. 98.
[35] See *The Economist* (1863), pp. 1381-1383 and pp. 1411-1413, as well as note 20 in chapter 1.
[36] *Ibid., passim*. As far as the author is concerned, his name was revealed when the article in *The Economist* was republished in the *Journal of the Statistical Society* (1864). It was, in fact, Newmarch, an expert on British statistics, who pointed out in his article that 'The rates of capitalisation can only be a matter of estimate'. See *The Economist* (1863), p. 1382.
[37] See *The Economist* (1863), p. 1413. The total average accumulation estimated by Newmarch was £130 million a year for the four-year period 1859-1862 (*ibid.*).
[38] See Giffen (1878).
[39] *Ibid.*, p. 3.

[40] *Are we consuming capital?* was in fact the title given to the article published the previous year, that is 1877, in *The Economist* (see note 16 in chapter 1). Giffen was actually to return to the question of the evaluation of Britain's domestic and international wealth in a large monograph that developed the content of the 1878 article for the relevant years; see Giffen (1889). Previously Giffen (1877) had dealt with financial markets.

[41] See *Nineteenth Report of the Commissioners...*, Parliamentary Papers (1876), Vol. 20, pp. 500 ff. It is common practice in research on this topic for the values which actually refer to the financial year that goes from April 1 of one year to March 31 of the following year to be attributed to the solar year; see p. 58. As a matter of fact, the data used by Giffen had been published in the *Eighteenth Report of the Commissioners......*, Parliamentary Papers (1875), Vol. 20, pp. 550 ff; furthermore, they were also presented in the *Twenty-eighth Report of the Commissioners...*, to which the *Complete tables of accounts of the duties from 1869-1870 to 1884-1885 inclusive* were attached, Parliamentary Papers, Vol. 22, Appendix C.

[42] Schedule C included the income from public domestic and foreign loans at fixed interest rates; although the *Report of the Commissioners* did not specify the amount of the two types of loans, it was not difficult to trace the national loans by consulting both official and unofficial sources. This is exactly what Giffen did, though not in an absolutely precise way, because the aggregate figure of £41.765 million for this income published in the *Nineteenth Report of the Commissioners* did not lead to Giffen's figure of £20.7 million which he obtained by subtracting the £21.737 million he attributed to income from public domestic securities owned by British citizens; see Giffen (1878), pp. 4-5.

[43] *Ibid.*, p. 7.

[44] There are numerous references to this in the *Report of the Commissioners*. One of these passages is particularly interesting for its singular discussion about tax frauds involving income in Schedule D. It recalls a publication in the United States that stated 'As to frauds on the Revenue, there are no reliable statistics. In England it is estimated by an able writer on taxation that the Government is defrauded of fully one-third of the Taxes due to it'. It also said, 'We do not think that in this country [United States] it will amount to more than one tenth, and much of that results from ignorance, rather than a desire to defraud'. This comment was received justifiably with irony by the drafters of the *Ninth Report of the Commissioners*. See Parliamentary Papers (1865), Vol. 27, p. 128.

[45] The analytical estimate of income from foreign investments in Giffen's Appendix amounted to £65.625 million (1878, p. 31), which is slightly different from the one presented for the same year, 1875, in a more aggregate form in his monograph of 1889. Here Giffen measured the international component of Britain's total wealth in both flows and stock. According to this estimate, the percentages of unidentified and identified income were about 58 per cent and 42 per cent of the total respectively and together they totalled £68.933 million. See Giffen (1889), Table B on p. 30.

[46] *Ibid*, part of Table A on p. 4, which included all the items making up the total wealth of Great Britain. The title of the table is quite different from the original. The year of reference is 1875, as Giffen had indicated, even though the data on the income refers to the financial year 1874-1875.

[47] It should be stressed that this led to a close approximation of the estimate made by Seyd for 1874. See sections 1.2 and 4.2.

[48] The total sum of foreign capital (£310.65 million), which was calculated in the same way as the 1875 estimate by means of a years' purchase of 25 for the first flow (£210.65 million) and 10 for the second flow (£100 million), had a purely indicative value, given the obvious gaps in the data, even for 1875. See Giffen (1878), part of Table B on p.11.

[49] Giffen (1889), part of Table A on p. 11. At this point it needs to be made absolutely clear that a great part of the unidentified income from abroad, as the *Report of the*

Commissioners had already shown, was hidden inside the rather miscellaneous item 'Businesses, Professions, &c., not otherwise detailed (including salaries of employés)', and therefore included in Schedule D. As a consequence, this is not just a question of evasion, as Giffen seemed to believe, but rather a problem of having to actually identify the foreign income in this item which could not be easily disaggregated, even though it was subject to taxation; see section 2.3.

[50] *Ibid.* As can be noted, the only variation in the years' purchases concerned the non-public securities of foreign countries and colonies. The coefficient for this component, in fact, passed from 15 to 20. Giffen did not consider the presence of foreign capital invested in Great Britain to be of any quantitative significance, though it would naturally affect the outcome of his estimate; see section 4.3.

[51] He himself recalled some cases of the tax law which authorized the non-declaration of some particular types of income earned abroad. A clear condemnation of real tax frauds, at least in Great Britain at that time, can be found by running through the *Report of the Commissioners*; see note 44. For an attempt to specifically quantify the amount of tax evasion on income from foreign investments, see Bowley (1895), pp. 244 ff.

[52] Information from the *Investor's Monthly Manual* and from the *Banking Supplement*, both supplements of *The Economist*, suggested a figure of more than £85 million as opposed to the £35 million indicated in official sources, namely the *Twenty-eighth Report of the Commissioners* of 1885, for the amount of income that could be attributed to securities, such as the income considered in Schedules C and D. See Giffen (1889), p. 27 and Table 1 of the Appendix. It is not specified, however, whether all the income indicated by private sources definitely belonged to residents in Great Britain.

[53] This is the difference between the figures of £85 million for 1885 and about £69 million for 1875. As in the case of 1875, Giffen's analytical estimate for 1885 also led to a figure of £85.3 million, which was more or less in line with the amount just mentioned. See Giffen (1889), Table 1 in the Appendix. As for the income attributed to loans made through the financial market, another publication in the same year reached the same results as Giffen's estimates; see Clarke (1878), p. 308.

[54] It is worth bearing in mind firstly that, if the amount of capital accumulated between 1875 and 1885 as indicated in Giffen's estimates is calculated in nominal terms, the total sum obtained is £252.425 million and secondly, that *The Economist* proposed an estimate of at least £275 million for capital invested by British residents in foreign shares and bonds just for the years 1874-1877; see *The Economist* (1878), p. 396.

[55] For these components, see Giffen (1889), pp. 41-42 and the tables in the Appendix. Giffen did not specify the evaluation criterion of the new issues which he referred to as 'actual new issues' (*ibid.*, p. 41).

[56] This research had been prepared by Giffen as a documented paper in the debate on the situation of Britain's international accounts; see Tiberi (1988), section 2.1. By referring to the years 1854-1880 he intended to show, as others had done, that this situation could not be considered simply through the deficits shown in the balance of trade, independently of the trend of invisible items; see Giffen (1882), especially section IV. Some remarks on the overall trend of the current account of Great Britain, limited to the years 1869-1872, were made in Giffen's first work on the accumulation of capital, as mentioned above. See Giffen (1878), p. 39.

[57] See Giffen (1882), p. 223. Giffen's eclecticism is noteworthy, because he never hesitated to use any instrument to improve the information on the phenomenon being studied.

[58] There was no sudden fall in foreign investments in the period between 1882 and 1885; on the contrary, as we have just seen, Giffen himself argued that capital had continued to accumulate abroad in these years. There had, however, been a fairly large number of cases

of partial or total insolvency of foreign debtors at the beginning of the 1870s. See *The Economist* (1876), pp. 393-395 and Clarke (1878), pp. 328 ff.

[59] See Bowley (1905), pp. 76-77.

[60] As mentioned above, Seyd had talked of about £600 million for 1854 which had been calculated 'with accurate estimates', though he did not leave any trace of them in his work; see Seyd (1878), p. 8 and section 1.2.

[61] He said, 'The figures which follow are new, and not so reliable, but agree with all available facts, and appear to be the only ones consistent with them', and that was all; see Bowley (1905), note 3 on p. 76.

[62] See Money (1903).

[63] *Ibid.*, p. 68.

[64] *Ibid.* Cautious or not, Money's estimate was sufficient to annoy protectionists who made their protests in the most widely-read newspapers; see Lawrence (1905).

[65] See Money (1911), p. 15.

[66] However, on the total flow of annual income, Money (*ibid.*) added, 'It is impossible to estimate precisely, but there is good reason to believe that it is not less than £140,000,000'. On identified and unidentified income, see, among others, Gregory (1928), pp. 132-133.

[67] The data would seem to suggest that a rate of return of 7.3 per cent had been hypothesized for this part of Britain's international wealth and therefore the years' purchase was about 14 (see note 6). *Ibid.*, p. 65.

[68] For example, by applying the years' purchase chosen by Giffen for 1885 to the data on the 1901-1902 income used by Money, the estimate obtained is about £300 million lower than Money's estimate of the stock of Britain's foreign capital.

[69] See *The Economist* (1911a, 1911b, 1911e).

[70] Porter's work, which had last been published in 1851, was in fact re-presented by Hirst in 1912 with all the necessary revisions (see bibliography).

[71] The bibliography only shows what are considered to be the most important articles on this subject in the magazine.

[72] See *The Economist* (1909a); we will deal with this in section 2.4.

[73] See also section 2.4; nor should we forget the quite frequent cases of debt defaulters, as is recalled quite often. On this topic, see *The Economist* (1909b), p. 439. Traces of petitions presented by damaged British citizens can be found in the Parliamentary Papers; see, for example, (1854c), Vol. 69, pp. 41-46. For an official comment on this topic, see Parliamentary Papers (1875), Vol. 11.

[74] See *The Economist* (1911e), p. 1088. It was shortly after this that Crammond re-proposed Giffen's method, using a similar disaggregation of British foreign assets; see section 2.3.

[75] *Ibid.*, p. 1087. The data is part of a table which contains the estimates of all the other components of British wealth (land, houses, industrial capital, public property, etc.).

[76] *Ibid.*, p. 1089. Hirst made no allowance for the existence of wealth owned by foreigners in Great Britain.

[77] In the only sentence added at the end of the article in *The Economist* that was republished in the new edition of Porter's book, Hirst himself said, 'Let us hope that fifty years hence a similar comparison will provide posterity with as good grounds for satisfaction as our retrospect in this chapter and in many preceding pages happily affords'. See Porter (1912), p. 705.

[78] See Crammond (1907, 1911, 1912, 1914, 1915) and Paish (1909, 1911, 1914).

[79] See Tiberi (1984), chapter 5 and (1988), sections 2.1 and 2.2.2.

[80] See Tiberi (1988), section 2.2.2 and chapter 3. For further basic information, see Speck (1993), chapters 5 and 7.

[81] This topic still arouses interest today with the growing internationalization of economic systems, and especially of their industrial activities. See Ietto-Gillies (1992), among others.

[82] In this section we will just consider the quantitative aspects.

[83] See Crammond (1907), p. 246.

[84] As Crammond scrupulously noted (*ibid.*, p. 248), except 'to make provision for accidental omissions as well as deliberate evasion'.

[85] In this particular case Crammond (*ibid.*) attributed £330 million of the £1,342 million of the total amount of securities to British owners.

[86] This item, 'Businesses, professions &c., not otherwise detailed (including salaries of employés)', can be found, for instance, in the *Fifty-seventh Report of the Commissioners....*, Parliamentary Papers (1914), Vol. 36, Table 115 on p. 415. Note that the unidentified income also included income hidden under various forms of tax evasion to which Giffen had drawn attention (see section 2.2).

[87] *Ibid.*, p. 422.

[88] See Nash (1880, 1881); on this author, see section 2.4.

[89] For example, for America the countries appeared in the following order: Canada, the United States, Mexico, etc., whereas for Europe some countries were grouped together like France, Germany, Holland, Belgium and Denmark, whilst others were considered separately, such as Spain, Portugal and Russia; see Crammond (1907), pp. 249-252.

[90] The five columns have the following headings: Government stocks; Railways; Corporation stocks, banking, financial, land, etc.; Mines; Miscellaneous. *Ibid.*

[91] Even though Crammond always spoke about a decade in his work, in actual fact the data presented refers to the end of the years 1897 and 1906 respectively, as Crammond himself specified (*ibid.*, p. 264), and consequently there are only nine years under consideration and not ten (*ibid., passim*).

[92] Crammond himself (*ibid.*, p. 253) indicated the assets of shipping freight, insurance, telegraph and business services. And investments, such as bank deposits, should also be included. It needs to be said that Crammond, who was more concerned with mid- and long-term investments, did not manage to account for 'private investments of British individuals in colonial and foreign land and other properties' (*ibid.*) in the same way, except by aggregation.

[93] *Ibid.*, Table on p. 260. The table has been simplified in part to make it more homogeneous with the other tables in the present book. On the question of the decade, see note 91 above.

[94] These problematic aspects of estimating financial assets will be dealt with at length in sections 2.4 and 2.5.

[95] See Crammond (1907), p. 269.

[96] See Trade Figures Committee (1926), p. 7 and Hobson (1963), p. 219.

[97] See *Forty-ninth Report of the Commissioners...*, Parliamentary Papers (1906), Vol. 26, pp. 613 ff.

[98] Some doubts may be expressed here, firstly, about the adoption of the figure for the stock of capital for 1906 which was reached only at the end of the year and to which a rate of 4.5 per cent was applied and secondly, about the choice of this rate of return that Crammond himself considered to be too cautious; see Crammond (1907), p. 267. It is equally evident, however, that it was not a simple task to identify a satisfactory average rate of interest in the presence of such a mixed group of assets and in the absence of reliable points of reference in some cases.

[99] See *Fiftieth Report of the Commissioners ....*, Parliamentary Papers (1907), Vol. 20, p. 625. Identified income was said to stand at £79,560,116 for the following financial year 1906-1907 too; see *Fifty-first Report of the Commissioners...*, Parliamentary Papers (1908), Vol. 24, p. 551.

[100] See Crammond (1907), p. 269.

[101] *Ibid.*

[102] The years' purchase corresponded to the rate of return of four per cent that was just slightly lower than the 4.5 per cent adopted for British foreign assets, because the returns that could be obtained at home were generally considered to be lower than those available abroad. This was also due to the composition of British debts which were mostly highly liquid. It is worth noting that Crammond made no allowance for very liquid debts, as for example bank deposits held by British residents abroad, even though the amount of these debts was not totally irrelevant and could therefore have completed the survey of all of Britain's assets and liabilities towards the rest of the world (see note 143 in chapter 1).

[103] The difference is about 3.2 per cent more for the evaluation at market prices which stood at £3,220 million as opposed to the £3,150 million at nominal values. Table 2.7 did not appear in Crammond's paper, but has been constructed by elaborating Crammond's information, including the rate of four per cent chosen by the author on the basis of what was said in note 102.

[104] See Crammond (1911).

[105] *Ibid.*, p. 45.

[106] On this part, see *ibid., passim.*

[107] There was no subdivision into sectors in this article.

[108] See *Fifty-third Report of the Commissioners...*, Parliamentary Papers (1910), Vol. 36; the exact figure was £88,837,393. *Ibid*, p. 1000.

[109] See Crammond (1911), p. 44. It is important to appreciate the essential role played by the rate of return applied to all types of income. To make this point clearer, it is sufficient to recall that the choice of different rates, such as 4.5 per cent and 5.5 per cent, would lead to estimates of the stock of capital abroad equal to £3,956 million and £3,236 million respectively. It should also be remembered that in his previous work Crammond had chosen a rate of return of 4.5 per cent on the whole stock of capital estimated at its nominal value to determine the flows of income from foreign investments for 1906; see p. 94.

[110] *Ibid.* p. 47.

[111] The balance of payments for the year 1910 was not presented with a clear indication of all the items in such a way that its balance could be calculated or, at least, approximately estimated. *Ibid.*, pp. 51-58.

[112] Given a rate of return of four per cent on the nominal value of foreign capital present in Great Britain, the value of x can be calculated at £375 million with a simple proportion (325:13=x:15). If the general upward tendency of the rates of return were taken into account and the rate of 4.2 per cent applied, the stock of foreign capital would fall to £357 million.

[113] This is the difference between the gross stock of British investments of £3,722 million and the stock of foreign capital accumulated in Great Britain equal to £375 million, according to the first estimate in the previous note.

[114] See Crammond (1912), pp. 420-425; (1914), pp. 798-807; (1915), pp. 205-206.

[115] See Crammond (1912), p. 421. It was on this occasion that he expressed his reluctance to make a complete estimate of the international accounts of Great Britain. As he wrote, 'It is quite impracticable to hope to submit a statement which will show an exact balance, because there are so many items which enter into the adjustment of the trade balance for which no reliable data are available'; *ibid.*

[116] According to Crammond's questionable approach, this figure coincided more or less with the total value of the subscriptions of foreign securities, although he was aware of a possible difference with the sum actually paid up; see Crammond (1907), *passim.*

[117] See Crammond (1912), p. 421. In point of fact Crammond did not give much information in this article about the sources of the values he gave to the items in his table, including those just mentioned in the text.

[118] See Crammond (1914).

[119] See *Fifty-fourth Report of the Commissioners....*, Parliamentary Papers, 1911, Vol. 29, pp. 239 ff. There are some small inaccuracies in the figures of the various currency inflows used by Crammond.

[120] For the first three items of identified income Crammond applied Giffen's years' purchase of 25 for government bonds and 20 for other securities and railway companies. For the residual item Crammond applied a multiplier of 15. Giffen had, in fact, introduced a residual item to take account of the income that had escaped identification and therefore was not included in *Schedules C and D;* the multiplier in this case was ten (see section 2.2).

[121] See Crammond (1912). The actual estimate was £2,936.8 million, the sum of some items in his Table on p. 424.

[122] *Ibid.*, p. 425. In the absence of precise indications from Crammond the estimate probably referred to the end of 1911 more or less.

[123] Crammond's estimate of £20 million for the income produced by foreign investments in Britain can be used to estimate their net stock in 1911 (see p. 74).

[124] See Crammond (1914).

[125] *Ibid.*, pp. 798-799.

[126] See *Fifty-sixth Report of the Commissioners....*, Parliamentary Papers (1913), Vol. 28, pp. 858 ff. Crammond's table contained, among other things, a rather significant error, because he attributed the sum of £50.828 million as the annual income of the item 'Foreign and colonial securities and coupons' instead of £40.829 million as indicated in the *Report*. See Crammond (1914), the Table on p. 803 and Table 110 in the *Report*.

[127] The broad description of the residual item (Income not brought home...) was less convincing than the one that Crammond had used in his previous work, where he had made a detailed calculation of the domestic wealth of only England and Wales. Here the heading of the item had contained two expressions, 'not brought home' followed by 'or not included above', which accounted more precisely both for the income hidden from the Inland Revenue because it was 'not brought home' and for the income declared to the Inland Revenue, but not identified because it was hidden in a miscellaneous aggregate. See Crammond (1912), p. 424.

[128] See Crammond (1914), p. 803.

[129] Crammond himself had shown that he was aware of this when dealing with the estimates of British overseas investments in the construction of the balance of payments of the country, as mentioned above. As for the calculation of the net wealth, see what has been said in note 123.

[130] See Crammond (1915). The two preceding articles of 1907 and 1911 that were published in the same journal were explicitly cited by Crammond, who ignored, however, his other two contributions of 1912 and 1914 examined above; *ibid.*, note on p. 205.

[131] *Ibid.*, p. 205.

[132] *Ibid.* This estimate by Crammond appeared in his next work; see Crammond (1917), pp. 32-33.

[133] The other piece of interesting information that he gave was the average annual income from these investments, which according to Crammond could be estimated at about £200 million, equal to an annual return of about 5.12 per cent. See Crammond (1915), p. 205. On the question of the yield of British foreign investments, see, among others, Lehfeldt (1913, 1914, 1915) and Edelstein (1976).

[134] In fact, Crammond wrote generically, 'On the eve of the outbreak of war'.

[135] These problems will be discussed further in section 2.4, quite independently of Crammond's estimate.

[136] See Paish (1909).

[137] *Ibid.*, pp. 466-467. The references for what follows are also to be found in Paish's paper.

[138] Paish did not mention what criteria had been used in these documents to evaluate various investments or to estimate the publicly known capital of private property. Nor did he mention any precautions taken to avoid double-counting in the estimates. However, there can be no doubt about his being aware of the problems involved in making these measurements (see section 3.2).

[139] In this work we will not dwell on the various qualitative aspects (sectors, geographical divisions, etc.) Paish highlighted.

[140] See Paish (1909), p. 475.

[141] See p. 73. Of course these percentages refer to quantified income from investments; other sources of foreign income, such as overseas bank deposits or capital invested abroad privately, are mentioned but not specifically quantified in the table by Paish, who just indicated a sum 'amounting to several hundred millions of pounds'. For the table, see Paish (1909), p. 472.

[142] *Ibid.*, pp. 472-473.

[143] See Tiberi (1988), chapter 2.

[144] The year was measured from July 1 of one year to June 30 of the following year. Paish gave no exact indication of whether it included issues made only in London or on all British markets.

[145] Other objections can be made about his approach, as happened in the rest of the discussion on Paish's work. For example, the difference that existed at times between the capital subscribed and that actually paid up; the presence of subscribers who were not resident in Great Britain or foreign purchasers of securities subscribed initially by British citizens; the total number of issues of securities resulting from a simple transformation of capital already held by private individuals. At the same time, it is worth noting the general consensus on Paish's estimates expressed by Crammond, Beaumont and Dilke who, with the benefit of their experience, made valuable contributions to the discussion. Lastly, Paish's own remarks in the discussion should also be noted because they provided useful information about his work. See Paish (1909), pp. 481-495 and later sections 2.4 and 3.2.

[146] See Paish (1911).

[147] *Ibid.*, p. 187.

[148] It has already been pointed out that these referred to the financial year ending March 31, 1907; see p. 77.

[149] See Paish (1911), p. 197.

[150] *Ibid.*, pp. 186-187. Unless Paish's hint can be considered as an explanation when he spoke of 'at least' £455 million for subscriptions made over the three-year period.

[151] The silence of Crammond and Paish on the subscriptions of capital made directly overseas by British residents is disconcerting. Although this capital may not have amounted to a particularly significant sum, it was mentioned in the pages of *The Economist* of the time, where allusions to the closely connected question of tax evasion were also made. See, for example, *The Economist* (1911c), p. 393; (1911d), p. 442.

[152] See Paish (1911), p. 187.

[153] In this sense it was correct to exclude from the estimates the value of the shares sold to their sellers at the time of issue (the so-called *vendors' shares*), as Paish pointed out at the end of the statistics on issues (*ibid.*, p. 172), and also the value of issues made to transform old loans into new loans (*conversion loans*). However, no similar allowance was made for the securities issued because their owners simply wished to change the nature of their previous assets without further expenditure.

[154] The issue of securities representing new investments underwritten on the London market over the three-year period 1908-1910 really amounted to about £517 million, whilst those of British ownership recognised by Paish (*ibid.*, p. 171) were correctly reduced to £455 million, as we have just seen.

[155] See Paish (1914).

[156] The table did not appear in this form in Paish's article, but it has been laid out using the information it contained. It is well to remember that the figure for 1907 corresponded more or less to the estimate of the financial capital owned, without the addition of capital invested privately or the deduction of capital owned in Great Britain by non-residents. Paish also provided information on the issues in 1907 which had been ignored to avoid double-counting, at least partially. The subscriptions for which Paish calculated the round figure of about one million pounds were calculated at issue prices, except for *conversion loans* and *vendors' shares*. Paish finally stated (*ibid.*, p. v) that 'the total is not less than £4,000,000,000', of which at least £300 million can be attributed to private investment.

[157] *Ibid.* As a matter of fact, the figure obtained from the sum of the amounts indicated for securities was £3,731,761,660, therefore £17,100,660 more than the figure of £3,714,661,000 given at the bottom of his table. This difference was ignored by Paish, probably because it was so small.

[158] In a fairly recent work, for example, an expert on this subject used Paish's three articles as a basis for his own research on the aggregate and disaggregated size of Britain's foreign investments in the years immediately preceding the First World War. See Corley (1994).

[159] This opinion will be discussed again later (see section 3.2) when the criticisms of Paish's work made by Arndt and more recently by Platt will be taken into consideration.

[160] See section 2.3.

[161] A quick glimpse at the issues of *The Economist*, the *Journal of the Statistical Society* or other specialist journals is sufficient to find occasional brief references to the volume of wealth accumulated abroad by Great Britain, especially in the form of securities. In fact, both official and unofficial publications provided an increasing amount of information about these, though there remained the problem of the quantification of international wealth that was not handled on the Stock Exchange.

[162] See London Statistical Society, (1827).

[163] *Ibid.*, p. 112.

[164] See *The Economist* (1870), p. 64. This piece was the exact copy of the article that had appeared previously in the *Money Market Review*.

[165] *Ibid.* The estimate that was proposed for all income from total investments in this article was of at least £28.5 million, although the author says (*ibid.*), 'We believe that this is considerably under the actual amount'.

[166] See Nash (1881), Table 1 and Appendix. This was the third edition of a work on all investments in both domestic and foreign securities. The part containing data on foreign investments had appeared anonymously in the *Bankers' Magazine* (1881).

[167] See Nash (1880), pp. 2-3. Nash also edited some editions of *Fenn's Compendium*, an important publication on British and foreign financial affairs.

[168] In actual fact, there exists a difference of £15 million between the totals in the table published in the *Bankers' Magazine* and the one in the third edition of the *Short Inquiry*, which was not explained by the author. This corresponds to a percentage that is well below one per cent of the total, but it rises to about three per cent if it is calculated for foreign investments only.

[169] The original table gave a total sum of £3,450 million that were mostly domestic financial assets. It included, however, a residual item of £400 million that was included in the table in the book. According to Nash's exemplification, this item also hid a quota of foreign wealth that could not be quantified separately. See *Bankers' Magazine* (1881), Table on p. 158 and Nash (1881), Table on p. 133. According to the criteria on which it was built, the total figure given in Table 2.10 represented an underestimation of the foreign assets of Great Britain. This is so, even if Nash himself had to admit that 'the nominal capital is no

adequate measure of a nation's debts'. See *Fenn's Compendium* (1883), p. XIV, as recalled in note 4.

[170] The figures given appeared in a table in Nash's book which was published shortly after the article in the *Bankers' Magazine*. See Nash (1881), Table on p. 133.

[171] See Nash (1881), p. 133.

[172] As documented by other authors, the Stock Exchanges operating in Great Britain increased both in number and size from the 1890s onwards without, however, seriously challenging the supremacy of the London Stock Exchange; see, among others, Cottrell (1975), pp. 24-25 and Edelstein (1982), Table 3.2.

[173] See *Bankers' Magazine* (1881), p. 158. An approximate estimate of the amount of foreign public debt securities quoted on the London Stock Exchange had been published in the *Commercial History and Review of 1869*, another supplement of *The Economist*.

[174] See Harris (1896), pp. 99-101.

[175] *Ibid.*, p. 100. The modest nature of Harris's estimate, at least from this point of view, was unquestionable, because nothing of any importance had happened in the years since Giffen's measurements to justify the halving of the sum attributed to private investments.

[176] See *The Economist* (1909a), p. 376.

[177] *Ibid.*

[178] *Ibid.*

[179] In fact, even though there is no precise information on this, the temporal reference of the two estimates should be quite close to the date of the publication of the journal and, therefore, it is reasonable to suppose the data refers to the end of 1908. It has to be remembered, however, that this magazine later proposed Hirst's estimate of £2,332 million for the stock of British international investments in the year 1909. Although this estimate was 'a minimum', as pointed out by the author, it was obtained by applying the method of the capitalization of the current income (see pp. 67-68).

[180] See *The Economist* (1909a), p. 376.

[181] From a quantitative point of view, the most important destinations can be considered to be the United States (£485 million and £400 million respectively), Australasia (£321 million and £450 million), Canada and North America (£305 million and £300 million), Argentina (£254 million and £300 million); *ibid.* The debate about the stock of British capital invested in India was held in *The Economist* with Keynes (1909a), p. 454 and (1909b) pp. 983-984, as well the authors of the two estimates, that is Beaumont (1909), pp. 520-521 and an anonymous *correspondent* (1909c), pp. 770-771. For a careful geographical classification of direct investments (as defined today), see Corley (1994), Table 3.

[182] See Speyer (1905), p. 369. The lack of empirical support emerged also in the debate that followed Speyer's conference; *ibid.*, pp. 392-393.

[183] See Hobson (1963), chapter VIII.

[184] For example, Hall considered this quota to be too high for the period 1895-1899 and too low for the last years of the series; see Hall (1957), p. 62. It can be supposed that, even if Hobson's series is unreliable for single years, it could be useful for giving a reasonable idea of the stock at the end of the period when the over- and under-estimates could be considered to compensate each other. In any case Hobson should be given credit for having understood the importance of the imperfections in the market to explain, at least in part, the presence of financial investments across various countries; see Hobson (1963), p. 234.

[185] In fact, information on the history of the securities was given in *The Economist*, as well as the *Investor's Monthly Manual* and the important annual supplement *Commercial History and Review*.

[186] This observation was also made by Simon, a great scholar of this subject, in an article which will be discussed later. See Simon (1967), p. 36. Naturally the most significant variable was the *called* capital rather than the nominal or issue value of the securities. For a

discussion of the mechanisms of the floating of securities on the British Stock Exchanges, see *The Economist* (1872), pp. 48-49 in the supplement *Commercial History and Review*.
[187] It is reasonable to suppose that this list, although at times very long, was incomplete and contained incorrect indications of foreign securities and domestic securities; on this point see, for example, Hall (1957), pp. 60 ff. It is worth noting the different heading used for the columns of data in the *Investor's Monthly Manual*, which referred to Great Britain, and in the *Commercial History and Review*, which referred to England only. The correct heading appeared to be the one in the *Manual*; however, the possible lack of data from British Stock Exchanges not actually located in England would have had a very limited effect on the total.
[188] There is some uncertainty here which is caused by Hobson's remarks about the area of the markets the data refers to: London, England or Great Britain. In fact, the *Investor's Monthly Manual* quoted by Hobson attributes the data to Great Britain (see note 187).
[189] See Hobson (1963), Table on p. 219. The column containing the data on the issues of domestic securities is of no interest here and therefore has been omitted from the table. Furthermore, the data on the export of capital in Hobson's original table has already been presented in Table 1.4 above. The information on the export of capital for the year 1913, which was missing in Hobson's original table, has been included here as indicated in note 54 of chapter 1.
[190] Some of these remarks could also refer to the measurement of capital actually invested in the country.
[191] On this point, which is generally neglected by scholars, see Kindersley (1931), p. 376.
[192] See Hobson (1963), pp. 209-210. On the specific question of the *conversions*, it is worth remembering the effort made over the years by those compiling the data to identify the conversion issues. The conversion issues then had to be divided into those that can be strictly defined as *conversions*, that is, they did not involve an actual expenditure of capital (*swap conversions*) and those that required an allocation of new capital (*export conversions*). See Hall (1957), p. 65 and Simon (1967a), p. 39. Hall spoke about *conversions* again (1958, *passim*) in response to the remarks made by Cairncross (1958, *passim*) about his 1957 article.
[193] Hobson, in fact, also included a graphic representation in his comments about the trends in the export of capital and the issues at home and abroad. See Hobson (1963), chapter VIII. On this point, see also pp. 95 ff.
[194] See Jenks (1971), p. 2.
[195] See Marshall (1834), p. 120*b*.
[196] See Jenks (1971), p. 64 and note 62 on pp. 356-357.
[197] Jenks, however, did not fail to express his scepticism about Bowley's estimate of Britain's stock of international wealth, which was more than twice the figure (£550 million) at the same point in time; see *ibid.*, p. 413. On this point, see section 4.2 below.
[198] See Jenks (1971), p. 335.
[199] At the bottom of the table Jenks himself (*ibid.*, p. 425) described the difficulty of dealing adequately at an empirical level with the problem of the partial issues (*partials*) that has already been mentioned, because the official sources did not give indications about the quota assigned to each market. Furthermore, neither the issues on other British Stock Exchanges nor possible subscriptions by non-residents were taken into consideration. Possible successive movements of the issues, such as refunds, defaults and purchases by non-residents, were also neglected. There were no indications about the stock existing at the end of 1859, nor on the volume of the flows of capital invested outside the financial markets. And lastly, the evaluation criteria adopted for the various parts included in the table are not clear.
[200] See Thomas (1967), p. 5.

[201] See Jenks (1971), Appendix D on p. 425. Jenks later presented the disaggregated series of securities issued by private companies that were in a column of an earlier table; *ibid.*, Appendix E on p. 426.

[202] See Ayres (1934).

[203] *Ibid.*, Table 7 on p. 38.

[204] *Ibid.*; the data in *The Economist* came from its supplement, *Commercial History and Review*: (1905), p. 6 and (1915), p. 333. Some changes have been made to the original table, such as the heading, the number of columns and some convenient rounding of figures.

[205] Cairncross (1975), pp. 182-186. Cairncross also mentioned a concise estimate of about £1,100 million for the end of 1880 (*ibid.*, p. 183). His estimate for 1870 has already been discussed (see section 1.5.3), whilst his 1885 estimate was almost the same as the one obtained by Giffen with the capitalization method, which included direct investments (Table 2.2).

[206] See Hall (1957, 1958, 1963, 1968).

[207] The heading favoured by the *Commercial History and Review* is 'capital created and issued', which stands together with the term 'actual money calls' to account for the funds that were actually paid up by underwriters. See the series in the annual supplement of *The Economist*.

[208] A very frequent case that has already been pointed out (see, for example, note 153) was the transformation of a firm into a joint stock company that led to the purchase of quite a large share packet by the firm's seller(s), the so-called *vendors' shares*, which the Stock Exchange's documentation tried to quantify. See Hall (1957), *passim*. It is easy to discern the repetitive nature of some of the criticisms levelled against the measurements proposed by different scholars.

[209] Among those taking part in the debate on this subject, other than Hall himself (1957, 1958), we can mention Lenfant (1951), Cairncross (1953, 1958) and Edelstein (1982).

[210] See Hall (1963, 1968), *passim*.

[211] See Hall (1957), Table II. The table is re-presented here only in part, with a changed heading. The presence of two figures for 1899 arises from the overlapping of the sets of figures in *The Economist* up to 1899 and of Ayres's series from 1899 onwards.

[212] See Segal and Simon (1961).

[213] See Simon (1967a, 1967b).

[214] See Segal and Simon (1961).

[215] The publications of the UNCTAD are worth noting on this question. Just after the end of the Second World War an official publication of the UN already stated, 'Direct investments – or "entrepreneurial" investments – [...] differ from so-called portfolio investments in that they involve the control of the foreign enterprise in which the investment is made'. See United Nations (1949), p. 18. On the other hand, Segal and Simon's definition seemed to suit the approach adopted by the authors of the time, as we have seen, for example in Crammond and Paish (see section 2.3).

[216] See Simon (1967a, 1967b).

[217] For the article published with Segal, the *Investor's Monthly Manual* was simply integrated with the *Stock Exchange Year Book* and *Official Intelligence*; see Segal and Simon (1961), p. 569. Later Simon, realizing the inadequacy of the data in these publications and following the example of Jenks, extended his empirical references noticeably; see Simon (1967a), p. 38. As Stone has pointed out recently, if both Jenks's and Segal and Simon's researches are taken into consideration, more than forty sources were consulted; see Stone (1999), pp. 19-20. It is possible to have an idea of the corrections introduced after Segal and Simon had consulted more publications by comparing the figure of about £1,933 million for *called* capital (Segal and Simon (1961), Appendix) with the

figure of approximately £1,700 million (Simon (1967), Table 2) for the period 1865-1894 covered by both works.

[218] See Edelstein (1982), pp. 15-16. This identity would need a further adjustment for the movements of bullion and the evaluation criteria of the individual items, especially if the aggregate series is being constructed over a number of years. For an interesting discussion on this subject, see Lenfant (1949), *passim*.

[219] See Simon (1967a), p. 35. And he had to add that he could not take into account the transfers of securities to non-residents, the redemption of financial debts and the issues of British securities abroad. Neither Simon, nor indeed many other authors, gave any importance to the sum of foreign financial assets lost through default by private and public debtors. On this question, in addition to the information provided by *The Economist* (see note 185) and its supplements, see Feis (1974), pp. 11-17. On the working of the British financial market at the beginning of the 20th century, see Lavington (1921) and de Cecco (1971, 1974, 1979).

[220] See Simon (1967b), p. 282.

[221] There is still some ambiguity between the nominal value and the issue value of the securities in this definition, which can be resolved in part, but not entirely, by looking carefully at the tables presented in the *Investor's Monthly Manual*. See Simon (1967a), p. 36 and notes 186 and 218. In fact, the term *created* capital is used by scholars, including Simon, in such a way as to avoid the other distinction made by the magazine between *created* capital, referring to newly formed firms, and *issued* capital, referring instead to the new issues of already existing firms. On the question of definitions, it is interesting to note Simon's preference for the term *called up* instead of *called*, which is used by other scholars.

[222] In the debate on this subject, Stone (1999), p. 33, always aiming at ever greater precision, rightly notes that the requests for the payment of capital underwritten could also have remained unanswered, thus affecting the actual amount of British capital exported.

[223] Hall had already illustrated the usefulness of a careful examination of the sources for the actual amount of *called* capital; see Hall (1957), *passim*.

[224] *Ibid.*, p. 4. Hall had concentrated on the specific case of mines; see *ibid.*, p. 63.

[225] This ratio is about 95 per cent, if just the years 1865-1894 are taken from Simon's 1967 article to compare the value of the ratio over a period of a similar length. On the particulars of this evaluation, see Simon (1967a), *passim*.

[226] See Simon (1967a), *passim*. On the quite substantial presence of foreign-owned British capital, believed to be in the order of £100-200 million at the time of the 1914-1918 war, see, among others, Thomas (1967), pp. 6-7; Davis and Huttenback (1985), p. 33 and Stone (1999), p. 32. It was only after the First World War that some scholars focussed more directly on an estimate of this important aggregate; see Kindersley (1929), pp. 10-11.

[227] On the persistent difficulty of obtaining data on this specific aspect, even after the First World War, see Kindersley (1929), p. 82 and Royal Institute of International Affairs (1937), pp. 337 ff.

[228] It is sufficient to recall the long list of assets that could be attributed to British residents in the pages of the *Report of the Commissioners* (see p. 70). On the specific part of direct investments in the stock of British foreign investments, see, among others, Svedberg (1978) and Corley (1994). On the definition of direct investments, see note 215.

[229] For example, it was Edelstein himself who considered a net credit of about £100 million in favour of Great Britain to be plausible, after drawing on the researches of Bloomfield (1963) and Lindert (1969). See Edelstein (1982), pp. 18-19.

[230] As Simon himself wrote (1967a, p. 53), these differences could be explained by the presence of 'movements in outstanding securities, redemptions and the short-term capital account'. Interesting comments on this point can be found in Ford (1958-1959), *passim*.

[231] A similar comparison, which had already been proposed by Hobson (see pp. 85-86), was presented in a graphic form by Cottrell (1975), figure 1 and by Edelstein (1982), figure 2.1. Edelstein commented on it by saying, 'The main drawback of Simon's estimates is that they are valued in nominal terms, not at the actual price paid by the first British purchaser' (*ibid.*, p. 16), which seems unfounded since it refers to Simon's estimates of *called up* capital. With regard to the years taken into consideration in Table 2.15, there are no figures for the years 1815-1864 for Imlah and for 1914 for Simon.

[232] Thanks are due to Francesco Carlucci and Alberto Bagnai of the Department of Public Economics, University of Rome 'La Sapienza'.

[233] This conclusion is derived from the calculation of the simple correlation coefficient, equal to 0.30, as well as the regression of the first differences in Simon's values over Imlah's, with R^2 equal to 0.09 and the Durbin-Watson statistic equal to 2.

[234] This result is confirmed by a co-integration analysis performed following Engle and Granger (1987). The computed CRADF statistic, equal to -4.35, rejects at the 1 per cent level the hypothesis of non co-integration.

[235] See Stone (1999), p. 4.

[236] This variation was also due to simple typing errors in the vast amount of data used by Simon, as Stone admitted (*ibid.*, p. 32).

[237] These qualitative aspects should be dealt with in a future research.

[238] See Davis and Huttenback (1985), p. 31; on this, see also *The Economist* (1911a), pp. 322-323. For later contributions by the two authors, see Davis and Huttenback (1986); an abridged version of this text was published in 1988.

[239] On this point, the statements of the Trade Figures Committee seem to be the most appropriate: (1926), pp. 2 ff. See also Lenfant (1949), part I and Butlin (1962), pp. 405-407.

[240] In fact, these studies also concentrated on the qualitative aspects of British financial expansion abroad, as did Segal and Simon, but they also introduced some new points that are not discussed here.

[241] This implies the particular broadening of the stock that includes these types of issues. On the sources consulted, see Davis and Huttenback (1986), p. IX.

[242] *Ibid.*, Table 1. It should be noted that Davis and Huttenback's last quinquennial period included the year 1914, which had been excluded from some of the previous tables for reasons of homogeneity, even when the data was available.

[243] What Davis and Huttenback (*ibid.*, p. 32) reported as missing, that is 'The finance transferred by non-public companies, by some public companies floating issues on provincial exchanges and by direct investment', also coincided roughly with what Simon mentioned (1967a), *passim.*

[244] In comparison with their objective of measuring financial aggregates that was conditioned by the limited data available, Davis and Huttenback (1985, p. 33) dared to claim, 'The series should be viewed as an index of the capital calls, and the actual totals are almost certainly higher than the figures reported'.

Chapter 3

The Sceptical Positions

3.1 Introduction

By the 1980s anyone wanting to learn about the volume of Great Britain's foreign investments before the First World War had a fairly wide range of useful information at hand, especially in view of the fact that the long historical period under consideration had not provided sufficient documentation, institutional or otherwise, for our scientific needs. This has meant that in the past many scholars have worked on the various estimates discussed above in the attempt to fill that void and propose satisfactory measurements of the flows and stocks of the wealth owned abroad by British residents.

In the process different methods have been adopted, which have traditionally been classified into the three basic methods referred to a number of times in the previous chapters. Nevertheless, as happens with any classification, it can be difficult at times to make all the elements under consideration fit into the various categories. In our particular case, it has been seen that some important contributions, such as Crammond's and Paish's, cannot be said to belong exactly to one of these three methods (see section 2.3). This has not prevented economic literature from providing, even if on a purely conjectural basis, a rich set of evaluations on the trend of Great Britain's foreign investments in the course of the century, and especially before the First World War. Indeed, the profound disruption the conflict had brought to life in many countries has led many scholars to focus their attention on data for the years immediately preceding the war.

The importance of this work, and in particular that of Paish and Imlah, becomes evident when a research aims specifically to estimate the value of the stock of Britain's foreign investments in that period. Although Paish and Imlah applied different methods, they both gave generally converging results. Paish, a contemporary of the period, had adopted a method (see section 2.3) that was marked by a certain degree of eclecticism, even though it remained essentially within the canons of the direct method. This method is to be interpreted in two ways, however; on the one hand, as static, that is, like a snapshot picture of the assets owned abroad by Great Britain at the end of 1907[1] and, on the other, as dynamic, because the estimates presented in later articles,[2] referring to the end of 1910 and 1913 respectively, were obtained by adding the flows of the issues of later years to those assets.[3]

Half a century later, following along the lines of those who had applied the so-called indirect method such as Hobson and Cairncross, Imlah presented within a much broader research work (see section 1.5.4) his own estimate of the same stock obtained as an aggregate of the balances on current account of the British balance of payments.

The estimates, which were quite similar in their final results, were received with widespread approval by experts in the field; in the case of Paish, his reputation is obviously of long standing, even though occasional doubts have been expressed about his estimates (see note 24 of this chapter). Only Platt, however, has enlarged upon these doubts, first with a short article and later in a more systematic work.[4]

3.2 Arndt and Platt

In his first contribution Platt explicitly declared that he aimed 'simply at correcting the overestimation which has arisen from calculations for the holding of overseas *securities* in Britain (i.e. the direct method)'.[5] In fact, he immediately specified that 'the divide [...] between direct and indirect estimates might suggest that indirect estimates themselves are due for revision'.[6]

Before re-examining the data, Platt made some general observations about what had influenced his work, though they are useful for anyone wishing to deal with this topic. In his opinion the reliability of the estimates of the stock of Britain's foreign wealth has to be considered in relation to many other correlated aspects, such as the size of British domestic investments and other countries' foreign investments, the development of financial markets, especially the London market, and the attitude of British investors over the years.

Platt gave a clear description of the main difficulties that the direct method encounters in determining the stock of foreign investments by making specific reference to the flows of security issues which cannot always be inferred from the various sources available. These difficulties included the presence of foreign subscriptions, the difference between nominal, subscribed and *called* capital, the instability of the market prices of many securities, the transfer of property made on the secondary markets and the repayments and defaults of debtors.[7]

These points had always been taken into account by those applying the direct method, such as Hobson, Hall, Segal and Simon, who, in any case, had not intended (as we have just seen in section 2.4) to propose an estimate of the stock of Britain's foreign investments in their researches, as Platt was well aware of. If they had wished to do so, they would have had to overcome the difficulties suggested by Platt and provide an estimate of other possible components of this stock (the so-called direct and short-term investments).

The main force of Platt's criticism fell on the estimate of the stock of foreign capital attributed to Great Britain about the 1870s. It has already been seen that the year 1870 had been chosen by many important scholars, including Hobson and Cairncross (see chapter 1), to begin their reconstructions using the indirect method. However, those applying the direct method (Segal and Simon; Davis and Huttenback) had also started their estimates just a few years earlier in 1865.

The choice of this period as a starting point could be partly random, but it is reasonable to suppose that it had been influenced by the greater amount of information, though still fragmentary, that was available from that time onwards. In fact, this information suggested the presence of a strong growth in British foreign investments in the first part of the 1870s that had to be taken into account in some way.[8]

For the year 1870 Platt concentrated on the estimate of £785 million proposed by Cairncross for 'Foreign securities' alone, of which £459 million accounted for government bonds and £326 million for other assets, such as railways, banks, public services, etc.[9] It was a snapshot evaluation, that we could also call an inventory hurriedly put together by Cairncross before proceeding with the more laborious task of reconstructing the current account of the balance of payments, which he did by following the procedure previously outlined by Hobson, with some changes in two important items (see section 1.5.3).

Hurriedly, however, does not mean superficially. To begin with, Cairncross had referred to various sources of information[10] and later given precise indications about some insurmountable gaps in these sources, as in the case of continental railways. He had talked knowingly of the difficulties arising from the presence of foreign investors and pointed out that most of the government bonds had not been estimated at their nominal value, but rather at their market value, therefore at 'prices well below par'.[11]

At a methodological level he had added an important note on the relevance of cross-checks in this kind of research. As far as his own direct estimate is concerned, it can be vindicated by the results obtained with the indirect method and by those of the estimate of capital income. For the first, in the absence of precise indications by Cairncross, it can be supposed that he was referring to two authors, Seyd and Jenks, who had previously made estimates with the indirect method for the years before 1870 (see sections 1.2 and 1.5.2).

In some parts of their works on the stock of Britain's foreign investments these scholars had actually indicated a sum of £1,100 million for 1872 and £1,200 million for 1875 respectively.[12] Even in view of the fact that these figures did not cover exactly the same aggregates used by the two authors, they did appear to be sufficiently compatible with Cairncross's estimate for 1870, which had to be increased by £250-300 million to cover investments made abroad by British citizens in the five years after 1870.[13]

For the second comparison Cairncross recalled that his estimate for the item of capital income included in the balance on current account for 1871 stood at £42 million. This amount is not far from the figure of more than £43 million that would have been produced with an average yield of 5.5 per cent on the £785 million of capital invested in financial assets alone in 1870 (see above), which would have been perfectly reasonable for that period.[14]

Platt, on the other hand, believed that he had to make a substantial cut of more than £160 million to the £459 million calculated by Cairncross for government bonds and made a revision based on market prices. It was a big quantitative revision, but not very convincing, as the difference between his criterion of evaluation and Cairncross's, which we have just discussed, was not very clear. Nor did he provide satisfactory arguments to explain the big reduction he made to Cairncross's estimate of £326 million in other assets to reach his own estimate of

£200 million.[15] The result presented by Platt as his estimate of the total stock of Britain's foreign capital amounted to £500 million.

This estimate was not only quite distant from Cairncross's used in the comparison, but also from other estimates that had been proposed for the years around 1870 and were quoted by Platt himself. As a consequence, this could lead to serious doubts about a number of other more or less elaborate estimates, including Giffen's (£1,048.3 million for 1875),[16] Hall's (£1,300 million for 1875) and Deane and Cole's (£1,000 million for 1875).[17]

At the same time, however, Platt gave some credit to estimates that diverged from his; on the one hand, the brief estimate in the *Money Market Review* of £570 million for 1870, republished in *The Economist* and already mentioned above (see p. 82) and on the other, Imlah's estimate of £692.3 million for 1870 that had been calculated with the indirect method. Platt commented on this last result by adding apodictically that '"indirect" estimates *must* produce a larger total because they include so many more elements than "direct" estimates', as his own estimate could be defined.[18]

In contrast Platt completely avoided the important question of the flows of income produced year by year by these investments, which had been introduced by Cairncross. The relevance of these flows is quite obvious because there is a direct functional and quantitative connection between the stock of capital owned and the total income obtained yearly. It can be supposed that Platt's silence derived not so much from the embarrassment of having to challenge Cairncross's estimates, but rather from the belief that the estimates of these flows would be implicitly discredited by his doubts about the estimates of the stock of foreign capital.

It should be added, however, that the estimates of this income made by other scholars (Giffen, Hobson, Imlah and Feinstein) are not far from Cairncross's (see section 1.5). But it is also true, as Platt quite rightly said, that 'some estimates are better than others'[19] and their quality cannot be established simply by a majority vote.

It is from this point of view we will now consider Platt's second and more ambitious contribution, that is his book of 1986, in which he made a critical review of the estimates that had been made for the stock of Britain's foreign investments before the First World War, as suggested by both the title and sub-title of the book. Among these estimates Platt took into consideration those made by the most accredited exponents, that is Paish and Imlah.[20]

Paish is considered to be the father *tout court* of the direct method,[21] followed by well known names like Simon, Davis and Huttenback (see section 2.4), though the latter were not 'concerned with the calculation of a stock estimate for Britain's overseas investments at any single date'.[22] In contrast, Imlah is viewed as the elaborator of the most complete series of the flows and stocks of these investments obtained by applying the indirect method, that is the 'balance of payments' method or rather, as Keynes said, and Platt remembered, the 'net investment' method, meaning the 'favourable balance of trade on income account'.[23]

Platt argued that the widespread recognition they both received in official and unofficial literature[24] generally originated from an uncritical acceptance of their results, whereas he believed it was proper to repeat and develop the critical observations made in his previous article.

In general it is fair to say that either method can produce satisfactory results. In the case of the direct method it is a question of identifying the foreign assets, both real and financial, that were owned by residents in a country, either as a result of a survey that can successfully follow each single asset throughout its life from birth to extinction or with a meticulous investigation revealing the assets each resident had stored away in a safe place, so to speak.

Naturally the physical identification of these assets, if it is in fact possible, does not resolve the problem of an economic estimate, since any value – historical, current, nominal or real, where available – can be applied. Certainly, some authors may be less careful about this problem than others and therefore occasional errors or some incongruities can appear in their work. Platt combined a more general critical approach with the more specific criticisms made against individual authors.

He expressed the same criticisms on the direct method that he had made in his article, only more forcefully. In particular, he drew attention to the presence of portfolio assets quoted on British Stock Exchanges but owned by foreign residents, since they were purchased at the time of their total or partial issue or on the secondary market. He also criticized the double-counting or over-estimates caused by the failure to make allowance for *vendors' shares, conversions*, refunds through sinking funds or other instruments, defaults, crossed shareholding and lastly the variations in values caused by fluctuations in the exchange rate and/or variations in prices.

The question is how to interpret these interesting observations made by Platt. Are they to be seen as an important technical warning to all those who apply the direct method or do they act as a premise for him to make a substantial quantitative revision to Paish's estimates and pick up on some of the comments made by discussants at the time of the presentation of Paish's first two works?[25] Indeed, could Keynes have been right when he suggested calling Paish's second work "'Estimated Amount of Capital Subscribed in London" rather than "Estimated Foreign Investments"'?[26]

In point of fact, Platt seems to have chosen the second alternative proposed in the first question and also to have accepted Keynes's opinion. Later he subjected Paish's estimates to a critical scrutiny, especially those for the year 1913, as he considered them to be the total amount of portfolio investments obtained by imperfectly applying the direct method and thus to contain 'instances [...] both of overestimation and of underestimation, of double counts and of elements important to "flow" figures but not to "stock"'.[27] Indeed he proposed a definition of portfolio investments that is no longer used today, but is more in line with the tradition of this type of research, that is 'long-term investment in the form of marketable securities'.[28]

In dealing with Paish's estimates Platt drew on and developed the critical remarks passed by Arndt, a German scholar of that time,[29] who had immediately expressed reservations about the possibility of profitably using the data on the issue of securities published in Great Britain in order to determine both the flows and stocks of the country's foreign investments.[30]

Arndt had shown very clearly how inadequate this documentation was for the following reasons: the failure to consider any investments other than securities, the presence of issues that could enable the conversion of existing investments, the increasingly widespread practice of issues floated at the same time in different countries, the questionable estimate of the actual values transferred abroad and the time gaps between statistical surveys and the moving of funds.

These defects, however, did not concern the main part of Paish's estimate, which had used other means to measure the stock in 1907 (see section 2.3). In any case, Arndt underestimated the precautions that Paish had taken to avoid these distortions when updating the 1907 estimate of the stock with the flows of investments in securities for the years up to 1913.[31]

This question will be discussed later, but first a detailed description will be given of the results proposed by Platt, who had been able to take into consideration not only Paish's work, but also Imlah's.

The corrections suggested by Platt clearly lowered, rather than raised, Paish's estimates and they were accompanied by well-grounded explanations, although they were not always adequately documented. Some are not of particular relevance here, such as the positive and negative variations made by Platt in order to make an exact comparison of the data up to the beginning of the war by updating his own estimate to July 31, 1914.

For the other corrections it is well to distinguish between those corrections intended to modify Paish's estimate for the period up to 1907 and those for the period 1907-1913, although some items in Platt's revision cannot be broken down in this way, because they were presented in an aggregate form over the two periods. Platt hoped this subdivision would focus attention on the two separate estimates presented by Paish for 1907 and 1913 and leave to one side his intermediate estimate published in 1911.[32]

This temporal subdivision introduces a crucial point for assessing the quality of Platt's revision, in so far as it raises the question of how consistent Paish was in his method when he was preparing his two estimates presented within a few years of each other.

Platt listed the items with his revised figures for Paish's estimates that he had obtained by applying either a higher or lower percentage, as indicated below.[33]

Two reductions were made to include the foreign ownership of securities, which represented foreign wealth, because Platt attributed a discretionary percentage to this type of property: one was eight per cent on Paish's estimate for the total amount of issues for the years 1908-1913 of about £1,038 million (see Table 3.2); the other was 15 per cent on Paish's estimate set at the end of 1907, which amounted to about £2,694 million (see Table 2.8). The total of the two reductions corresponded to £487 million, that is £83 million and £404 million respectively. As Platt himself recalled (1986, p. 31), Paish had set the percentage of foreign assets 'of one kind and another' invested in British companies at ten per cent (1909, p. 473). He added in the course of the subsequent discussion that this percentage had been chosen following information received about income subject to Income Tax that had been earned by non-residents on foreign investments originating in British financial markets. As a consequence the question of the presence of foreign capital in Great Britain, even if it was not purely marginal, was dropped from the Paish-Platt comparison and therefore did not contribute in any way to a clearer definition of the net credit position of Great Britain towards the rest of the world.[34]

Another aspect explored by Platt was the presence of issues floated on more than one market, the so-called *partials*. Platt first confirmed Paish's statement that he had made allowance for them in his 1907 estimate, but later argued that Paish's series did not adequately reflect the decline in the importance of the London market, also for foreign investors ('drift'), in this type of operation during the turbulent years between 1908-1913. It was necessary, therefore, to make a negative adjustment of 15 per cent to Paish's aggregate for the period in question (£1,038 million), which amounted to about £150 million.

Attention also needs to be paid to the operations made on the secondary market during the estimation of both the flows and the stocks of the aggregates of financial assets. In Platt's opinion, Paish's evaluation of the total stock of foreign assets for 1907 (about £2,694 million) had not taken them into account. Therefore, yet another negative adjustment of at least five per cent to this figure was necessary, that is about £135 million of financial assets transferred from British residents to non-residents and classified as 'Unidentified foreign repurchases on the secondary market'.[35]

A smaller adjustment concerned the repatriation and redemption of part of the debt in the period 1908-1913, for which Platt used the maximum percentage fixed by Kindersley in the early 1930s for the British economy.[36] Thus, by applying a percentage of 1.5 per cent to the aggregate already used (£1,038 million), a further sum of £16 million had to be deducted.

A larger but less elegant reduction was made by Platt through the item 'Losses and defaults'. In this case he drew on Edelstein's work,[37] which had proposed an adjustment to British credits in the order of £500 million, that is £450 million for companies and £50 million for governments, for the years 1870-1914. After assuming that gains and losses on capital account should be considered to be more or less at the same level throughout the period, Platt reduced Edelstein's figure to £350 million without further explanation.

The last two reductions Platt made are not the result of a proportional calculation, but of the quantification of the persistent gap between nominal (or subscribed) capital and capital actually *called*, which, as we have already seen, had dominated the attention of those applying the direct method (see section 2.4).

Platt used two distinct items to substantiate this phenomenon. With the first he intended to represent the non-payment of capital owed for unsuccessful issues and, above all, the presence of so-called underwriting.[38] With the second he wanted to specifically measure the physiological difference between capital issues and money calls. As Platt pointed out, both items concerned only the flows of financial assets that took place in the last years of the period (1908-1914 for the first and 1908-1913 for the second) and were set at £100 million and £30 million respectively, with a strong dose of arbitrariness. In this way he drew to a close the series of his downward adjustments.

Although Platt made fewer upward adjustments to Paish's estimates of financial assets, they are equally worthy of attention.

The reason for the first adjustment was quite straightforward. Platt wanted to update the estimate of Britain's foreign wealth to the outbreak of the First World War, just as he had done for the items with a downward adjustment. This involved adding the new capital *called* between January 1, 1914 and July 31, 1914 to Paish's estimate which referred to the end of 1913. Platt's estimate, net of the deductions to be made to the figures of the new issues that appeared in official sources, stood at £70 million.

There are two other important aggregates that need to be considered to complete the analysis because they represent the investments made by British residents in financial assets abroad outside the traditional and dominant market of London. These two items, which were on the increase, referred, on the one hand, to British purchases of securities in domestic and foreign Stock Exchanges other than London and, on the other, to the purchases of unregistered securities. The figures proposed by Platt and intended to cover the whole period 1870-1914 were £65 million and £50 million respectively, for a total of £115 million.[39]

After this long but necessary review of the revisions to the figures for financial assets, that is the so-called portfolio investments, there remains just one last important revision to be noted, that is the adjustment to the so-called direct investments. Platt proposed an upward revision to the very rough estimate that had been set at the sum of £300 million in Paish's articles of 1911 and 1914. This aggregate covers a very wide range of assets, including loans, mortgages, other forms of financing, the purchase of land, property, etc.[40] and therefore Platt's proposal of £500 million for this type of investment, £200 million more than Paish's, seems reasonable, even though it is not backed by adequate documentation.

Bearing in mind all the adjustments made, Platt's new estimate appears to suggest a total of £3,132 million for the stock of British foreign investments on July 31, 1914, as can be seen in Table 3.1,[41] as opposed to Paish's estimate of 'not less than £4,000,000,000' for the end of 1913.[42]

If the figures presented in the table are re-aggregated in a different way, even with simple approximations owing to some inexact time references in the revisions, the reduction of 25 per cent suggested by Platt has the greatest impact, amounting to more than £800 million, on portfolio investments which Paish had estimated to be approximately £2,700 million for the end of 1907.[43] Obviously this adjustment made by Platt also affects his estimate of the stock which referred to July 31, 1914, unlike Paish's which referred to the end of 1913.

Platt's work involved a wide-scale revision and therefore inevitably included the work of Imlah, the most representative exponent of those applying the indirect method (see section 1.5.4). Platt expressed his reservations on the method in general and more specifically on some essential aspects of Imlah's estimates.

To begin with, Platt discussed the characteristics of the indirect method by comparing it with the direct method and expressed a balanced and constructive opinion on a possible choice between one or the other:

The argument depends, as much as anything else, on what questions are asked, and what answers are expected.[44]

So, for example, the indirect method

cannot supply an amount for the capital floated in London on a particular date; it does not indicate to which country it went, in what volume and for what purpose; it cannot show who bought the issues, at what rate and when.[45]

Table 3.1 Great Britain's stock of investment overseas, 31 July 1914 (rounded millions of pounds)

	A portfolio	B direct	(A+B) Total
Paish's estimates for 31 December 1913	3,715	300	4,015
PORTFOLIO INVESTMENT			
Reductions			
Foreign share of London subscriptions, 1908-1913	83		
Foreign share of London subscriptions to 31 December 1907	404		
Partials and 'drift'	150		
Unidentified foreign repurchases on the secondary market to 31 December 1907	135		
Repatriation and redemption, 1908-1913	16		
Losses and defaults 1870-1914	350		
Failed issues and deficiencies in underwriting, 1908-1914	100		
Issues less money calls (companies) 1908-1913	30		
Total	(-) 1,268		
Increases			
New issues (colonial and foreign) 1 Jan. to 31 July 1914	70		
British purchases of securities in exchanges other than London	65		
Purchases of unregistered securities	50		
Total	(+) 185		
DIRECT INVESTMENT			
Increase		200	
Great Britain's stock of investment overseas 31 July 1914	2,632	500	3,132

Source: Platt (1986), Table 2.3.

To support this point of view, he recalls Morgenstern's, Kindersley's and Wilkins's opinions (see bibliography) which were expressed in similar terms, even though they were formed in different scientific contexts. He then cited Pollard, whose criticisms appeared altogether too harsh on the scholars who had worked on an estimate of the stock of Britain's foreign investments for the years preceding the First World War by applying the various methods we have discussed.[46]

It is true, in fact, that there was no general convergence of estimates obtained by scholars, especially between those estimates made by strictly applying the direct method, as for example Hall's or Simon and Segal's quoted by Pollard, and Imlah's estimate obtained by using the indirect method. Indeed, the presence of a substantial gap between the evaluations made with the various methods is actually due to some of the difficulties the direct method faces in identifying certain important elements (foreign assets purchased on the primary and secondary markets, the allocation of the so-called *partials*, short-term assets, direct investments, etc.), which Pollard himself mentioned and have already been discussed at length in section 2.4.

As a consequence, this means having to enter into the merits of the work of the various authors in order to verify its quality and avoid resorting to general impressions, as Platt did (see note 18). In fact, when working on Imlah's lengthy calculations, Platt adopted the same analytical procedure followed in his examination of Paish's estimate, except more succinctly. He therefore concentrated on some of the crucial aspects of Imlah's reconstruction of the invisible items in the balance on current account, that is the various components of 'Business services' and 'Balance on interest and dividends'.[47]

In the almost total absence of official or unofficial data these items had been quantified by Imlah with his own adjustments or by using the method of other authors who had worked on this problem. Naturally the remaining gaps were filled by combining the empirical material that each author had managed to collect with a strong dose of discretion, thus reaching a synthesis whose absolute reliability can be considered as somewhat doubtful.

In this situation, however, unless an author can be proved unreliable, any attempt on his part to verify the quality of his own work through comparisons of hypotheses, methods and results of other scholars should be considered positively. And this is exactly what Imlah did. After having chosen to work on a very wide time horizon, perhaps with unwarranted courage, he skilfully and cautiously extended the fragments of information available to the whole period.[48]

Platt, himself, conducted his re-examination of a part of Imlah's work by simply indicating the numerous, apparently randomly chosen, moments with references to percentages, rates, amounts, etc. And so his revisions of Imlah's estimates (see section 1.5.4) were made at 2.5 per cent of the total value of British trade already chosen by Giffen to take into account different financial services in particular and at five per cent of a similar aggregate for profits obtained mostly with business services adopted by Jenks, who in turn had drawn on Bourne. Shipping income was calculated again on the basis of Giffen's freight rates, whilst the computation of income from foreign investments followed the approach suggested by Hobson.[49]

Platt's opinions were occasionally wide of the mark, as for example when he dryly stated, without any explanation, that Bourne was 'an unreliable source',[50] or when he recalled the difficulty of calculating earnings from shipping, of which everybody was well aware,[51] and again when he simply mentioned that the total of

Imlah's items that he took into consideration 'reaches the gigantic sum of £11.5 billion, and the potential for error is therefore immense'.[52]

In point of fact, an error could be with either a positive or a negative sign and could also lead to values that compensate each other. This latter situation, which was not actually documented, was assumed as a useful hypothesis, thus enabling Imlah to present his series as a dynamic reconstruction of the values of the stock without considering the gains and losses on capital account. Admittedly this is not strictly a question of errors cancelling each other out, but rather variations in the value of certain economic items which could be supposed to follow symmetrical trends.

Among other things, this hypothesis, which Imlah made for the whole century of his analysis, was simply confirmed by Platt who did not believe it necessary to revise Paish's estimates, either for the effects of variations in exchange rates or in the market prices of securities.[53]

Having said this, Platt's obviously evasive position on Imlah's work could be explained quite convincingly by the fact that, even in the middle of a discussion of the application of the direct method, Platt himself had to rely on percentages and absolute values obtained by using his own sense of responsibility as a scholar, rather than by following indisputable methodological canons.

In light of these remarks and of the recognition given to Imlah's reconstruction for the years up to 1870 (see p. 122), the following statement by Platt is rather puzzling:

> some day, somewhere, it may be possible to assemble sufficiently satisfactory data from which the 'indirect' method may be rehabilitated.

And even more perplexing:

> If we are to construct what remains the object of this book – a stock figure for British investment abroad on the eve of the First World War – we must return to the 'direct' method and, at least as a starting point, to Sir George Paish.[54]

At this point we will return to Platt's revision of Paish's work, bearing in mind not only his seriously argued case for this drastic adjustment of about 25 per cent of the estimated value, but also the strong reservations expressed by Kennedy and Feinstein about Platt in their reviews of his book.[55]

First of all, there is no reason why Paish's intention to keep an eye on the net foreign wealth of Great Britain in all his papers should be questioned. Paish's almost pleonastic use of the adjective 'net' would appear to indicate his awareness of the existence of quite significant flows and stocks of financial and real assets owned by non-residents in Great Britain, at least for the years before the First World War, which could not be ignored in an empirical study aiming to measure that wealth. Some similar, but not identical, remarks can be found here and there in other parts of his writings, but his general intention was quite clear, especially when some people expressed their doubts about it.[56]

Having said this, however, it seems quite legitimate to reflect on the extent to which Paish remained true to his intention in all his works (see also section 2.3). In his first paper, the procedure followed by Paish seems to have been first to identify all the flows of income coming from British capital invested abroad in both official and unofficial documents. In a second phase, with the help of this important information, he ran through the same sources to list all the components of British residents' foreign portfolios.

Alongside this list Paish drew up an estimate based on the following criteria: market prices for government bonds, the nominal value for other bonds and, for companies, the value of the capital raised and recorded in their balance sheets and therefore not their market value.[57]

As a result the size of the stock was fixed at more than £2,693 million, which can be defined as gross because a part of this wealth was owned by non-residents and produced an income subject to Income Tax in Great Britain and therefore was included in the figures he used from the *Report of the Commissioners*, as Paish pointed out.

On the basis of the research conducted on this subject Paish believed he could reasonably propose a figure of ten per cent of the total and therefore of about £270 million for the part belonging to non-residents. On the other hand, Paish added that there were assets producing income from abroad, such as those grouped as a set of assets under the heading of direct investments that were not represented by securities quoted on the Stock Exchange. Furthermore, these assets were of such a size that he was persuaded to propose a specific stock of £500 million and to state that:

> the figure of 2,700,000,000*l.* of British capital invested abroad was, if anything, an under-statement, but he only wished to place before the members a figure for which he had documentary evidence.[58]

Paish proceeded in a different way with the calculations in his two later works, that is he moved from the snapshot direct method to the dynamic one, but always keeping the tiller firmly directed at the quantification of the net stock of British foreign wealth (see pp. 79-80). Inevitably this change affected the linearity of the procedure. The variations in the stock of 1907 that had emerged from a fairly detailed estimate could in fact be found by checking the movements of the financial assets in the years that followed. However, Paish acknowledged that a fundamental drawback of this procedure was not being able to repeat the previous analytical study, because 'the work of going through 3,000 and 4,000 companies' reports was enormous, and therefore he had to take the new issues of capital as indicating the amount subscribed in the last three years'.[59]

What Paish stated in the course of the discussion of his second paper also applies to his last contribution of 1914, which was even shorter on information about the procedure, but more important as far as its content was concerned, because it included the measurement of the stock at the end of 1913. The outbreak of the war the following year turned it into an historical document, regardless of its specific merits. This should not deter from assessing the quality of Paish's last estimate; indeed it should encourage it. And from this point of view it is only right to point out the inadequate support given by the data, even if, as we shall see, it does not substantially affect the final conclusions he reached.

The intermediate measurement for the stock of 1910 presented in the 1911 paper can, to all intents and purposes, be put to one side, because in his last paper of 1914 Paish practically re-presented the same series of new issues for the years 1908, 1909 and 1910 to update the previous estimate of the 1907 stock (see Table 2.9). The series is given for the whole set of years in Table 3.2.[60]

Table 3.2 Great Britain's flows of foreign investments through subscriptions on financial markets, 1908-1913 (pounds)*

Year	Flows
1908	145,878,300
1909	182,408,050
1910	189,053,705
1911	163,972,455
1912	160,042,544
1913	196,608,600
Total	1,037,963,654

*Calculated at prices of issue, and excluding all conversion loans and shares issued to vendors.

Source: Paish (1914), Table p. V.

The procedure that Paish followed to estimate the stock for the end of 1913 started with the estimate of the portfolio investments which he had prepared for 1907, that is about £2,700 million. To this he added not only the £1,000 million and more that appears in Table 3.2, but also £300 million of 'capital privately placed abroad' so that 'the total is not less than £4,000,000,000'.[61]

In view of this brief statement, it is undeniable that this procedure was carried out as if it were made with the bold thrusts of a sabre rather than with the fine strokes of a foil, but this does not alter Paish's notable conciseness that has been illustrated above. Nevertheless, it is worth noting some important elements. To start with, throughout his second paper Paish was conscious of the need to take account of the presence of foreign capital and proposed once again an adjustment of about ten per cent to the values identified, thus adopting the same percentage he had used in his first work.[62] However, there is no way of knowing to what extent this criterion, correct at least in principle, though controversial in the application of a discretionary percentage, had effectively been maintained in the 1914 measurements, as Paish made no mention of it.

Some rather peculiar ambiguities, however, emerge from a close perusal of this data: for example, the data for 1909 and 1913, but not for the other years, practically coincided with those that the *Commercial History and Review*, an annual supplement of *The Economist*, attributed to the set of issued and *created* securities underwritten by British investors on all home and foreign markets, including the flows directed towards investments inside the country.[63]

At the same time it must be remembered that the total sum proposed by Paish for the years 1908-1913 falls more or less in line with the estimates of other scholars who were later to adopt other methods in order to account for the dynamics of the foreign flows of British capital for the same years (see Table 3.2).[64]

Two other scholars made important contributions which need to be mentioned at this point because they add greater credibility in a more or less direct way to Paish's estimates. Firstly, Crammond, whose work is articulated over a number of papers, was particularly careful to avoid falling into the trap of an estimate based essentially on financial assets and proposed similar amounts to Paish.[65] And secondly there is Feis, who used Paish's estimate for 1913 in one of his works and suggested two upward adjustments to the British assets held in Russia and Turkey, leading in this way to an estimate of about £4,050 million for the stock.[66]

Table 3.3 Estimates of British foreign investments by various authors, 1908-1913 (rounded millions of pounds)

Author	Estimate
Ayres	1,016
Cairncross	919
Feinstein	1,108
Hobson	998
Imlah	1,076
Paish	1,038
Simon	1,108

Sources: our elaboration of data in other tables in the text; Ayres, Table 2.13; Cairncross, Table 1.8; Feinstein, Table 1.11; Hobson, Table 1.4; Imlah, Table 1.10; Paish, Table 3.2; Simon, Table 2.15.

There was also what might be called a small 'reserve fund' available to Paish's estimates which should not be forgotten. He himself had declared explicitly in the course of his first two works that he had not taken into consideration either the value that could reasonably be assigned to British shipping as a partial foreign asset or the value of the assets that were not actually producing income at that time, although 'capital, other than that placed in loans, rarely becomes fully productive until several years after it is expended'.[67]

What this seems to mean is that for reasons that can be imagined but not accepted, Paish had actually produced another sabre blow to the estimate of the stock of British foreign investments in an article on other questions.[68] It was certainly a well-centred hit, since he used his excellent command of the subject to make his synthesis for the years 1908-1913, which was certainly concise, but not sufficiently so to avoid being tainted by a presumed lack of precision in his measurement of *partials*, repayments, defaults, transfers on the secondary market, etc.

What remains of Platt's critical study at this point? Frankly, very little, because the criticism levelled against the years before 1907 did not bear upon Paish's correct approach at a logical level. As for the criticism against the later years, although it highlights a certain grossness in the scholar's work, it has not revealed any particularly relevant errors. For the first period, in fact, since Paish wanted to measure the stock of assets as sources of income up to the end of the last year 1907, it follows that all phenomena preceding that period had to be excluded from the estimate. These included purchases on the secondary market, the allocation of *partials*, the defaults of debtors or the evaporation of loan procedures, all of which Platt had used to build his revision.

The different, but higher, quota of wealth ownership attributed to non-British residents by Platt (15 per cent as opposed to Paish's ten per cent), which led to a correction of £135 million (that is five per cent of the £2,700 million of stock for 1907), could stand logically speaking. But, apart from the fact that there also exist arguments in favour of Paish's estimate, the £200 million of direct investments that Platt himself seemed ready to add to Paish's final estimate could also be interpreted as a way of counterbalancing these discretionary evaluations (see Table 3.1).

3.3 Madden and Foreman-Peck

Madden passed some very pertinent critical remarks on Imlah's work in Appendix 1 of his book about a very specific aspect of Britain's foreign investments.[69] Understandably these remarks only appear in the extensive and well-documented appendix in which Madden dealt with the empirical question of the estimates of Britain's foreign investments which had inevitably emerged as an important topic in the course of his research.[70] These estimates indicated the presence of a larger number of scholars adopting the indirect method, including Imlah, at the time of Madden's writing.[71]

We know that whoever opted for this method, not surprisingly also called 'the balance of payments method', had to cope with a manifest lack of data, especially for the invisible items that constituted a considerable part of the British current account.[72]

Madden gave account of the numerous attempts made by the scholars of the time (Bourne, Newmarch, Seyd, Giffen, etc.) to fill the gaps with their estimates, encouraged among other things by the debate still raging between protectionists and freetraders who had both discovered the then almost unknown and unfavourable trend of the country's foreign accounts as a topic of discussion about the 1870s. But Madden felt obliged to declare as a matter of precaution that the diversity of the criteria and the results proposed should 'be used cautiously in view of the possibility that these investigators were not free from bias'.[73]

Leaving aside these possible prejudices, it has to be said that the difficulties facing scholars lay in the very nature of things and it could have tempted them to resort to an inevitable dose of discretion. For Imlah, however, the scholar closest to our times, it is reasonable to suppose (see section 1.5.4) that the discretionary choices made in the construction of his series were guided by the familiar figures often quoted from estimates that had been made in the past by other scholars for the period he was covering, that is from 1816 to 1913.

The basic values necessary for the construction of the balance on current account, that is the trade balance (exports, re-exports, imports), had already been through a series of vicissitudes that had not left them entirely transparent, even after official sources had adopted merchants' declarations as the criterion for their data from 1870 onwards. Nor could indications from the f.o.b. criterion for exports and re-exports and the c.i.f. criterion for imports be considered as conclusive.

Unfortunately it is not just a question of the inevitable dose of unreliability, inaccuracy and carelessness inherent in human nature, but of the essential fact that research carried out in archives cannot give an absolute indication of the economic-accounting content of the figures indicated by merchants. One example will be sufficient to illustrate the situation: should the value declared by exporters be considered as only the manufacturer's price or that price plus the freight, insurance and other business services up to the time of loading?[74]

A scholar effectively runs the risk of double-counting when he is calculating some of the invisible items perhaps classified under different names (commissions, earnings from foreign trade, etc.) and he fixes a higher percentage to increase the volume of exports or a generally lower percentage to decrease the imports in order to account for the income earned by British residents in the various services accompanying trade.[75]

In particular, in the case of Imlah, it should be remembered that he identified three sub-items in the one specific item of 'Business services' in the invisible account: a) profits on foreign trade and services; b) insurance, brokerage, commissions, etc.; c) net credit from shipping.[76]

As far as the first two items are concerned, Imlah made a very original choice that has no equivalent in the literature (papers, articles, editorials, etc.) on this subject that had tried to quantify this wide and heterogeneous area of the invisible items in various ways.[77] In short, what he did was to apply two different percentages to the first and second sub-items, both of which referred to the total value of foreign trade (including re-exports and excluding bullion movements). The first sub-item included not only those activities connected in some way with the transfer of goods (the handling of goods, banking operations, etc.), but also completely distinct elements (British administrative services paid for by foreign institutions, the savings and pensions of public functionaries working abroad), whereas the second sub-item covered other important aspects of the profession of business and financial services (insurance, brokerage, etc.).

The two percentages adopted by Imlah followed an unusual pattern over the years: for the longest period, 1819-1879, they were at five per cent (after Jenks) and 2.5 per cent (after Giffen) respectively; before and after this period they were revised upwards (1816-1818) and downwards twice (1880-1892 and 1893-1913), although one was always twice as high as the other.[78]

Even in the face of this complex empirical framework invented by Imlah to measure various and often intangible phenomena, Madden's legitimate but insurmountable doubt about whether there is some double-counting in 'Profits on foreign trade and services' appears to be marginal in comparison with the other perplexities that could arise from Imlah's immense work (see section 1.5.4).

Quite independently of Madden, Foreman-Peck recently expressed his own reservations on this particular sub-item used by Imlah.[79] He made a comparison of the Board of Trade's estimates for 1907, 1910 and 1913 (see section 1.5.1) with Imlah's for the same years.

It has already been pointed out (see p. 20) how the Board of Trade's figures deserve attention because they represented the first official application of the residual method to the measurement of the annual flows of British foreign investments. And yet they can only be of limited importance in the debate on the estimates of the stock of these investments.[80]

In fact, the only original aspect of the Board of Trade's contribution was the item concerning freight. For the rest, its balance on current account appeared very schematic and heavily indebted to other sources, such as Giffen and Paish. And following in the steps of Giffen who had moved along similar lines in one of his last works,[81] the Board of Trade proposed to update this estimate and to introduce a new entry called 'miscellaneous items', to which another part of the currency inflows were assigned (see Table 1.6). On the whole, however, the Board of Trade's calculation of the flow realized in this field was noticeably lower than the flow estimated by Imlah.

It is reasonable to suppose that this divergence can be explained by the particular meticulousness of Imlah's research.[82] However, there remain some legitimate questions that Foreman-Peck raised about the size of the sub-item 'Profits on foreign trade and services', which he described as 'arguably the most doubtful aspect of Imlah's reconstruction'.[83]

At the same time it should be noted that the main source of this currency flow had been identified by men of great practical experience, such as McKay and Bourne (see section 1.2), and had also been used by Jenks (see section 1.5.2). At least for one part of foreign trade, this involved, as Madden himself explained 'the assumed difference between the manufacturer's price to the exporter and the exporter's price to the foreign buyer'.[84]

Therefore there exist real and convincing arguments to explain a large part of the credit side of Britain's balance of payments which Imlah measured (see p. 32) by applying a variable percentage to the total value of traded goods.

Of course there are good reasons for expressing legitimate doubts, as indeed Platt did for example. He spoke of 'very slender and subjective grounds'[85] in Imlah's estimate. In any case Foreman-Peck, who was aware of Platt's doubts, worked out a procedure which took into account the fall in currency inflows from 'Profits on foreign trade and services' and led, *ceteris paribus*, to a revision of Imlah's stock of British foreign investments for 1913.

However, he also showed how similar values to Imlah's for the 1913 stock could be reached by making up for the fall in these inflows with an increase in the flows of income from foreign investments under the hypothesis of a higher rate of return than the one adopted by Imlah.[86]

The level required for this rate, that is more than eight per cent, seems somewhat exaggerated in comparison with the set of estimates proposed by other scholars (see note 133 in chapter 2). But, on reflection, it is not unreasonable to suppose that some inflows could be recovered to square Imlah's accounts by revising the rate of return on foreign investments he had applied for the first years of the 20th century. In fact, the amounts attributed to the item 'Net income from overseas investments' in the Board of Trade's estimates used by Foreman-Peck were actually higher than those presented by Imlah for all three years under consideration (1907, 1910 and 1913).[87]

Equally successful at a logical, rather than at a strictly quantitative, level are Madden's critical remarks about the presence of double-counting in Imlah's estimate, because these profits on foreign trade and services can also be found, at least in part, amongst the unidentified capital income that Imlah included in another item 'Balance on interest and dividends'. Drawing on the intellectual ability of Paish and Hobson, Imlah once again (see section 1.5.4) had to accommodate an aggregation of currency flows, which certainly existed but was of an uncertain quantity, resulting from a component of British foreign wealth. And, once more, it cannot be established beyond doubt whether the activities linked to the traded goods identified by Paish among the sources of currency inflows from investments did not also produce 'Profits on foreign trade and services', which Imlah measured separately.[88]

Another controversial point was the third sub-item, that is the earnings from shipping, which have already been mentioned when discussing North and Heston's critical remarks about Imlah's estimate that Platt, in turn, had recalled (see note 51). Madden also dealt with this point briefly, but gave greater weight to Cairncross's measurement which used an index of freight rates in order to take account of these earnings in time, whilst Imlah used an index of import prices that was certainly less appropriate. The difference that can be quantified this time was of £50 million for the years 1870-1890, which is a fairly significant figure because, as Madden pointed out, even if this amount were considered available only from 1880 onwards with a reasonable rate of return of five per cent, it would lead to a difference of £250 million in the measurement of the stock of capital in 1913.[89]

Imlah seemed to have foreseen these criticisms because he expressed his concern about the distorting effect of using an index of import prices which had a more upward dynamic trend than freight rates and could lead to an overestimation of the earnings from shipping at least for most of the second part of the period in his estimate. At the same time he maintained that it was not easy to construct an index of freight rates in the first part of the period owing to the lack of documentation. Nevertheless, the data available in this period suggests a stronger downward trend of import prices than freight rates, thus creating the basis of a compensatory mechanism throughout the whole period of his analysis.

In response to Imlah it could be said that it would have been better to improve the estimates of the single periods rather than rely on the distorted values compensating each other. In the same way certain conclusions about the measurement of capital accumulated abroad by British residents can be reached by collecting pieces from the mosaic of criticisms, just as Madden did.[90] In fact, in an extremely pragmatic approach he suggested adopting Imlah's estimates for 1870-

1873 and Cairncross's for the other years, but with a preference for the more moderate evaluations.

Furthermore, he used Imlah's estimates for both the stock at the beginning of the twenty-year period of his research, that is £390 million for 1860, and the flows throughout the 1860s until 1873, but Cairncross's estimates for the years after 1873, to propose a figure of £1,050 million for 1880 as his own estimate of the stock of British capital invested abroad. This was slightly lower than his 1875 figure that had been valued at £1,070 million in his own eclectic series.[91]

Although the possible effects of these lower figures on the estimates for 1913, particular on Imlah's, are self-evident, Madden did not discuss the question at length,[92] but succinctly wrote:

> It is possible to state with some degree of accuracy whether capital abroad increased between 1870 and 1913 by £1,830m. or £3,275m. with the evidence supporting the former rather than the latter figure.[93]

We feel that we cannot agree with Madden's conclusion entirely, with all due respect for his pungent remarks on some of the components of Imlah's overall plan. From a strictly accounting point of view, it should be pointed out that the total balance on current account for the period between the beginning of 1870 and the end of 1913 was £2,417 million according to Cairncross (see Table 1.9) and £3,340.2 million according to Imlah (see Table 1.10).[94]

Furthermore, Imlah's estimate of the volume of British foreign investments could actually be reached by revising two of his important hypotheses affecting the quantitative results. The first concerned the stock of capital at the end of 1815, the year his study on the accumulation of capital begins. The ten million pounds proposed can justifiably be increased by an appreciable amount (see sections 2.2 and 2.4).

The second involves the invisible items, especially the two sub-items of 'Business services' which Madden discussed in a very forthright manner. It is reasonable to suppose that the percentages adopted by Imlah and others had to be revised, but it is perhaps equally reasonable to suppose that Imlah's decision to eliminate the bullion movements, which were fairly substantial over the whole period, from the calculation of the commissions on the amount of foreign trade had been too drastic. Even then a large amount would still have to be 'recovered' with the flows assigned to 'Business services' among the invisible items.[95]

To sum up, we are convinced that Imlah's contribution should be judged within the context of the literature that has dealt with this subject in different eras and in different ways. This is, in fact, what he did when he was looking for valid points to support his work (see section 1.5.4). In this sense we believe Platt's negative opinion of pooling resources in research in this way should be overruled, not out of any sense of meta-scientific solidarity, but as a statement in favour of a correct method to deal with a very important, but challenging, area of study.

3.4 Conclusions

This chapter has focussed on the scholars who have proposed a downward revision of the values attributed to the flows and stocks of Britain's foreign investments by the most important authors discussed in the previous chapters, and in particular Imlah and Paish. If the revisions were made first to the flows, then the size of the stocks was, as a consequence, affected too; in this case the doubts raised concern the results obtained with the indirect method. By contrast, when the focus of attention was on the stocks, this led to a review of the estimates obtained with the direct method. It should be noted once again that Paish's work, which has also been subjected to revisions, should in actual fact be considered an eclectic approach (see section 2.3), in so far as his estimates were obtained by combining the dynamics of the financial assets with the capitalization of the income flows.

The main interest of this chapter lies in Platt's research work in this field (see section 3.2), which critically dealt with the measurements that in his opinion had overestimated the values of the stocks of British foreign investments at particular points in time before the First World War.

Platt proposed substantial revisions to estimates for both the initial and the final phases of the period he was dealing with, that is from 1870 to July 1914. For the initial year, 1870, he critically revised Cairncross's estimate of £785 million obtained with the direct method, which only accounted for assets in the form of securities, and proposed an alternative estimate of £500 million. Credit has been given to Platt's approach, which intended to question an important stage in the quantitative evolution of Great Britain's foreign investments, but it has also been pointed out why his estimate must, nevertheless, be considered of limited reliability, especially as it was in net contrast with the conclusions reached by other scholars for this period.

For the years before the First World War Platt made a broader and more precise investigation into the results obtained by Paish, who had used a mixed methodology and whose work has generally enjoyed a broad consensus.

However, this general agreement was not unanimous, because Arndt, a German economist and a contemporary of Paish, had already expressed some reservations about his work, which Platt was to draw on and develop. They concerned Paish's estimate of Britain's stock of foreign investments in 1907 and his estimate of the flows for the following years, which he had then used to update the initial figure of the stock to the end of 1913.

These criticisms focussed on the general characteristics of the direct method, whose reliability is questionable (see section 2.4) when it is used to determine either the flows or the stocks of foreign investments, and even more so when it is weakened further by errors made by those applying the method. Information from the financial market about the so-called portfolio investments, which is the very essence of the direct method, cannot directly and accurately represent either the wealth accumulated abroad by the residents of a country or trace year by year the dynamics of that wealth.

Therefore Platt examined Paish's figures very closely and suggested a set of corrections which are mostly downwards, but also occasionally upwards. The downward revisions were made to the following items: the financial assets belonging to non-residents underwritten on the primary market in Great Britain or abroad (*partials*), repurchases on the secondary market, repatriation, redemption, losses and defaults, failed issues and deficiencies in underwriting, and issues less money calls. The upward revisions concerned the financial assets included by British residents in their portfolio, but not reported by Paish for various reasons, and a large amount of the so-called direct investments that Platt believed Paish had underestimated.

The result of this detailed check was a new estimate of British foreign investments which Platt set at £3,132 million on 31st July, 1914 (Table 3.1), a much lower figure than the one of 'not less than £4,000,000,000' indicated by Paish for the end of 1913.

Platt also took it upon himself to revise Imlah's retrospective estimate, which had been reached by identifying the stock of British foreign investments by the indirect or residual method and was fixed at £3,988.4 million. This figure was in fact very close to the one presented by Paish. Platt worked in particular on certain items on current account, namely the 'Balance on business services' and the 'Balance on interest and dividends', which had taken up quite a large part of Imlah's reconstruction and their preparation had involved some rather discretional, and therefore debatable, choices.

Nevertheless, it has been suggested that a careful reading of the documentation on Paish's work, including the debates following the presentation of his first two papers and the numerous endorsements given to it by experts of the subject, provides solid arguments against the critical observations made by Platt. In fact, Paish seemed to be well aware that his task was to reach an estimate of the net foreign wealth owned by British residents and his empirical analysis was intelligently conducted in order to choose the data that was appropriate to the fulfilment of this task, though some minor errors were made.

As for Imlah, it can be confidently said that Platt's doubts are inevitably justified in such a broad analysis that required numerous discretionary moves; nevertheless, the choices Imlah made were almost always backed by authoritative references to the literature on the subject. Admittedly the literature also contains important contributions from other sceptics, as for example Madden and Foreman-Peck, who concentrated their criticisms on Imlah's item of 'Profits on foreign trade and services'.

Imlah's estimate does, in fact, lend itself to two types of comments, both of which are relevant; the first is about the overestimation arising from the percentages on the value of foreign trade and the other about the double-counting of earnings attributed to this item that also appear under another item of capital income, especially the so-called 'unidentified income', according to the terminology of the *Commissioners' Report*.

It has been argued in the course of the chapter (see section 3.3) that Imlah's estimates of the flows for the item 'Profits on foreign trade and services' and consequently their effects on the most important estimates of the stocks calculated annually until the years immediately before the First World War should be accepted as reliable enough and are comparable with Paish's estimates. Although

Imlah's series would appear to have been overestimated in certain aspects, it could recover much of its credibility thanks to the valid reasons given to support an upward revision of the initial stock of £10 million he chose for the end of 1815, as suggested by Foreman-Peck.

In the light of these observations, which have touched all the fundamental contributions made by the scholars engaged in research on the quantitative evolution of British foreign investments, the last chapter of this book will attempt to trace the path that led this country to 1913, a date which is considered almost unanimously by experts of the subject to be crucial because it marks the beginning of the decline of Great Britain's supreme power in the world.

Notes

[1] See Paish (1909). The original crossed and systematic use of information on both the size of the various items of British foreign wealth and of the various types of income that it produced has led us to define Paish's approach as eclectic, rather like Crammond's (see section 2.3).

[2] See Paish (1911, 1914).

[3] We will dwell further on the procedure followed by Paish shortly; see also section 2.3. It should be remembered, however, that the estimate of the annual flows had been made 'at prices of issue, and excluding all conversion loans and shares issued to vendors. See Paish (1914), p. v.

[4] See Platt (1980, 1986).

[5] See Platt (1980), p. 12.

[6] *Ibid.*

[7] See Platt (1980), *passim*. Platt's narration of some emblematic events surrounding foreign securities issued on both British and foreign markets was very interesting and extensive.

[8] It was, in fact, Platt's article that provided evidence of this; *ibid.*, *passim*. He wrote that '1870 has here been chosen in preference to 1875 because the early seventies were a period of intense boom in overseas investment'; *ibid.*, p. 13.

[9] See Cairncross (1953), pp. 182-183 and section 2.4.

[10] He indicated *Fenn's Compendium* and Jenks; *ibid.*, p. 182.

[11] *Ibid.*; however, continental railway companies did not represent a large part of the total.

[12] See Seyd (1878), p. 6 and Jenks (1971), p. 335. In point of fact, Seyd gave roughly the same value for the stock in 1874 (*ibid.*, p. 8). This is not a clamorous contradiction, however, because he attributed a further accumulation of just £53 million to the years 1873-1874; see Table 2.1 and section 4.2.

[13] Cairncross's estimates were of about the same size; see Table 1.8.

[14] On this point it seems legitimate to ask whether Cairncross's estimate of capital income was not reached quite independently of the value of the stock he attributed to 1870.

[15] It is certainly not convincing to criticize Cairncross by picking on one single element from Hall's estimate (1963, Table 4), which generally was not that far from Cairncross's. See Platt (1980), p. 13.

[16] See Table 2.1. Giffen should be remembered as the scholar who made the greatest contribution to the method of capitalizing income from investments to measure the total and the foreign wealth of Great Britain; see section 2.2.

[17] See Platt (1980), pp. 12-13. The data referred to by Platt can be found in Hall (1963), Table 4 and Deane and Cole (1969), Table 71, respectively. This last table also includes data on 1865 and 1885 taken from Giffen, as remembered by the authors.

[18] Platt (1980), p. 14. And he also added, as a warning in advance, 'Indeed, the matching of an "indirect" estimate with a "direct" estimate should more properly be regarded as a cause for alarm than satisfaction' (*ibid.*).

[19] *Ibid.*, p. 10. It should also be said, however, that in the course of his article, but in a different context, Platt gave a list of the rates of return on many securities at that time which appear to be entirely compatible with the average rate of return of 5.5 per cent proposed by Cairncross. To support his own estimates, Cairncross repeatedly insisted on the more advantageous returns available on foreign investments than on domestic investments. The large reduction in the stock suggested by Platt had to be compatible with the figures for the flows of income that it produced. On this topic, see, among others, Kennedy (1974) and Edelstein (1976).

[20] See Platt (1986). As a matter of fact, Platt expressed his own reservations about qualitative (such as geographical and functional) estimates (*ibid.*, part III), which are not taken into consideration here.

[21] It is a good idea to bear in mind the doubts expressed at the beginning of this chapter about a rigid categorization of methodology and what was said in section 2.3. In fact Paish was cited here as being a rather eclectic author as far as his method was concerned.

[22] See Platt (1986), p. 17. Platt appropriately included Kindersley among those who applied the direct method. However, his numerous papers aimed to provide estimates of British foreign investments in the period between the two World Wars, that is at the time he was writing (see bibliography).

[23] The actual expression used by Keynes is consonant with the terminology in vogue at that time (*ibid.*, p. 5). Naturally the method was compatible with the presence of unfavourable balances in some years.

[24] Among others, support for Paish came from the *Board of Trade Journal* (1923), *League of Nations* (1924), *Royal Institute of Economic Affairs* (1937), *United Nations* (1949) and for Imlah from Kuznets (1961), Deane and Cole (1969) and Mitchell (1988).

[25] The first two papers were presented by Paish in meetings at the Royal Statistical Society which traditionally provided for a discussion with the authors. The third paper was an editorial in the *Statist*, an important financial journal in Britain (see section 2.3).

[26] For Keynes's comment at the presentation of Paish's work, see Paish (1911), p. 195 and Platt (1986), p. 9.

[27] *Ibid.*, p. 31.

[28] See Platt (1986), p. 4. Naturally for Paish, as for Platt, the overall estimate had to include the so-called direct investments, the 'capital invested privately that did not pass through a public stock exchange' (*ibid.*, p. 5), which were very difficult to quantify, but certainly were not a modest amount.

[29] See Arndt (1915).

[30] *Ibid.*, pp. 300 ff.

[31] Arndt recalled how Speyer and Gayer approved of Paish's measurement of the stock. Gayer actually considered the estimate to be cautious, whilst Arndt proposed an estimate of about £3,000 million for 1914. Although it was not supported by adequate reasoning, Platt was to propose a similar estimate in 1986; see Arndt (1915), p. 311 and Table 3.1.

[32] See Platt, chapter 2.

[33] *Ibid.*, pp. 57-59. For some corrected items, Platt generically included 1914 as a final year; *ibid.*

[34] A particularly authoritative author on this and other questions was Kindersley (see note 227 in chapter 2), who, after a specific investigation, had set the share of British property at

79 per cent of total financial assets, and not just foreign assets, quoted on the London market in 1926; see Kindersley (1929), pp. 10-11. The unquestionable fall in this share had been in great part due to the expenditure incurred by Great Britain during the First World War. On this topic, see *Parliamentary Papers* (1919).

[35] Like many other scholars, Platt minimized the importance of the secondary market for British investors, who were considered to be interested almost exclusively in new issues; see Platt (1986), p. 53. In any case, the simple transfer of foreign financial assets from one British resident to another is irrelevant, as far as this book is concerned.

[36] See Kindersley, (1931), pp. 378-381. In fact, both the reference percentage and aggregate chosen by Platt did not correspond exactly to those selected by Kindersley.

[37] See Edelstein (1976), p. 298.

[38] In a special appendix Platt illustrated the widespread practice in British markets by which important financial bodies (for example, insurance and trust companies) underwrote securities that were not floated on the market. These bodies operated in this way on commission and then waited, at times for quite considerable periods, for favourable conditions to appear before floating the securities on the market. See Platt (1986), p. 1.

[39] Fortunately the figures in question were not particularly large, but it should be said that Platt was less lucid than usual in this passage. The time reference of these two additions to Paish's packet was not very clear in fact and there is some confusion over direct investments. Platt stated that the £65 million in question allowed 'both for direct investment until August 1914 and for a portion of provincial investment incorporated in Paish's figures, to the end of 1907'. However, he immediately proposed a sizeable adjustment of £200 million to the direct investments without specifying the year or period of reference. See Platt (1986), p. 59.

[40] It is perhaps worth noting that one of the forms of direct investments in Great Britain at that time was what Stopford defined as 'expatriate' investments, that is the sums of capital provided by the home country to its industrious emigrants. See Stopford (1974) and Platt (1986), p. 56. Paish had, in fact, not given many details about the components of these direct investments; see also Madden (1985), p. 364.

[41] See Platt (1986), Table 2.3. Once again in this case some marginal adjustments have been made to the original table.

[42] See Paish (1914), p. v.

[43] See Paish (1909), *passim* and section 2.3 above, especially Table 2.8.

[44] See Platt (1986), p. 18.

[45] *Ibid.*, pp. 18-19.

[46] 'It may, of course, be that by some miracle all these divergences cancelled out, but suspicion must remain that there has been a certain amount of fudging to achieve the recorded overall agreement, especially since the values for the intermediate years differ widely'. See Pollard (1985), pp. 492-493.

[47] See Platt (1986), pp. 20-21.

[48] On Imlah, apart from his main work of 1958, see Tiberi (1992), chapter 4 and section 1.5.4 above.

[49] See Platt (1986), pp. 20-21.

[50] It should be remembered that Bourne had been one of the first interesting analysts of the current account of Great Britain. He had tried to reconstruct its trend in a number of works by integrating the little official data available with his own estimates; see bibliography and Tiberi (1988), section 2.1.

[51] It was on the very question of shipping income that North and Heston (1960) expressed strong doubts about a substantial overestimate in Imlah's series. Platt referred to this source generally, but not on this specific point, in one of his notes (1986), note 80.

[52] *Ibid.*, p. 21.

[53] *Ibid.*, pp. 40-44; however, it should be pointed out that Platt was mainly referring to the last decades before the First World War.

[54] *Ibid.*, p. 22. The authoritativeness of the group applying the indirect method, such as Seyd, Shaw-Lefevre, Hobson, Jenks, Cairncross, Imlah and Feinstein (see chapter 1), does not seem to have curbed Platt's critical tone.

[55] See Kennedy (1987) and Feinstein (1990).

[56] This is the case of the responses to remarks passed during the discussion of his first two works; see Paish (1909), pp. 489 ff and Paish (1911), p. 397 ff. Keynes's observations on the second work have already been mentioned above (see p. 123).

[57] These are the indications given by Paish in the course of the discussion of his second paper to explain the procedure followed in the first. See Paish (1911), p. 197 and p.79 above.

[58] See Paish (1909), pp. 490-491.

[59] See Paish (1911), p. 198.

[60] The difference that existed between the measurements for the years 1909 and 1910 in the two papers is absolutely irrelevant; see Paish (1911), Table on p. 171 and Paish (1914), Table on p. v. This table also contains the estimate of new issues for 1907 (about £89 million), but this information will be left out of later comments that presume the existence of a stock estimate made by Paish in his first work with reference to the end of 1907. It is hoped that at least for this point an obvious duplication can be avoided. The aggregate values of the series given in Table 3.2 appeared in two distinct tables in Paish, based on a division according to geographical area and sector. *Ibid.*, pp. v-vi.

[61] *Ibid.*, p. v.

[62] In this work the figure of more than £516 million for the three-year period 1908-1910 was reduced to £455 million; see Paish (1911), p. 71.

[63] We are talking about one of the most important sources for those applying the direct method (see section 2.4); it is also true, however, that the reconstruction of the data from the *Commercial History and Review* made by Ayres (see Table 2.13) for those years, which represent a particularly dynamic period for British foreign investments, set domestic investments at only 9.5 per cent of total investments in 1909 and 16 per cent in 1913. Paish's consequent overestimate would, therefore, amount to less than £50 million.

[64] It is worth noting that the choice of the issue price and the exclusion of *conversions* and *vendors' shares* made by Paish certainly helped to keep his estimate under control.

[65] See Crammond (1907, 1911, 1912, 1914, 1915), as well as section 2.3. To check on the consistency of Crammond's methodology, see especially his article of 1907.

[66] See Feis (1974), pp. 23-24.

[67] See Paish (1909), p. 473; for Paish's other estimates that persuaded him to declare that 'If he had erred it had been on the side of conservatism' (*ibid.*, p. 494), see Paish (1909, 1911), *passim*. Cairncross was among those who were sceptical; when writing about Paish's estimates, he said, 'His calculations probably had an upward bias'. See Cairncross (1975), p. 186.

[68] In fact, whilst the first two works concentrated on Britain's foreign investments, the third, as suggested by the title itself, had a broader subject matter which also concerned foreign investments, but not exclusively; see Paish (1914).

[69] See Madden (1985).

[70] *Ibid.*, pp. viii-ix.

[71] Imlah's article of 1952 (see bibliography), and not his 1958 book, was taken into consideration. This happened because the Appendix had obviously not been reviewed by Madden at the time of the publication of his book, although it had originally been prepared for a Ph.D thesis at Cambridge (UK) in 1957; as for Imlah's estimates, however, his basic data underwent only very marginal revisions in the move from the article to the book.

[72] See Tiberi (1984, 1988, 1992).

[73] See Madden (1985), p. 345. The references given in the previous note may also be useful for this subject.

[74] It should be borne in mind that similar examples can be proposed both for imports and re-exports; *ibid.*, pp. 344 ff. on this topic. See, among others, Deane and Cole (1969), *passim*.

[75] Some scholars have preferred to proceed with one single percentage for the total value of traded goods.

[76] See Imlah (1958), pp. 47-56 and section 1.5.4. above.

[77] See Madden (1985), Appendix 1 and Tiberi (1988), chapter 2.

[78] See Imlah (1958), pp. 47-48. Imlah should be given credit for trying to support his long research with plausible explanations, even if inevitably they were not overwhelmingly convincing. Among these explanations, the need to take account of similar operations made by foreigners with the subsequent outflows of currency for Great Britain. See section 1.5.4.

[79] See Foreman-Peck (1989), Table 2 and *passim*.

[80] For these variables, the Board of Trade more or less used Paish's estimates; see Board of Trade (1923), pp. 384-385.

[81] See Giffen (1904). In this paper Giffen collected the set of currency receipts from business services under the one item 'Commissions and brokerage', a fundamental component of that part of the balance of payments, that he himself had called 'invisible exports'; see Giffen (1882), p. 219. Giffen assigned a 'moderately estimated' sum of £20 million to this item for 1902, which was much lower than Imlah's estimates for similar services by British operators (see Table 1.10).

[82] In any case, long before Imlah, Hobson had explored the broad and heterogeneous area of British invisible items, but in greater depth than Giffen and the Board of Trade. Some useful points on this topic can be found in almost all the publications of the period (see bibliography).

[83] See Foreman-Peck (1989), p. 362.

[84] See Madden (1985), p. 353. In fact, before McKay and Bourne, Williamson was the first to note the currency receipts favourable to Great Britain that could be hidden amongst the values of the imports. See *The Economist* (1877), p. 217.

[85] See Platt (1986), p. 20.

[86] See Foreman-Peck (1989), Table 2.

[87] *Ibid.*, Table 1.

[88] Madden's remark about this was not conclusive, because it was theoretically possible to distinguish between the profits earned by the certainly very large number of companies engaged in business services in Great Britain and those earned from investments overseas by similar companies based in foreign countries. See Madden (1985), pp. 363-364.

[89] *Ibid.*, p. 343.

[90] Here we have not dwelt on other aspects of Madden's well documented review.

[91] See Madden (1985), p. 376. It is useful to remember that, firstly, in the period studied by Madden (1860-1880) a comparison between Cairncross and Imlah is possible only for 1870-1880; secondly, Platt preferred Imlah's estimate for the 1870 stock to Cairncross's; and lastly, Imlah's estimates referred to those in the 1952 article and not the 1958 book (see note 71).

[92] Only occasionally did Madden express any doubts about Paish not taking sufficient account of the frequent *conversions* of family companies into joint stock companies quoted on the Stock Exchange in his first work of 1907. This emphasis, however, was not really necessary because we have already seen how Paish was aware of the risk of double-counting on that side.

[93] See Madden (1985), p. 376. On this point, there are interesting results to be found in Foreman-Peck who suggested alternative views of the evolution of the stock of British

foreign investments. These pictures revolve around the estimate proposed by Imlah for the stock of British foreign capital at the beginning of 1816, that is £10 million (see section 1.5.4). This stock was reduced to zero only in two cases of the simulation, whilst in another it was increased to £12 million. See Foreman-Peck (1989), Table 2.

[94] In fact, the figure of £1,830 million proposed by Madden appeared in Cairncross's book, but referred to a period of time that did not go beyond 1911. See Cairncross (1975), p. 184.

[95] The nominal value of gold and silver movements in bullion and coins over the whole period before the First World War was in the order of a few thousand million pounds. See the various annual issues of the *Statistical Abstract for the United Kingdom*.

Chapter 4

The Outcome of a Long
Collective Work

4.1 Introduction

The numerous studies that have been discussed so far all attempt to give a quantitative evaluation of Great Britain's flows and stocks of international investments in the years before the outbreak of the First World War in 1914. Some have concentrated on this specific aspect of the phenomenon, whilst others have broadened their analysis to include equally important elements that, for the sake of simplicity, we can define as qualitative (geographical distribution and/or sectoral composition, type, etc.).

As far as the so-called quantitative aspect is concerned, it has been shown how three basic methods have been adopted over the years by various authors in the elaboration of their estimates. These studies have either centred principally on 1913, the year immediately preceding the beginning of the war, or have covered a number of decades in both the 19th and 20th centuries, with the addition of the years 1911-1913, and in some cases also 1914, to complete the period studied.

The First World War had such an emotional impact on the world that scholars consider it to be an historical watershed. Indeed, most of the literature on the strictly economic issues of the period maintains that the war gave rise to a radically new order in the world economy. It interrupted a process of growing interdependence and integration of the various economic systems within an institutional framework which generally rested on the canons of free trade and of the gold standard, of which Great Britain was its principal advocate. Furthermore, the war created the conditions that provoked a sharp regression in this process, which would be resumed only after the Second World War and in very different circumstances.[1]

It is reasonable to suppose that the events surrounding the expansion of Great Britain's economy overseas attracted great interest and that the quantification, for single years or accumulatively, of British foreign investments acquired a symbolic significance. In particular, the value of the stock of foreign investments in the possession of various countries on the eve of the First World War has been interpreted, more or less explicitly, as a reflection of their relative economic power. Naturally, the need to further our knowledge means that not only the movement of capital, but also of goods and people, and more generally of other economic indicators, have to be placed correctly in time and space so that other objectives can be pursued.[2]

Although the focal point of this work remains firmly anchored to the activities of Great Britain as an international investor, it also wants to develop the point raised at the end of the previous chapter about the presence of a large number of scholars engaged in this subject. By reviewing their work it is hoped to bestow greater historical depth on the topic and, at the same time, to recover a sense of the combined effort that has been made by these scholars, including those slightly discordant voices and regardless of the method adopted by each individual author, and thus give greater overall empirical validity to their work.

To do so, the various estimates proposed need to be examined carefully in order to ascertain whether it is possible to realistically trace the trend of British foreign investments. A good example was set by Staley and by a leader writer of *The Economist*, who as usual remained anonymous; both of them believed it appropriate to remember in their works some of the significant moments of that collective legacy mentioned above.[3]

For the sake of clarity, it has been decided to present the material that has been collected and discussed so far in two distinct periods; the first goes up to 1870 and the second to the outbreak of the First World War. For technical reasons this choice is not entirely arbitrary. In fact, from 1871 onwards, as recalled above (see section 1.2), all international trade flows were recorded in the *Annual Statement* according to the value declared by merchants, thus providing a valuable empirical platform, at least for those applying the indirect method.

4.2 The points of reference in the years up to 1870

There is in fact no continuous documentation for the first decades of the 19th century; occasionally fragments of information can be found that may not necessarily be considered contradictory, but they nevertheless fail to provide totally reliable indications. This is the period for which Imlah searched, with great determination, for economic clues that testify to the international presence of Great Britain. In order to compute the currency flows produced by capital invested abroad among the items in the balance on current account, it was necessary to quantify the initial net value of assets owned by British residents in other parts of the world.

He did so very cautiously because he was working on a period of time in which the amount of resources actually transferred from one country to another was very limited, at least in its absolute value. This was also true of Great Britain, which actually applied abroad for finance on various occasions, both on behalf of its government and of individual citizens. Indeed, traces of references to foreign creditors can be found in the official documents[4] of the time, though they are contradicted by information from reliable sources which escaped the notice of the usually attentive Imlah.

A good solid introduction to the question can be found with Giffen, whom we have already met (see section 2.2) as an authoritative exponent of the capitalization method, in which the various annual returns are capitalized in order to calculate the total wealth of Great Britain including, as a specific component, the stock of foreign investments.

It is worth remembering that Giffen held the post of Head of the Statistical Department at the Board of Trade for many years, and as such he certainly had access to an unprecedented quantity of data. As for the quality of his professional work, numerous tributes have been made to his vast research work,[5] but it will be sufficient to quote the one that appeared in an article in *The Economist*. Here the author mentioned the names of many scholars of the early 19th century, whose estimates had been acknowledged, though critically, by Giffen in his book on the evolution of the total volume of British capital in the course of the 19th century (see section 2.2). The author of the article remarked that 'the estimates are corrected by Sir Robert Giffen, so that they are the more valuable for comparative and scientific purposes'.[6]

At the very end of the 18th century Beeke proposed an estimate of at least £100 million for British foreign stock. The author can be criticized for the shortage of data he provided, but not for the lucidity of his approach;[7] in at least two passages of his paper there emerges, in fact, a clear perception of the presence of foreign capital as a corrective item in the estimate of the annual income and, consequently, of net British-owned stock.[8] The £100 million he proposed should not be quoted just as a counter argument to the criticisms of overestimation made against the whole of Imlah's series, and in particular in the later years (see section 3.3), but rather as an acceptable measurement of the net foreign wealth of Great Britain at that time.

The next important contribution was made by Colquhoun and it was particularly interesting for two reasons; firstly, because he proposed an estimate of about £5 million as 'foreign income [...] for the support of Proprietors and other Persons residing in Great Britain and Ireland'[9] which, if capitalized with a totally plausible years' purchase of 20, would result in almost £100 million. Secondly, and appropriately, Colquhoun himself made a rather rare quantitative observation, not just about the favourable state of the balance on current account, but also about one of the ways in which Great Britain, particularly at certain times and in certain parts of the world, accumulated wealth overseas.

After listing all the wealth of the British empire, he wrote:

> Of this immense property the Colonies and Dependencies taken from the enemy during the present war, exclusive of ships and other floating property captured since 1792, amount by estimate to £106,917,190! The captures on sea and land may probably amount to fifty or sixty millions more.[10]

It has already been pointed out what an impact, *ceteris paribus*, a substantial increase in the initial stock can have on Imlah's series (see section 3.3) through the systematic growth of the item 'Balance on interest and dividends' and, consequently, of the balance on current account from which, in the indirect method, the annual flows and stocks of British foreign capital are derived. Therefore the following statement by Imlah is relevant, but not conclusive:

All in all, the foreign capital placed in Britain may have equalled the gross amount of British investment abroad in 1815.[11]

Nor does the sum of £96 million for 1827 indicated by the London Statistical Society seem to bring any support to Imlah's estimate, even though it comes close to the £100 million that appears in Imlah's series for these years. This sum, as Staley pointed out,[12] corresponds only to loans granted to foreign governments between 1816 and 1825. In the light of what Beeke and Colquhoun stated, it is certainly too low to represent the stock of Britain's foreign wealth, as indeed is the figure proposed by Imlah.

One other interesting, but brief quantitative foray into the first decades of the century is the estimate made by Seyd. His work will be discussed later, but in the meantime, suffice it to say that he attributed a stock of between £100 million and £200 million to Great Britain in 1816 without giving much documentation and clarification to prove the reliability of his data.[13]

Another expert of the time whose estimate did not coincide with Imlah's, as Imlah himself acknowledged, is Marshall. In fact, the first time he applied the emerging norms of international accounting, which he certainly did not explain, he quoted a figure of £100 million as the total for British foreign loans for the years around 1816-1830, which is more than 15 per cent higher than the amount calculated by Imlah.[14] Certainly Marshall's estimate is not sufficient to define the total stock of Britain's foreign investments, but it is yet another source which raises doubts about the excessive caution with which Imlah seems to have constructed his series for the first decades of the 19th century.

Due consideration should also be given to the estimate proposed by Jenks, even if Imlah himself described it as 'limited in content',[15] because Jenks played a very important role in quantifying the movements of capital invested abroad by British residents and, in this particular context, pioneered retrospective work which has since been developed by other scholars, including Imlah himself.[16] His calculation for 1830 can be considered the second estimate of the stock of British foreign investments to be obtained using the direct method after the one made by the London Statistical Society. However, also in this case the calculation is incomplete, because Jenks identified only some of the components of the stock, namely the securities of governments and mining companies issued publicly between 1815 and 1830, whose value is estimated to be about £83 million.

Jenks's work is short on documentation, though it seems reasonable to presume that, in line with his advice to follow closely the history of each share, he prepared his estimate by aggregating data on the new issues that he had gathered from the financial sources of the time. However, it has been seen above (sections 2.3 and 3.2) how much additional information (on evaluation criteria, the presence of foreign capital, defaults, *conversions*, etc.)[17] is required to make this procedure more reliable. In fact, British capital was already placed in very many sectors (public works, business and financial services, plantations, etc.) which did not appear in Jenks's list of items, so that Imlah's suggestion of just rounding Jenks's figures upwards by 20 per cent, that is by adding 1.5 per cent to the 18.5 per cent

Paish had suggested in his 1907 estimate for the so-called direct investments as opposed to portfolio investments, cannot be considered as satisfactory.[18]

In other words, Imlah tried in a rather exaggerated manner to find some point of contact with one of the few estimates proposed for this period by placing his total aggregate figure of about £100 million for the balances in the period 1815-1830 alongside a similar figure that he obtained by adapting Jenks's estimates.

Jenks did, however, provide a little more information when he suggested another estimate of the stock of Britain's foreign wealth for the year 1854. Yet, it was once again only partially satisfactory, because, in keeping with the procedure followed by the direct method, he presented the data about different financial assets mixing geographical and sectoral criteria,[19] and also neglecting evaluation criteria, the possible presence of foreign capital at home, and so on.

Nevertheless, just sufficient elements are supplied to make his estimate admissible as an application of the direct method and he proposed a figure ranging between £195 million and £230 million. This is a fairly big difference, but not sufficient to be sharply criticized in view of the limited sources available.

Jenks's estimate should, nevertheless, be taken into consideration so that British direct investments, on the one hand, and foreign capital in Britain on the other, can be accounted for, even if along general lines only. This means, for example as Imlah pointed out, that Jenks's stock should be increased by 20 per cent for the first item and the new stock reduced by ten per cent for the second item, thus obtaining a net stock for 1854 that fluctuates between £211 million and £254 million. These figures come close to Imlah's estimates of £228.9 million and £234.7 million for capital accumulated in 1853 and 1854 respectively, and the difference with Jenks's estimates still remains acceptable.

Imlah does not try to hide his liking for Jenks's estimates which tend to attribute the same kind of rhythms to the accumulation of Britain's wealth overseas as his own. However, the same doubts that were expressed about Jenks's estimate for 1830 may be raised here again about the percentages chosen for the adjustment. Furthermore, in this case there are two other estimates available in the literature on this period more or less that have to be taken into consideration. The first is Bowley's which indicates £550 million for 1854 as a first estimate of the stock, updated for the years 1860, 1875, 1880 and 1890 with the figures of £750 million, £1,400 million, £1,500 million and £2,000 million respectively.[20] Obviously the size of the difference between Bowley's, Jenks's and Imlah's estimates is particularly striking, but this would seem to confirm what was said above about Imlah's figures being too low. It should be noted, however, that Bowley produced neither direct nor indirect documentation to substantiate his estimates for 1854 or, indeed, for the following years.

In point of fact Bowley's work is substantiated, but only from an objective point of view, by the second estimate which was made by Seyd, an observer of the time. Seyd has already been remembered, alongside Shaw-Lefevre, as having correctly introduced the procedure based on the measurement of the balance on current account used to calculate the flows of resources that could be invested abroad annually (see section 1.2).

In fact Seyd presented his very own estimate in so far as he calculated the current account starting from a figure of £600 million as the estimate of the stock of British foreign wealth for 1854, from which he derived, as part of the current account, the series of annual income until 1877 at a profit rate of six per cent per year, as already seen (Table 1.1). Once again the aggregate result is not sufficiently documented, but it does place another question mark over the series of stocks calculated by Imlah, especially as it comes from an expert of the time.[21]

It is obvious, therefore, that Seyd's and Imlah's overseas income estimates for the years 1854-1877[22] diverge greatly, especially in the early years of this period. Later, however, all the items included in the current account have a compensatory effect on each other, making Imlah's total estimate almost always higher than Seyd's. In this way the total of the balances on current account for the period is about £878 million for Imlah and £708 million for Seyd.[23]

Consequently a new situation arises with the estimates of the stock: Seyd presented a figure of £1,026 million for 1877, the last year of the period examined, which is, in fact, close to Imlah's estimate of approximately £1,100 million for the same year (see Tables 1.1 and 1.10).

There are, therefore, two very divergent estimates for the year 1854 and two comparatively convergent estimates for the later date. Imlah put forward his own explanation for this in order to give greater prominence to the second rather than the first result. He believed that Seyd worked backwards in his calculations, using his estimate of £1,100 million for 1874 as the base figure for capital invested abroad, a figure which Imlah himself recognised to be more valid because it was better documented. From this stock, Seyd was supposed to have subtracted the total of the annual balances on current account that he had calculated, but, as these figures were much lower than the real ones according to Imlah, he overestimated the stock for 1854.[24]

According to Imlah, Seyd's stock for 1874 needs to be adjusted, but not in the way suggested for Jenks. Imlah believed that the value presented by Seyd can, in fact, be considered comprehensive of all British investments, including those in the merchant navy.

Indeed, within the framework of the research on British foreign investments Seyd adopted an original position on this point, because he believed that the resources employed in shipping should be included in the aggregate, in so far as they can be considered invested overseas, thus contributing more to inflows under the item of income from foreign capital and less to those under shipping and other business services. This position seems very plausible, but so does the opposite position held by most other scholars who prefer to keep shipping capital outside the stock.[25]

This question has to be resolved within the conventions of accounting and, above all, by avoiding any risk of double-counting. It is reasonable, however, to subtract the value attributed to the merchant navy as a component of Britain's foreign wealth from Seyd's estimate, as Imlah did, in order to reach an estimate of the stock which was structurally similar to that of other authors. Therefore, £160 million were deducted from the £1,100 million estimated by Seyd, leaving a total of £940 million. According to Imlah, a further reduction of ten per cent (following

Jenks) still had to be made, thus reducing the stock calculated by Seyd to £846 million. This adjustment, net of the total of the balances on current account, also affected the value of the stock for 1854, which was considered excessive by Imlah; '£600 millions would reduce to between £500 and £550 millions of true foreign investment'.[26]

However, there appears to be some incongruity in Imlah's argument. To begin with, one may not agree with Seyd's approach, but it would be very surprising if Imlah himself disagreed with it, since Seyd, albeit in a less ambitious research programme than Imlah's, actually anticipated his method, in which the initial stock of capital is estimated first and then, moving from this basic source of income, the series of balances on current account is constructed for the subsequent years in order to trace the evolution of the initial stock. This is exactly what Seyd intended doing and consequently it seems too contrived to suggest, as Imlah did, that he was inverting the time direction.

Secondly, no explanation was given of how this inversion of the calculation process could actually be done for the whole series of capital income, that is starting from the last, and not the first, stock of capital. Thirdly, Imlah did not explain why, in Seyd's case, a given percentage of the stock, for instance 20 per cent, is not added to the estimate of £1,100 million in order to quantify British direct investments, since this operation would have markedly increased the gap between Seyd's and Imlah's stock estimates even for 1874;[27] nor did he provide any documentation about the £160 million which was deducted as the value of shipping capital.[28] Lastly, it is hard to understand how, after starting from Seyd's revised estimate of £846 million and deducting the aggregate balances on current account calculated at £521 million by Seyd for the years 1854-1874, the estimate is reduced only to a figure of £500-550 million, which is considerably higher than the one Seyd would have reached, according to Imlah's re-elaboration, that is about £300 million (see Table 1.2).

It seems possible, therefore, to conclude that Seyd's estimates, which can be considered fairly reliable, give good cause for a critical reflection on how Imlah traced the evolution of the stock of British foreign capital.

The last document of particular interest for the years around 1870 is an article published in the annual supplement of *The Economist*, the *Commercial History and Review of 1869*,[29] which gave an account of the stock of British foreign investments, but it was limited, as seen above (see section 2.4), to publicly issued securities of foreign countries and of the colonies.

The estimate, which was based on the nominal value,[30] aimed to represent only the gross assets of British residents with reference to the year 1869 and was set at £570 million, of which £500 million were in foreign securities and £70 million in colonial securities. After consulting other sources, such as Jenks and Cairncross (see sections 1.5.2 and 1.5.3), it can be seen that many other investments had been made by British residents in railways, public works, business services, etc. for a total of a few hundred million pounds. Even allowing for the deduction of a certain amount of investments belonging to foreign subjects, the stock of wealth as proposed by this source was clearly above the £648.2 million calculated by Imlah for the end of 1869 (see Table 1.10) and therefore some credit should also be given, for example, to Cairncross's partial estimate of £785 million for the end of 1870 (see section 2.4).[31]

4.3 The period preceding the First World War

This second period which refers to the years after 1870 has already been touched upon during the discussion of Bowley's, Jenks's and Seyd's works; in any case the subdivision used was not intended to group the different authors into a single period, since many of them have covered a much broader time horizon in their reconstructions of the era. This is true, for example, of Giffen who only dealt briefly with the first period, whilst most of his research concentrated on the last decades of the 19th century.

As mentioned above, the systematic use of the method which determines the total value of wealth owned by British residents at a given moment by capitalizing the annual returns on the wealth at so many years' purchase was introduced by Newmarch. Nevertheless, his article in *The Economist*, at that time anonymous, reserved an absolutely minimal space for the measurement of the stock of British foreign investments.[32]

In point of fact, the capitalization method requires a knowledge of the income flows in order to calculate the capital they come from and Giffen himself had had to deal with this problem in his later works (see section 2.2) when he adopted Newmarch's approach. The data for many components of British domestic capital was provided by tax documentation, whilst information about income from capital abroad was either non-existent or at least incomplete before the publication of the *Report of the Commissioners* started in the financial year 1877-1878.[33]

Giffen can be seen to move cautiously in his estimate because he lists only two specific items for foreign capital among the total amount of British capital for 1865. The first, income from government securities, could be easily identified and Giffen estimated the amount of wealth invested in them to be more than £210 million, whereas the other, the foreign investments not included in Schedules C and D of Income Tax, an area as yet unexplored by the tax authorities, was estimated at £100 million of capital, which he obtained by capitalizing a supposed income of £10 million at ten years' purchase.[34]

Giffen's estimates, which were made at ten-year intervals, became more sophisticated for the year 1875, when he tried to give a more analytical description of the flows of capital income and proposed an estimate of about £1,048 million for the stock of foreign capital.[35]

It has to be noted, however, that Giffen was at pains to identify the income which actually belonged to British residents. He tried to limit that shady area of capital invested abroad directly by private businessmen by making an estimate of the income earned by both trading and insurance companies, as well as by depositors abroad. However, no mention was made of any possible presence, in any form, of foreign capital in Great Britain, the amount of which would certainly have affected the net stock of foreign wealth.

This is not in itself wrong, because Giffen could possibly have intended to calculate the gross, and not necessarily the net, wealth of Great Britain. Indeed there is a statement by Giffen which suggests that he believed the amount of foreign capital in Great Britain was, statistically speaking, irrelevant. In fact, when he was explaining the reason why the national debt did not appear in his calculations of domestic wealth, he wrote that it would be incorrect as it could be said to be held entirely inside the country, 'whereas we should have to deduct it if it were held by foreigners'.[36] This comment refers to the national debt, but at this point it is reasonable to suppose that Giffen, like many other scholars, always considered the amount of any type of wealth owned by non-residents in Britain to be rather modest.

Giffen's estimate can be considered unsatisfactory, but it cannot be corrected simply within the usual accounting norms by adding or deducting sums which he believed to have taken more or less into account, as for example, by fixing the amount of investments not identified by the tax authorities under Schedules C and D at £400 million in order to complete the estimate of the stock of international wealth owned by British residents or by ignoring the existence of foreign assets in Britain because it is considered statistically irrelevant.

The accounting method adopted by Giffen serves to confirm the important estimate he proposed for the stock of 1875. In fact he provided an estimate for both the income from investments abroad for 1875 and the new issues of capital, though only for government and railway securities for the years 1876-1885.

These additional calculations were not presented in a categorical form as far as the figures were concerned. Indeed, with regard to the issues of capital, Giffen mentioned other items that would be necessary to give greater precision to his series: the inclusion of other capital flows invested in the form of securities or through private channels; the calculation of the amounts effectively invested and not just subscribed; the evaluation of loans lost through insolvency, etc. Nevertheless, he wanted to give the idea of a plausible picture for his estimate of Britain's foreign wealth as a component of the total wealth of the country, which he also re-elaborated later for 1885.[37]

Certainly his choice of the years' purchase, which varies from one component of foreign wealth to another, and even from one period to another, is open to question, but this variation is an essential characteristic of the method. In fact, Giffen's estimate of £1,048.3 million for 1875 is fairly credible and Imlah's estimates (see Table 1.10) stand up well to the comparison both for 1874 (£1,014 million) and 1875 (£1,065.3 million), as the difference is only marginal.[38]

This convergence, however, occurs only for the year 1875, because Giffen's subsequent estimate for 1885 and those made by Hirst using the same method for 1895, 1905 and 1909 no longer coincide with Imlah's estimates (see Tables 1.10 and 2.4).

Giffen's estimate for 1885 moves along the same lines as those defined for 1865 and 1875, even though in the first case foreign wealth was not particularly relevant. However, the additional sum of £250 million accumulated over the ten years between 1876-1885 is more or less equally spread over all the items, namely 'Public funds', 'Foreign and colonial securities',[39] 'Railways out of the United

Kingdom' and 'Foreign investments not in Schedules C or D', thus giving rise to a stock of £1,300.7 million (see Table 2.2).[40] It is also worth remembering that Cairncross's estimate for 1885 fixed the total of British foreign investments at £1300 million, though it only included securities (see section 2.4).

For the same year Imlah, who recorded a favourable trend in the balances on current account especially in the five years from 1881-1885, fixed the stock at £1,497.2 million; the difference of about an extra 15 per cent, this time in Imlah's estimate, is certainly significant.[41]

This difference should be considered as even greater because, on the one hand, there is no reason to increase Giffen's estimate since his approach covered all the positive components of foreign wealth. There could, on the other hand, be cause to revise the estimate downwards because Giffen himself briefly mentioned 'the capital called in from abroad, of which we have heard so much'.[42] However, there are not sufficient traces of this flow in the records to transform the stock from gross to net.

In fact, in this phase Giffen's position raises some concern because he suggested, admittedly in a less rigorous context, an estimate of £1,500 million (see p. 65) for the stock of Britain's foreign investments for 1882 which is not compatible with his own estimates for the period 1875-1885, when there was, in his opinion, an increasingly intensive accumulation of wealth abroad.

These misgivings about the type of research introduced by Giffen increase with the estimates for the years 1895, 1905 and 1909 made by Hirst using the same method. Hirst actually proposed estimates for overseas investments which were poorly supported by irrelevant documentation and in stark contrast to the precise data provided by Giffen. The fact is that these values are well below the estimates presented by other authors for this period and can be considered to be of only limited credibility, as indeed Hirst himself implied when he wrote that they represented 'a minimum rather than a maximum' (see p. 67).

Obviously this distortion is not only a consequence of the method adopted because, as will be remembered below, Crammond obtained very different results by applying Giffen's method for the year 1912. But it must be admitted that Giffen's important methodological opening has not had a systematic and fruitful follow-up.

An almost symmetrical position was taken by Bowley, another eminent scholar of the British economy, whose relatively higher estimates were not backed by appropriate empirical proof. His presentation proceeded correctly by using the connection between the dynamics of the stocks and the dynamics of the flows in the intermediate years, but no analytical explanation was given for the content of either the stocks or the flows. Instead Bowley asked the reader to trust his figures because they 'agree with all available facts'.[43] As far as the stock itself is concerned, Bowley provided an estimate of about £1,400 million for 1875 and £2,000 million for 1890.[44]

Nevertheless, Bowley's work deserves to be examined carefully because it was cited by Hobson, who has already been remembered for his studies on problems connected with the movement of capital, both in general and particularly in the British case (see sections 1.3 and 2.4). It has been seen that the main empirical part of Hobson's work focussed on the determination of capital flows from 1870 onwards by adopting the indirect or residual method, although he did not pay much attention to the connection between his research on the flows and the trend of the stocks.

It seems very unlikely, however, that he did not keep a check on the compatibility of his calculations on the flows with those made by other experts on the stocks at the beginning and the end of the period studied. But it is true that Hobson's aggregate balances on current account, which amount to £2,524 million for 1870-1913, do not at first glance represent a satisfactory link to Paish's stock estimates. This can mean that either the estimates made by Hobson, who expressed no opinion about the initial stock of 1870, are in fact too circumspect, as Imlah believed,[45] or there is a common train of thought, which is neither explicit nor coherent, running through Bowley's, Hobson's and Paish's work. Hobson, in fact, quoted Bowley and borrowed from Paish's work for the important part concerning the item about capital income in the current account. It is not unreasonable to suppose, therefore, that he kept an eye on the stocks measured by them as an indirect and implicit check on his work, although he did not want to go into details on this point.[46]

In the first decade of this second phase, a concise, but well-documented description of Britain's position in relation to other countries was finally provided by Nash. Few people were able to understand the evolution of British financial assets as Nash did. He listed, in fact, as separate items all the assets held in the form of securities in order to represent the rich assortment of British property overseas, but 'only estimated in the rough, for no exact data are ascertainable'.[47]

The basic limitation to Nash's contribution is more qualitative than quantitative in a certain sense, since the aggregate he proposed was not intended to represent the stock of all the net foreign wealth of Britain. In fact he was aware of the presence of capital held by foreigners and of other assets which were not considered in his work, but were owned abroad by resident Britons; consequently Nash quite correctly presented his table for 1880 as an 'Estimate of British investments in home and foreign securities'.[48]

His estimate of investments in foreign securities stood at £1,250 million,[49] but this figure, for the reasons mentioned above, should be appreciably increased because it does not correspond to a complete calculation of the stocks which could be made with the direct method itself. However, here another point implicitly emerges in favour of the opinion formed in this book that Imlah's view was too cautious in approximately the first half of his research, in which the total volume of the stock was valued at £1,190.4 million at the end of 1880 (see Table 1.10).

In that period, especially 1885, there is, on the other hand, a remarkable agreement between Imlah's estimate of £1,497.2 million for accumulated flows (see Table 1.10) and Cairncross's £1,300 million which included only portfolio investments by British residents (see section 2.4).

Table 4.1 Estimates of British foreign investments, calculated with various methods, 1799-1914
(rounded figures in millions of pounds)[a]

Year	Indirect method		Capitalization of annual income		Direct method		Eclectic method		No method	
	Authors	Estimates	Authors	Estimates	Authors	Estimates	Authors	Estimates	Authors	Estimates
1799			Beeke	100					Imlah	10
1815										
1816									Seyd	100-200
1825					LSS[b]	96			Bowley	550
1830					Jenks	83			Seyd	600
1854	Imlah	234.7			Jenks	195-230			Bowley	750
1860					*Economist*[c]	570				
1869					Cairncross	785				
1870	Imlah	692.3			Platt	500				
1875			Giffen	1,048.3			Jenks	1,200	Bowley	1,400
1877	Seyd	1,026								
	Shaw-Lefevre	1,046								
1880	Imlah	1,190.4			Nash	1,250	Madden	1,070	Bowley	1,500
1885	Imlah	1,935.1	Giffen	1,300.7	Cairncross	1,100				
1890					Cairncross	1,300			Bowley	2,000
1892					Harris	1,698				
1895			*Economist*[d]	1,600						
1897							Crammond	2,400-2,550		
1900	Imlah	2,396.9								
1902			Money	2,000						
1904									Speyer	2,500
1905			*Economist*[d]	2,025						
1906							Crammond	3,150-3,220		
1907			Money	2,637			Paish	2,935		

Year	Author		Economist[d]	Economist[c]	Author	Crammond
1908				3,050		3,560
				2,750		
1909	Imlah	3,370.1	2,332			
1910					Paish	3,500
					Crammond	3,722
1912	Crammond		3,800			
1913	Cairncross	3,173.9			Crammond	3,904
	Feinstein	4,165			Feis	4,050
	Hobson[r]	2,524			Paish	4,000
	Imlah	3,988.4				
1914	Arndt			3,000		
	Davis-Huttenback[h]			3,164.7		
				3,945.3		
				4,778.6		
	Platt[g]			3,132		
	Simon[h]			4,081.8		
	Stone[h]			4,079.3		

a. The data normally refers to the end of the year indicated; further details, especially about the possible distinction between gross and net stock, can be found in the text.

b. The London Statistical Society. The partial estimate concerns the years 1816-1825.

c. The estimate is taken from the Money Market Review.

d. The article is attributed to Hirst.

e. The first estimate belongs to an anonymous correspondent; the second to Beaumont.

f. The estimate refers to the years 1870-1913.

g. The estimate refers to 31 July 1914.

h. The estimates refer to the years 1865-1914; Davis and Huttenback's were prepared using three different criteria.

Sources: the first numbers are the years the estimates refer to; the number in brackets is the year the estimate was published.

Arndt: 1914 (1915); Beeke: 1799 (1800); Bowley: 1854, 1860, 1875, 1880, 1890 (1905); Cairncross: 1870, 1880, 1885, 1913 (1975); Crammond: 1897, 1906 (1907); 1908, 1910 (1911); 1912 (1914); 1913 (1915); Davis-Huttenback: 1865-1914 (1985); *Economist*: 1895, 1905, 1909 (1911e); 1908 (1909a); Feinstein: 1913 (1988); Feis: 1913 (1974); Giffen: 1875, 1885 (1889); Harris: 1892 (1896); Hobson: 1870-1913 (1963); Imlah: 1815, 1854, 1870, 1880, 1890, 1900, 1910, 1913 (1958); Jenks: 1830, 1854, 1875 (1971); London Statistical Society: 1816-1825 (1827); Madden: 1880 (1985); Money: 1902 (1903); 1907 (1911); Nash: 1880 (1881); Paish: 1907 (1909); 1910 (1911); 1913 (1914); Platt: 1870 (1880); 1914 (1986); Seyd: 1816, 1854, 1877 (1878); Shaw-Lefevre: 1877 (1878); Simon: 1865-1914 (1967); Speyer: 1904 (1905); Stone: 1865-1914 (1999)

In point of fact, the convergence of Imlah's 'vertical' and Paish's 'horizontal' calculations, which certainly did not occur purely by chance, would probably have happened in any case, if the pace of the accumulation of British foreign wealth in Imlah's long series had increased throughout most of the period before eventually slowing down in the latter part.

Madden's reservations about the estimate of the items 'Profits on foreign trade and services' and 'Net credits from shipping' elaborated by Imlah for the second period were not unfounded, but it can also be argued that Imlah most noticeably underestimated the item 'Balance on interest and dividends'. To be more specific, the currency flows derived from the returns on the annual, either gross or net, stock of British foreign investments could have had a higher value, for example, in the years 1875 and 1885, which had been estimated at £68.9 million and £84.8 million by Giffen, as compared to Imlah's figures of £57.8 million and £70.3 million. And, more generally, as noted on a number of occasions (see, in particular, section. 4.2), Imlah probably underestimated the capital accumulated abroad by British residents.

There are a number of other scholars who could deservedly take part in this imaginary meeting around a conference table where each one would be invited to present his estimates as indicated in Table 4.1. As far as Imlah is concerned, his ideal colleague would be Feinstein who worked with a similar approach, though on a shorter period of time, and made only small quantitative adjustments to his series.[50]

More people would probably feel greater affinity with Paish, not least of all Crammond, a versatile scholar of British foreign investments who is also remembered for having re-proposed Giffen's approach in one of his papers. The total stock calculated by Crammond on the basis of the partial data on the financial year 1911-1912 published in the *Report of the Commissioners* stood at about £3,800 million. The value of the stock of wealth held by non-resident Britons should be deducted from this figure to obtain an estimate of net British investments abroad.[51]

On this point, Crammond has already been seen to have considered British debts to amount to approximately ten per cent of gross assets. This would reduce his estimate by about £400 million, but still leave it close to Paish's and Imlah's. More generally, it has also been shown that Crammond's estimates for the stock of British foreign investments, obtained with a more personal approach, always proved to be more or less in line with Paish's (see section 2.3).

Other scholars who would also receive an invitation to this meeting would include, first of all, Feis, who in his lengthy work referred almost exclusively to Paish's estimate, making just a slight adjustment upwards[52] and with the only reservation that he did not always trouble himself to specify whether his calculations were to be considered net of British wealth belonging to non-residents.

Two other experts who would be worthy of an invitation were mentioned in an article in *The Economist*,[53] one explicitly named as Beaumont and the other referred to simply as *A correspondent*. They both indicated estimates for the year 1908 which are very similar to Crammond's, Paish's and Imlah's, though the author of the article did not give details about the methods adopted by the two experts.[54]

It is easy to imagine that professional pride or an awkward disposition would induce these scholars to boast greater precision in their own estimates than in their colleagues'. However, in the end they would probably come to the wise decision not to waste time searching for a definitive estimate which would, in any case, be impossible to find, and instead share the mutual satisfaction of having helped to build up a broad and sound consensus on the estimates that have placed the net stock of British foreign investments on the eve of the First World War at about £4,000 million (see Table 4.1).[55]

This estimate for the end of the period, which can take its place alongside the most valid estimates collected for the previous years in Table 4.1, obviously represents a convincing and reliable point of arrival for our knowledge of the flows and stocks of British foreign investments in that long historical phase. At the same time, it should also be viewed as a point of departure for the many other questions which have already been studied, but still need further investigation.

As far as the first aspect is concerned, the description provided by this survey of the evolution of these variables, especially by Imlah and Paish, lends support to the many contributions that have stressed the importance of foreign investments in Britain's economy. Even Platt, after his substantial revision of about 25% made to these estimates, only briefly mentioned the possibility that this revision could cast doubts on the ascendancy of Great Britain in the field of foreign investments.[56]

Moreover, according to the authoritative source of the United Nations, Great Britain covered about 41% of the world total of international credits in 1913. Platt's revision, therefore, could not affect the dominant position of Britain in relation to other countries, in view of the fact that the second position in the United Nations' classification was held by France with 20% of this total.[57]

With regard to the second aspect it is to be hoped that other disaggregated characteristics of these investments, which have been only briefly mentioned in this book, will be brought to light or studied in greater depth. Research may focus on, for example, a more accurate calculation of what are called direct investments nowadays, that is investments connected with gaining control of important foreign companies; the geographical distribution and/or sectoral composition of all investments; a clear definition of the relationship between the countries making and receiving the investments;[58] the interdependence of these investments and Britain's exports; and so on.

Nevertheless, it is well to remember that the international position of the economic system of a country cannot be measured just through its foreign investments. This is true in general, but particularly so for imperial Britain which was well integrated into the world economy with its imports and exports of goods, its extraordinary network of business services (shipping, insurance, banks, etc.), its migratory movements and the fundamental role it played in establishing the rules regulating the workings of the world economy which were based on the two cornerstones of free trade and the gold standard.[59]

And lastly, due consideration should also be given to the heated, though intermittent, debate on the actual economic benefits deriving from the imperial experience of Britain.[60]

There are many reasons, therefore, for proposing once again the idea of a new point of departure for future intellectual forays, which could also involve the author of this book.

Notes

[1] On the other hand, it should be remembered that many important countries, including the United States and Germany, adopted protectionist policies at the same time as pursuing a course of remarkable expansion in international relations. These policies emerged towards the end of the 19th century, but they became more widespread in the years between the two World Wars; see Tiberi (1999).

[2] *Ibid.* The bibliography at the end of the book may be useful for those who are interested in both this subject and the topic mentioned in the note above.

[3] See Staley (1935), pp. 524-525. The estimates he quoted begin with the £93 million indicated by the London Statistical Society for the year 1827 and end with Kindersley's estimate for 1932. For the years which concern us directly, the list concludes with Crammond's calculation for 1913-1914 (see Table 4.1). The table from *The Economist* begins with Jenks's estimate for 1854 and finishes with Kindersley's for 1934. The last estimate for the years before the First World War belongs to Feis for 1913 (see Table 4.1). The name of Hobson appears in this table and he was erroneously attributed estimates which were actually made by Hirst, using Giffen's method (see section 2.2).

[4] These are the Parliamentary Papers of 1808 and 1814-1815; see Imlah (1958), p. 66 and note 33 in chapter 2.

[5] See the bibliography in Tiberi (1988, 1992).

[6] See *The Economist* (1911b), p. 380. As we know Hirst was the author of the article which contained the updated series of estimates of British wealth that had been elaborated by Giffen (see note 70 in chapter 2); it must be added that Giffen, in turn, had followed Newmarch's example. The book cited is Giffen (1889).

[7] The context in which he presented his work discussing the possible tax revenue from the planned introduction of Income Tax by Pitt would suggest that the amount indicated resulted from the capitalization of the presumed income from capital abroad. See Beeke (1800), *passim* and section 2.2.

[8] *Ivi*, pp. 43 and 45.

[9] See Colquhoun (1814), p. 185.

[10] *Ivi*, p. 52. In light of Colquhoun's statement it is interesting to note the euphemistic flavour this type of appropriation acquired within the aggregates marked simply as direct investments or portfolio investments. It is on the basis of these aggregates that the foreign wealth of Great Britain was supposed to be identified somehow.

[11] See Imlah (1958), p. 60.

[12] See Staley (1935), p. 524. He added, in fact, that 'Total foreign investment would be much larger' (*ibid.*). With regard to the London Statistical Society, it has to be pointed out that the estimate of £93 million indicated in note 3 has been increased to £96 million after a close examination of the source.

[13] See Seyd (1878), p. 4.

[14] In fact, the aggregate for the balances on current account calculated by Imlah for the same period amounts to about £86 million. See Imlah (1958), p. 67.

[15] See Imlah (1958), p.67.

[16] It has already been mentioned that Jenks's academic background differed greatly from that of the other scholars we have met in the course of this work (see section 1.5.2); nevertheless, it has also been seen that Jenks tried to work with great discretion at an empirical level, using procedures from both the direct and the indirect method as necessary (see section 2.4).

[17] As Imlah noted, Jenks obviously gave considerable attention to the repatriation of securities, a point which is often ignored, thus giving rise to imperfections in the application of the direct method. See Imlah (1958), note 45.

[18] Paish had, in fact, placed the figure of £500 million of direct investments alongside the £2,700 million of foreign wealth representing securities (see section 2.3). However, in his last work Paish spoke of at least £300 million, later revised upwards by Platt; see sections 2.3 and 3.2.

[19] This estimate included, for example, the United States, Spain, Portugal and South America; government securities issued in France, Belgium, Holland and Russia and the French and Belgian railways; see Jenks (1971), p. 413. An aside by Imlah (1958, p. 68) seems to refer to Jenks's estimate as *called* and not simply as *created* capital, thus maintaining the definitions proposed by those who applied the direct method (see section 2.4). Indeed Jenks seemed to be very aware of the importance of this distinction, but he was obliged to juggle as best he could with data that sometimes prevented him from keeping to it. See Jenks (1971), p. 425.

[20] See Bowley (1905), pp. 76-77.

[21] In any case, Imlah himself considered Seyd's estimate to be completely independent of Bowley's. See Imlah (1958), p. 69.

[22] Imlah also calculated income from overseas investments in that period by applying a variable interest rate, but it was generally lower than Seyd's 6 per cent. *Ivi*, pp. 59-64.

[23] A comparison of the values in the item of income from abroad calculated by Shaw-Lefevre and Imlah for the period 1865-1877 also shows Shaw-Lefevre's estimates to be generally lower, though they do not contain convincing information about the stock of foreign wealth acquired by Great Britain at the end of 1864, which produced flows of income in the years following 1865. Shaw-Lefevre's and Imlah's aggregate balances on current account do not differ greatly for the years in question: £579 million for the first (see Table 1.2) and £652.7 million for the second (see Table 2.10).

[24] See Imlah (1958), p. 69. In this context Imlah also noted a misprint (or an error?) in Seyd's work, in which the estimate of £1,100 million of stock was attributed both to 1872 and 1874. In fact the estimate for 1874 amounts to £1,126 million by summing the balances on current account to the initial stock of £600 million. Imlah himself, in any case, created further misunderstandings because in a note he spoke of the end of 1873 as a possible base figure from which Seyd could have started moving backwards; see Imlah (1958), note 49. The year 1874 seems more credible and is therefore used in the following discussion.

[25] See Seyd (1878), p. 4.

[26] See Imlah (1958), p. 69.

[27] In the absence of any indication from Imlah himself, it may be that he did not intend to make that correction to Seyd's data, because they were obtained partially with the indirect method; however, even in this case, at least the value of the stock suggested by Seyd for 1854 should be increased.

[28] Seyd, in fact, placed the total value of all ships between £70 million and £75 million; see Seyd (1878), p. 6.

[29] See *The Economist* (1870), p. 64.

[30] It has been seen, however, with Crammond that the estimate at market prices does not give values that are very far removed from those made at nominal prices (see section 2.3). It has also been seen with Simon (see section 2.4) that the difference between *created* and *called* capital does not have any particular quantitative relevance in the measurement of stocks.

[31] For example, according to Giffen's estimate made only a few years later in 1875, the income derived from foreign investments that was not identified by the Inland Revenue amounted to £40 million; see Giffen (1878), p. 8 and section 2.2. With regard to Cairncross, it is worth noting his estimate of British foreign assets was contested by Platt (see section 3.2).

[32] The few references made in the article are by no means sufficient to draw up an estimate of this stock. See *The Economist* (1863), *passim.* It should be remembered that the article was reprinted later with a note by the author in the *Journal of the Statistical Society* (1864), pp. 118-127.

[33] See Parliamentary Papers (1881), p. 116 ff.

[34] Obviously Giffen, applying a years' purchase of 10, considered this type of investment to be particularly profitable, though risky; see Giffen (1878), p. 11. For the content of Schedules C and D, see section 2.2.

[35] See Giffen (1889), Table B on p. 30 and Table 2.1 in this book.

[36] *Ivi*, p. 21.

[37] *Ivi*, p. 41-42. Furthermore, Giffen, to his credit, made regular analyses on the trend of the current accounts of his country; see Tiberi (1988), section 2.1.

[38] In fact there remains a certain ambiguity in the choice of the year of reference, given that the capitalized income used by Giffen was found in the Income Tax records for the financial year 1874-1875.

[39] An increase in both the annual income (from £6.836 million to £9.589 million) and the number of years' purchase (from 15 to 20) produces a higher total for this item; this last variation is due to a decrease in the rate of return on the securities in question.

[40] See Giffen (1889), Tables A and B.

[41] The positive effect of the item 'Net credits from shipping', which is affected by the import price index, is felt over the five-year period in Imlah's series; see sections 1.5.4 and 3.3.

[42] See Giffen (1889), p. 41.

[43] See note 61 in chapter 2. Bowley often drew on Giffen's research in other parts of his work.

[44] See Bowley (1905), p. 77.

[45] For Imlah, the inadequacy of Hobson's estimates mostly concerns the 'Total profits on foreign trade', an item which was very controversial, as seen in section 3.3. Cairncross also obtained results that were only slightly lower than Hobson's, although he was not as indifferent towards the implications of his results for the stock estimates. For Hobson's and Cairncross's estimates, see Tiberi (1988, 1992), as well as sections 1.3 and 1.5.3.

[46] Douglas also considered a common train of thought between Bowley, Hobson and Paish and quantified its possible consequences in terms of the estimates of the stock at various deadlines. See Douglas (1930), pp. 673-674.

[47] See *Bankers' Magazine* (1881), p. 158. This very short article, which appeared anonymously (see section 2.4) in the journal, belongs to Nash who published other well-documented works on financial assets circulating in Great Britain's Stock Exchanges at this time; see Nash (1880, 1881).

[48] See *Bankers' Magazine* (1881), p. 158. The table refers to the gross financial wealth of Great Britain, represented partly by some easily identifiable items of securities typical of the

country's foreign investments; in this book, Table 2.10 shows only the data referring to these last items.

[49] Giffen's mention of £1,500 million of stock for the beginning of the 1880s may well have been inspired by Nash's authoritative estimate.

[50] Indeed, after the reservations expressed above about some of the elements in Imlah's series, the similarity between Imlah's and Feinstein's series can raise some doubts about the latter's work. As far as the trend of British foreign investments is concerned, Feinstein concentrated on Britain's accounts with foreign countries in this analytical way only for the period 1870-1913. Feinstein, instead, was to address the need to compare his figures with those produced by others for the preceding period elsewhere; see Feinstein (1988).

[51] Crammond used the same division of Great Britain's foreign assets into four items as Giffen had done, but changed their names slightly (see section 2.3). It should be noted that Crammond's estimates given in Table 4.1 do not refer to the net, but rather the gross, figure for British foreign investments. The reason for this is that the estimates of the second aggregate are more complete for all the various periods than the estimates of the first one.

[52] For Feis's higher estimate of British investments in Russia and Turkey, see p. 132.

[53] See *The Economist* (1909a), p. 377.

[54] At least one item, the British assets in India, estimated to be £470 million by *A correspondent* and £500 million by Beaumont, was in point of fact questioned by Keynes (see p. 184). It is perhaps appropriate to remember, however, that in Paish's 1913 table the item 'India and Ceylon' recorded about £379 million, which was the result of recent positive accumulations. See Paish (1914), p. v.

[55] It must also be added that this estimate appears to be compatible with Kindersley's estimate of British foreign wealth about the 1930s, considering the disinvestments that Great Britain had undertaken to meet its financial obligations during the First World War; see Feinstein (1990), p. 294. On the events concerning the dollar and sterling during the First World War, see Parliamentary Papers (1919). On the evolution of the situation of Britain's international accounts after the war, see, among others, *The Economist* (1930), Parliamentary Papers (1930-31) and Foot (1972).

[56] 'The downvaluation, if not quite so dramatic as for 1870, is more precise and perhaps as challenging. Naturally, total investment in 1914 was much larger, Britain's economy more deeply implicated, and the consequences of downvaluation greater in influence and effect', see Platt (1986), p. 4. But Platt himself in the course of his work did not follow up this statement and just explained how, in his opinion, the overestimates of foreign investments were influenced by the controversy between protectionists and free traders, which had flared up again at the beginning of the 20th century; (*ibid.*, chapter 3).

[57] See United Nations (1949), p. 1.

[58] On this point the definitions of 'formal' and 'informal' empire proposed by some authors still seem helpful. See Gallagher and Robinson (1953). In fact, the suggestions coming from other fields than economics can be very important, starting from the classical work produced by Seeley in the 19th century; see Seeley (1971).

[59] See Saul (1960); Kirby (1981), chapter 1; Tiberi (1999), section 2 and Mathias (2001), pp. 15-20.

[60] Without forgetting the doubts generally raised about the basically counterfactual arguments, which appear in this debate. See, among others, Harley and McCloskey (1981), chapter 3; O'Brien (1988); Foreman-Peck (1989); Edelstein (1994).

Bibliography

Books and journals

Arndt, P. (1915), 'Neue Beiträge zur Frage der Kapitalanlage im Auslande', in *Zeitschrift für Sozialwissenschaft*, paper subdivided into six parts over the year.

Ayres, G.L. (1934), *Fluctuations in New Capital Issues on the London Capital Market, 1899 to 1933*, unpublished M.Sc. thesis, University of London.

Bankers' Magazine (1881), 'An Estimate of the British Investments, Principal and Interest', Vol. 41, March. The article was credited to R.L. Nash.

Bastable, C.F. (1903), *The Theory of International Trade with Some of Its Applications to Economic Policy*, 4th edition, Macmillan, London (1st edition 1887).

Beaumont, H. (1909), 'Investments in India. A Letter to the Editor', *Economist*, Vol. 68 (3419), March 6.

Beeke, B.D. (1800), *Observations on the Produce of the Income Tax, and on Its Proportion to the Whole Income of Great Britain*, Wright, London (1st edition 1800).

Bloomfield, A.I. (1963), *Short-Term Capital Movements under the Pre-1914 Gold Standard*, Princeton Studies in International Finance No. 11, Princeton University, Princeton.

Bourne, S. (1875), 'The Progress of Our Foreign Trade, Imports and Exports, during the Past Twenty Years', *Journal of the Statistical Society*, Vol. 38, part II, June, reprinted in S. Bourne (1880), *Trade, Population and Food. A Series of Papers on Economic Statistics*, Bell, London.

Bourne, S. (1877), 'The Growing Preponderance of Imports over Exports in the Foreign and Colonial Trade of the United Kingdom', *Journal of the Statistical Society*, Vol. 40, part I, March; reprinted in *Trade, Population and Food...*, *op. cit.*

Bourne, S. (1889), 'On Variations in the Volume and Value of Exports and Imports of the United Kingdom in Recent Years', *Journal of the Royal Statistical Society*, Vol. 52, part III, May.

Bourne, S. (1893), 'Progress of the External Trade of the United Kingdom in Recent Years', *Journal of the Royal Statistical Society*, Vol. 56, part II, June.

Bowley, A.L. (1895), 'Changes in Average Wages (Nominal and Real) in the United Kingdom between 1860 and 1891', *Journal of the Royal Statistical Society*, Vol. 58, part II, June.

Bowley, A.L. (1905), *A Short Account of England's Foreign Trade in the Nineteenth Century. Its Economic and Social Results*, 2nd edition, Allen & Unwin, London (1st edition 1893).

Brezis, E.S. (1995), 'Foreign Capital Flows in the Century of Britain's Industrial Revolution: New Estimates, Controlled Conjectures', *Economic History Review*, Vol. 48 (1), February.

Brezis, E.S. (1997), 'Did Foreign Capital Flows Finance the Industrial Revolution? A Reply', *Economic History Review*, Vol. 50 (1), February.

Burdett, H.C. (ed.) (1882), *Burdett's Official Intelligence...*, editions from various years, Couchman & Co., London.

Butlin, N.G. (1962), *Australian Domestic Product, Investment and Foreign Borrowing, 1861-1938/39*, Cambridge University Press, Cambridge.

Cairnes, J.E. (1873), 'Political Economy and Laissez Faire', in J.E. Cairnes, *Essays in Political Economy, Theoretical and Applied*, Macmillan, London.

Cairnes, J.E. (1874), *Some Leading Principles of Political Economy Newly Expounded*, Macmillan, London.

Cairncross, A.K. (1958), 'The English Capital Market before 1914', *Economica*, Vol. 25 (98), May.

Cairncross, A.K. (1975), *Home and Foreign Investment, 1870-1913. Studies in Capital Accumulation*, Kelley, Clifton (reprint of the 1st edition, University Press, Cambridge, 1953).

Clarke, H. (1878), 'On the Debts of Sovereign and Quasi-Sovereign States', *Journal of the Statistical Society*, Vol. 41, part II, June.

Colquhoun, P. (1814), *A Treatise on the Wealth, Power, and Resources of the British Empire...*, Mawman, London, (2nd edition 1815).

Commercial History and Review, annual supplement of *The Economist*, various issues.

Corley, T.A.B. (1994) 'Britain's Overseas Investments in 1914 Revisited', *Business History*, Vol. 36 (1), January.

Cottrell, P.L. (1975), *British Overseas Investment in the Nineteenth Century*, Macmillan, London.

Crammond, E. (1907), 'British Investments Abroad', *Quarterly Review*, Vol. 207 (412), July.

Crammond, E. (1911), 'British Investments Abroad', *Quarterly Review*, Vol. 215 (428), July.

Crammond, E. (1912), 'England's Economic Position and Her Financial Relations with Scotland and Ireland', *Nineteenth Century*, Vol. 71 (421), March.

Crammond, E. (1914), 'The Economic Relations of the British and German Empires', *Journal of the Royal Statistical Society*, Vol. 77, part VIII, July.

Crammond, E. (1915), 'The Economic Position of the Allied Powers', *Quarterly Review*, Vol. 224 (444), July.

Crammond, E. (1917), *The British Shipping Industry*, Constable, London.

Davis, L.E. and Huttenback, R.A. (1985), 'The Export of British Finance, 1865-1914', in A.R. Porter and R.F. Holland, *Money, Finance and Empire, 1790-1960*, Cass, London.

Davis, L.E. and Huttenback, R.A. (1986), *Mammon and the Pursuit of Empire. The Political Economy of British Imperialism, 1860-1912*, with the assistance of S.G. Davis, Cambridge University Press, Cambridge; abridged edition: *Mammon and the Pursuit of Empire. The Economics of British Imperialism*, Cambridge University Press, Cambridge, 1988.

Deane, P. and Cole, W.A. (1969), *British Economic Growth, 1688-1959*, University Press, Cambridge (1st edition 1962).

de Cecco, M. (1971), *Economia e finanza internazionale dal 1890 al 1914*, Laterza, Bari.

de Cecco, M. (1974), *Money and Empire. The International Gold Standard, 1890-1914*, Blackwell, Oxford.

de Cecco, M. (1979), *Moneta e impero. Il sistema finanziario internazionale dal 1890 al 1914*, Einaudi, Torino.

de Finetti, B. (1955), *Lezioni di matematica finanziaria*, Edizioni Ricerche, Roma.

Devons, E. (1950), 'Dollars from Investment?', *Manchester Guardian*, I. 'Britain's Experience', January 18; II. 'Postponing the Problem', January 19.

Douglas, P.H. (1930), 'An Estimate of the Growth of Capital in the United Kingdom, 1865-1909', *American Journal of Economic and Business History*, Vol. 2, August.

Edelstein, M. (1976), 'Realized Rates of Return on U.K. Home and Overseas Portfolio Investment in the Age of High Imperialism', *Explorations in Economic History*, 13 (3), July.

Edelstein, M. (1982), *Overseas Investment in the Age of High Imperialism. The United Kingdom, 1850-1914*, Methuen & Co., London.

Edelstein, M. (1994), 'Imperialism: Cost and Benefit', in R.C. Floud and D.N. McCloskey (eds), *The Economic History of Britain since 1700*, 2nd edition, Vol. 2, Cambridge University Press, Cambridge.

Engle, R.F. and Granger, C.W.J. (1987), 'Co-integration and Error Correction: Representation, Estimation and Testing', *Econometrica*, Vol. 55 (2), March.

Feinstein, C.H. (1972), *National Income, Expenditure and Output of the United Kingdom, 1855-1965*, University Press, Cambridge.

Feinstein, C.H. (1978), 'Capital Formation in Great Britain', in P. Mathias and M.M. Postan (eds), *The Cambridge Economic History of Europe*, Vol. VII, part I, Cambridge University Press, Cambridge.

Feinstein, C.H. (1988), 'Sources and Methods of Estimation for Domestic Reproducible Fixed Assets, Stocks and Works in Progress, Overseas Assets, and Land', in C.H. Feinstein and S. Pollard (eds), *Studies in Capital Formation in the United Kingdom, 1750-1920*, Clarendon Press, Oxford.

Feinstein, C.H. (1990), 'Britain's Overseas Investments in 1913', *Economic History Review*, 2nd series, Vol. 43 (2).

Feis, H. (1974), *Europe the World's Banker, 1870-1914. An Account of European Foreign Investment and the Connection of World Finance with Diplomacy before the War*, with an introduction by C.P. Howland and a new introduction by the author, Kelley, Clifton, (reprint of the 1st edition, Yale University Press, New Haven, 1930).

Fenn, C. (ed.) (1837), *A Compendium of the English and Foreign Funds*, Sherwood, London (in the course of time this publication, also known as *Fenn on the Funds*, was edited by other authors, including R.L. Nash, and published by different publishing houses).

Foot, M.D.K.W. (1972), 'The Balance of Payments in the Inter-War Period', *Bank of England Quarterly Bulletin*, Vol. 12 (3), September.

Ford, A.G. (1958-59), 'The Transfer of British Foreign Lending, 1870-1913', *Economic History Review*, 2nd series, Vol. 11 (2).

Foreman-Peck, J. (1989), 'Foreign Investment and Imperial Exploitation: Balance of Payments Reconstruction for Nineteenth-Century Britain and India', *Economic History Review*, 2nd series, Vol. 42 (3); reprinted in J. Foreman-Peck (ed.) (1998), *Historical Foundations of Globalization*, Elgar, Cheltenham.

Foster, J.L. (1804), *An Essay on the Principle of Commercial Exchanges*, Hatchard, London.

Gallagher, J. and Robinson, R. (1953), 'The Imperialism of Free Trade', *Economic History Review*, 2nd series, Vol. 6 (1), August.

Gandolfo, G. (1994), *Corso di economia internazionale*, 2 Vols., 2nd edition , UTET, Torino (1st edition 1989).

Giffen, R. (1877), *Stock Exchange Securities: An Essay on the General Causes of Fluctuations in Their Price*, Bell, London.

Giffen, R. (1878), 'Recent Accumulations of Capital in the United Kingdom', *Journal of the Statistical Society*, Vol. 41, part I, March; reprinted in R. Giffen (1880), *Essays in Finance*, 1st series, Bell, London.

Giffen, R. (1882), 'The Use of Import and Export Statistics', *Journal of the Royal Statistical Society*, Vol. 45, part II, June; reprinted in R. Giffen (1886), *Essays in Finance*, 2nd series, Bell, London.

Giffen, R. (1889), *The Growth of Capital*, Bell, London.

Giffen, R. (1899), 'The Excess of Imports', *Journal of the Royal Statistical Society*, Vol. 62, part I, March.

Giffen, R. (1904), 'The Present Economic Conditions and Outlook for the United Kingdom' in R. Giffen, *Economic Inquiries and Studies*, Vol. II, Bell, London.

Gnesutta, C. (1983), *Lineamenti di contabilità economica nazionale*, La Nuova Italia Scientifica, Roma.

Goschen, G.J. (1861), *The Theory of Foreign Exchanges*, Pitman, London.

Gregory, T.E. (1928), 'Great Britain and Foreign Investments', in G. Cassel, T.E. Gregory, R.R. Kuczynski and H.K. Norton, *Foreign Investment*, Lectures on the Harris Foundation, University Press, Chicago.

Hall, A.R. (1957), 'A Note on the English Capital Market as a Source of Funds for Home Investment before 1914', *Economica*, Vol. 24 (93), February.

Hall, A.R. (1958), 'The English Capital Market before 1914: A Reply', *Economica*, Vol. 25 (100), November.

Hall, A.R. (1963), *The London Capital Market and Australia, 1870-1914*, The Australian National University, Canberra.

Hall, A.R. (1968), 'Introduction', to A.R. Hall (ed.), *The Export of Capital from Britain, 1870-1914*, Methuen & Co., London.

Harley, C.K. and McCloskey, D.N. (1981), 'Foreign Trade: Competition and the Expanding International Economy', in R.C. Floud and D.N. McCloskey (eds), *The Economic History of Britain since 1700*, 1st edition, Vol. 2, Cambridge University Press, Cambridge.

Harris, C.A. (1896), 'Foreign Investments', entry in R.H.I. Palgrave (ed.), *Dictionary of Political Economy*, Vol. II, Macmillan, London.

Hobson, C.K. (1963), *The Export of Capital*, with an introduction by R. Harrod, Constable, London (1st edition 1914).

Hobson, C.K. (1921), 'The Measurement of the Balance of Trade', *Economica*, Vol. 1 (2), May.

Ietto-Gillies, G. (1992), *International Production. Trends, Theories, Effects*, Polity Press, Cambridge.

Imlah, A.H. (1948), 'Real Values in British Foreign Trade, 1798-1853', *Journal of Economic History*, Vol. 8 (2), November.

Imlah, A.H. (1950), 'The Terms of Trade of the United Kingdom, 1798-1913', *Journal of Economic History*, Vol. 10 (2), November.

Imlah, A.H. (1952), 'British Balance of Payments and Export of Capital, 1816-1913', *Economic History Review*, 2nd series, Vol. 5 (2), December.

Imlah, A.H. (1958), *Economic Elements in the "Pax Britannica". Studies in British Foreign Trade in the Nineteenth Century*, Harvard University Press, Cambridge (Mass.), reprinted by Russell & Russell, New York, 1969.

Investor's Monthly Manual, monthly supplement to *The Economist*, various issues.

Jenks, L.H. (1944), 'British Experience with Foreign Investments', *The Tasks of Economic History*, a supplemental issue of *Journal of Economic History*, Vol. 4, December.

Jenks, L.H. (1971), *The Migration of British Capital to 1875*, Nelson, London (1st edition, Knopf, New York, 1927).

Kennedy, W.P. (1974), 'Foreign Investment, Trade and Growth in the United Kingdom, 1870-1913', *Explorations in Economic History*, Vol. 11 (4), Summer.

Kennedy, W.P. (1987), 'Review of "Britain's Investment Overseas on the Eve of the First World War: The Use and Abuse of Numbers" by D.C.M. Platt', *Economic History Review*, 2nd series, Vol. 40 (2).

Keynes, J.M. (1909a), 'British Investments in India. A Letter to the Editor', *The Economist*, Vol. 68 (3418), February 27.

Keynes, J.M. (1909b), 'British Investments in India. A Letter to the Editor', *The Economist*, Vol. 68 (3428), May 8.

Kindersley, R.M. (1929), 'A New Study of British Foreign Investments', *Economic Journal*, Vol. 39 (153), March.

Kindersley, R.M. (1930), 'British Foreign Investments in 1928', *Economic Journal*, Vol. 40 (158), June.

Kindersley, R.M. (1931), 'British Foreign Investments in 1929', *Economic Journal*, Vol. 41 (163), September.

Kindersley, R.M. (1932), 'British Foreign Investments in 1930', *Economic Journal*, Vol. 42 (166), June.

Kirby, M.W. (1981), *The Decline of British Economic Power since 1870*, Allen & Unwin, London.

Kuznets, S. (1961), 'Quantitative Aspects of the Economic Growth of Nations: VI. Long-Term Trends in Capital Formation', *Economic Development and Cultural Change*, Vol. 9 (4), part II, July.

Lavington, M.A. (1921), *The English Capital Market*, Methuen & Co., London.

Lawrence, J. (1905), 'Letter to the Editor', *The Times*, April 22.

Lawrence, J. (1909), 'Letter to the Editor', *The Times*, March 18.

Lehfeldt, R.A. (1913), 'The Rate of Interest on British and Foreign Investments', *Journal of the Royal Statistical Society*, Vol. 76, part II, January; part IV, March.

Lehfeldt, R.A. (1914), 'The Rate of Interest on British and Foreign Investments', *Journal of the Royal Statistical Society*, Vol. 77, part IV, March.

Lehfeldt, R.A. (1915), 'The Rate of Interest on British and Foreign Investments', *Journal of the Royal Statistical Society*, Vol. 78, part III, May.

Lenfant, J.H. (1949), *British Capital Export, 1900-1913*, unpublished Ph.D. thesis, University of London.

Lenfant, J.H. (1951), 'Great Britain's Capital Formation,1865-1914', *Economica*, Vol. 18 (70), May.

Lindert, P. (1969), *Key Currencies and Gold, 1900-1913*, Princeton Studies in International Finance No. 24, Princeton University, Princeton.

London Statistical Society (1827), *Statistical Illustrations of the British Empire*, Effingham Wilson, London.

Lowe, J. (1822), *The Present State of England in Regard to Agriculture, Trade, and Finance; With a Comparison of the Prospects of England and France*, Richardson, London.

Madden, J.J. (1985), *British Investment in the United States, 1860-1880*, Garland, New York.

Mathias, P. (2001), 'Europe in the XXth Century: A Commentary on Events in the Context of Finance and Banking', *Journal of European Economic History*, special issue on: *Financial Systems in Europe in the XXth-Century: Factors of Crisis, Stability and Growth*.

McKay, A.D. (1877), 'Letter to the Editor', *The Economist*, Vol. 35 (1789), December 8.

Messenger, J.A. (1865), *Memorandum*, Parliamentary Papers, Vol. 50; reprinted in *Journal of the Statistical Society*, part II, June.

Mitchell, B.R. (1988), *British Historical Statistics*, Cambridge University Press, Cambridge.

Money Chiozza, L.G. (1903), *Elements of the Fiscal Problem*, King, London.

Money Chiozza, L.G. (1911), *Riches and Poverty (1910)*, 2nd edition, Methuen & Co., London (1st edition 1905).

Morgan, E.V. (1952), *Studies in British Financial Policy, 1914-25*, Macmillan, London.

Morgenstern, O. (1959), *International Financial Transactions and Business Cycles*, Princeton University Press, Princeton.

Nash, R.C. (1997), 'The Balance of Payments and Foreign Capital Flows in Eighteenth-Century England: A Comment', *Economic History Review*, Vol. 50 (1), February.

Nash, R.L. (1881*)*, *A Short Inquiry into the Profitable Nature of Our Investments*, 3rd edition, Wilson, London (1st edition 1880).

Newmarch, W. (1878), 'On the Progress of the Foreign Trade of the United Kingdom since 1856, with Especial Reference to the Effects Produced upon it by the Protectionist Tariffs of Other Countries', *Journal of the Statistical Society*, Vol. 41, part II, June.

Nicholson, J.S. (1963), 'Balance of Trade', in H. Higgs (ed.), *Palgrave's Dictionary of Political Economy*, Vol. I, Kelley, New York (1st edition, 1894-1899; revised edition, 1925-1926).

North, D. and Heston, A. (1960), 'The Estimation of Shipping Earnings in Historical Studies of the Balance of Payments', *Canadian Journal of Economics and Political Science*, Vol. 26 (1), February.

O'Brien, P.K. (1988), 'The Costs and Benefits of British Imperialism 1846-1914', *Past and Present*, no. 120, August.

Oppers, S.E. (1993), 'The Interest Rate Effect of Dutch Money in Eighteenth-Century', *Journal of Economic History*, Vol. 53 (1), March.

Paish, G. (1909), 'Great Britain's Capital Investments in Other Lands', *Journal of the Royal Statistical Society*, Vol. 72, part III, September.

Paish, G. (1911*)*, 'Great Britain's Capital Investments in Individual Colonial and Foreign Countries', *Journal of the Royal Statistical Society*, Vol. 74, part II, June.

Paish, G. (1914), 'The Export of Capital and the Cost of Living', *Statist*, Vol. 79 (1877), February.

Palgrave, R.H.I. (1894), 'Commerce', entry in R.H.I. Palgrave (ed.), *Dictionary of Political Economy*, Vol. I, Macmillan, London.

Phelps Brown, E.H. and Handfield-Jones, S.J. (1952), 'The Climacteric of the 1890's. Studies in the Expanding Economy', *Oxford Economic Papers*, new series, Vol. 4 (3), October.

Pitt, W. (1808), *The Speeches of the Right Honourable William Pitt in the House of Commons*, Vol. II, Longman, London.

Platt, D.C.M. (1980), 'British Portfolio Investment Overseas before 1870: Some Doubts', *Economic History Review*, 2nd series, Vol. 33 (1), February.

Platt, D.C.M. (1986), *Britain's Investment Overseas on the Eve of the First World War. The Use and Abuse of Numbers*, Macmillan, London.

Pollard, S. (1985), 'Capital Exports, 1870-1914: Harmful or Beneficial?', *Economic History Review*, 2nd series, Vol. 38 (4), November.

Pollard, S. (1989), *Britain's Prime and Britain's Decline. The British Economy 1870-1914*, Arnold, London.

Porter, G.R. (1912), *The Progress of the Nation in Its Various Social and Economic Relations from the Beginning of the Nineteenth Century*, updated version edited by F.W. Hirst of the 3rd edition, Methuen, London (original 3rd edition, Murray, London, 1851).

Prest, A.R. and Adams, A.A. (1954), *Consumers' Expenditure in the United Kingdom, 1900-1919*, University Press, Cambridge.

Rathbone, W. (1877), 'Waste not, Want not. A Letter to the Editor', *The Economist*, Vol. 35 (1787), November 24.

Rose, G. (1799), *A Brief Examination into the Increase of the Revenue, Commerce, and Manufactures, of Great Britain, from 1792 to 1799*, Wright, London.

Royal Institute of International Affairs (1937), *The Problem of International Investment*, Oxford University Press, London.

Saul, S.B. (1960), *Studies in British Overseas Trade, 1870-1914*, Liverpool University Press, Liverpool.

Schlote, W. (1938), *Entwicklung und Strukturwandlungen des englischen Aussenhandels von 1700 bis zur Gegenwart*, Jena, 1938 (English translation: *British Overseas Trade. From 1700 to the 1930s*, Greenwood Press, Westport, 1952).

Schooling, J.H. (1911), *The British Trade Book. A Survey of the Home Production...*, 4th edition, with a preface by W.J. Ashley, Murray, London (1st edition 1905).

Seeley, J. R. (1971), *The Expansion of England*, edited and with an introduction by J. Gross, University of Chicago Press, Chicago (1st edition, Macmillan, 1883).

Segal, H.H. and Simon, M. (1961), 'British Foreign Capital Issues, 1865-1894', *Journal of Economic History*, Vol. 21 (4), December.

Seyd, E. (1876), 'The Fall in the Price of Silver, Its Consequences and Their Possible Avoidance', *Journal of the Society of Arts*, Vol. 24 (1216), March 10.

Seyd, E. (1878), 'Our Wealth in Relation to Imports and Exports, and the Causes of Decline in the Latter', *Journal of the Society of Arts*, Vol. 26 (1324), April 5; reprinted in E. Seyd (1878), *The Wealth and Commerce of Nations, and the Question of Silver...*, Fisher, London.

Shaw-Lefevre, G.J. (1878), 'The Opening Address', as President of the Statistical Society, *Journal of the Statistical Society*, Vol. 41, part IV, September.

Simon, M. (1967a), 'The Pattern of New British Portfolio Foreign Investment, 1865-1914', in J.H. Adler (ed.), *Capital Movements and Economic Development*, Macmillan, London and later in A.R. Hall (ed.) (1968), *The Export of Capital from Britain, 1870-1914*, Methuen & Co., London.

Simon, M. (1967b), 'The Enterprise and Industrial Composition of New British Portfolio Foreign Investment, 1865-1914', *Journal of Development Studies*, Vol. 3 (3), April.

Skinner, T. (ed.) (1875), *The Stock Exchange Year Book*, editions from a number of years, Cassell, London.

Speck, W.A. (1993), *A Concise History of Britain, 1707-1975*, Cambridge University Press, Cambridge.

Speyer, E. (1905), 'Some Aspects of National Finance', *Institute of Bankers*, Vol. 26, part VII, October.

Spicer, E.E. and Pegler, E.C. (1916), *Income Tax in Relation to Accounts*, 4th edition, Lynch & Co., London.

Staley, E. (1935), *War and the Private Investor. A Study in the Relations of International Politics and International Private Investment*, with an introduction by A. Salter, Doubleday, New York.

Stamp, J.C. (1916), *British Incomes and Property: The Application of Official Statistics to Economic Problems*, King, London.

Stamp, J.C. (1918), 'An Estimate of the Capital Wealth of the United Kingdom in Private Hands', *Economic Journal*, Vol. 28 (111), September.

Steuart, J. (1805), *The Works, Political, Metaphysical, and Chronological...*, edited by his son, Vol. III, Cadell and Davies, London.

Stock Exchange Year Book..., see Skinner T.

Stone, I. (1999), *The Global Export of Capital from Great Britain, 1865-1914*, St. Martin's Press, New York.

Stopford, J. (1974), 'The Origins of British Based Multinational Manufacturing Enterprises', *Business History Review*, Vol. 48 (3), Autumn.

Svedberg, P. (1978), 'The Portfolio-Direct Composition of Private Foreign Investment in 1914 Revisited', *Economic Journal*, Vol. 88 (352), December.

Sykes, E. (1932), *Banking and Currency*, 7th edition, Butterworth & Co., London (1st edition 1904).

The Economist (1863), 'The Annual Accumulations of Capital in the United Kingdom', I. Vol. 21 (1059), December 12; II. Vol. 21 (1060), December 19; reprinted under the name of W. Newmarch, *Journal of the Statistical Society* (1864), Vol. 32, part I, March.

The Economist (1870), 'Extent of British Investments in Foreign Loans', in the supplement *Commercial History and Review*, Vol. 28 (1385), March 12.

The Economist (1871), 'English and French Money Market in 1870', in the supplement *Commercial History and Review*, Vol. 29 (1437), March 11.

The Economist (1872), 'The Money Markets in 1871', in the supplement *Commercial History and Review*, Vol. 30 (1490), March 16.

The Economist (1876), 'The Fall in Speculative Foreign Stocks', Vol. 34 (1701), April 1.

The Economist (1877a), 'The Large Excess of Our Imports over Our Exports', Vol. 35 (1746), February 10.

The Economist (1877b), 'Imports and Exports', Vol. 35 (1785), November 10.

The Economist (1877c), 'Are We Consuming Our Capital?', I. Vol. 35 (1790), December 15; II. Vol. 35 (1791), December 22.

The Economist (1877d), 'Imports and Exports, Two Letters to the Editor of C. and a Merchant', Vol. 35 (1791), December 22.

The Economist (1878), 'Income Tax on British, Indian, Colonial, and Foreign Stocks', Vol. 36 (1806), April 6.

The Economist (1906), 'Our Income from Investments Abroad', Vol. 64 (3291), September 22.

The Economist (1907), 'The Security for Brewery Debenture Stocks', Vol. 65 (3342), September 14.

The Economist (1909a), 'Our Investments Abroad', Vol. 68 (3417), February 20.

The Economist (1909b), 'The Corporation of Foreign Bondholders', Vol. 68 (3418), February 27.

The Economist (1909c), 'British Investments in India. A Letter to the Editor of "A Correspondent"', Vol. 68 (3418), April 10.

The Economist (1910), 'Inland Revenue and Capital Abroad', Vol. 71 (3499), September 17.

The Economist (1911a), 'The Growth of Wealth and Capital, I. ', Vol. 72 (3521), February 18.

The Economist (1911b), 'The Growth of Capital, 1800 to 1885', Vol. 73 (3547), August 19.

The Economist (1911c), 'A Letter to the Editor of an "Anxious Investor', Vol. 73 (3547), August 19.

The Economist (1911d), 'A Letter to the Editor of X', Vol. 73 (3548), August 26.

The Economist (1911e) 'The Growth of British Capital from the Year 1885 to 1909', Vol. 73 (3561), November 25. The articles of the same year marked with the letters a, b and e, belong to F.W. Hirst.

The Economist (1930), 'British Capital Abroad', Vol. 111: I. (4547), October 18; II. (4548), October 25; III. (4549), November 1; IV. (4551), November 15.

The Economist (1931a), 'Britain's Balance of Trade', Vol. 113 (4594), September 12.

The Economist (1931b), 'Britain's Balance of Trade', Vol. 113 (4591), August 22.

The Economist (1931c), 'Britain's Balance of Payments', Vol. 113 (4607), December 12.

The Economist (1937), 'British Capital Abroad', Vol. 129 (4917), November 20.

The Times (1877), 'The Excess of Imports', December 7; reprinted in *Journal of Statistical Society*, Vol. 41, March.

The Times (1898), 'Mr. Ritchie on British Trade', November 25, 28 and 29.

The Times (1905), 'Editorial', May 18.

The Times (1909), 'Foreign Investments', March 18.

Thomas, B. (1967), 'The Historical Record of International Capital Movements to 1913', in J.H. Adler (ed.), *Capital Movements and Economic Development*, Macmillan, London.

Tiberi, M. (1980), *Investimenti internazionali e sviluppo del sistema capitalistico. Parte introduttiva*, Kappa, Roma.

Tiberi, M. (1984), *Investimenti internazionali e sviluppo del sistema capitalistico. L'evoluzione degli scambi commerciali della Gran Bretagna (1700-1913)*, Kappa, Roma.

Tiberi, M. (1988), *Investimenti internazionali e sviluppo del sistema capitalistico. Le partite invisibili della Gran Bretagna fino alla prima guerra mondiale*, Kappa, Roma.

Tiberi, M. (1992), *Investimenti internazionali e sviluppo del sistema capitalistico. Dalle partite invisibili alla bilancia dei pagamenti della Gran Bretagna fino alla prima guerra mondiale: il contributo degli economisti contemporanei*, Kappa, Roma.

Tiberi, M. (1999), 'Uno sguardo di fine secolo all'economia mondiale', in N. Acocella, G.M. Rey and M. Tiberi (eds), *Saggi di politica economica in onore di Federico Caffè*, Vol. III, Angeli, Milano.

Wilkins, M. (1989), *The History of Foreign Investment in the United States to 1914*, Harvard University Press, Cambridge (Mass.).

Williamson, S. (1877), 'A Letter to the Editor', *Economist*, Vol. 35 (1748), February 24.

Official publications

Great Britain

Board of Trade (1920a), 'The Balance of Trade. An Estimate of "Invisible Exports"', *Board of Trade Journal*, Vol. 104 (1207), January 15.

Board of Trade (1920b), 'The Balance of Trade. An Estimate of "Invisible Exports"', *Board of Trade Journal*, Vol. 105 (1237), August 12.

Board of Trade (1921), 'Shipping Earnings and the Balance of Trade. Comparison of 1920 with 1913', *Board of Trade Journal*, Vol. 106 (1262), February 3.

Board of Trade (1923), 'The Balance of Trade in 1922. Investment Abroad and Shipping Earnings', *Board of Trade Journal*, Vol. 110 (1374), March 29.

Board of Trade (1927), 'The Balance of Trade. The Years 1924, 1925, and 1926', *Board of Trade Journal*, Vol. 118 (1573), January 27.

Board of Trade (1932), 'The Balance of Trade. The Years 1929, 1930, and 1931', *Board of Trade Journal*, Vol. 128 (1837), February 18.

Customs and Inland Revenue Act (1885), (48 & 49 Vict. Ch. 51) in *The Public General Acts Passed in the Forty-Eighth and Forty-Ninth Years of the Reign of Her Majesty Queen Victoria...*, Eyre and Spottiswoode, London.

Marshall, J. (1834), *A Digest of All the Accounts Relating to the Population, Productions, Revenues,...of the United Kingdom of Great Britain and Ireland...*, part II, London.

Parliamentary Papers (1808), *An Account of All Exemptions Granted to Foreigners*, Vol. 6.

Parliamentary Papers (1814-15), *Amounts of Exemptions Granted to Foreigners*, Vol. 10.

Parliamentary Papers (1831-32), *Report from the Committee of Secrecy on the Bank of England Charter; With the Minutes of Evidence, Appendix and Index*, Vol. 6.

Parliamentary Papers (1854a), *An Account of All Sums of Money Paid or Advanced by Way of Loan, Subsidy, or Otherwise, to Any Foreign State, from the Year 1792 up to the Present Time, Distinguishing the Amounts Paid in Each Year*, Vol. 39.

Parliamentary Papers (1854b), *Loans, & c. to Foreign States*, Vol. 39.

Parliamentary Papers (1854c), *Correspondence between Great Britain and Foreign Powers, and Communications from the British Government to Claimants, Relative to Loans Made by British Subjects, 1847-1853*, Vol. 49.

Parliamentary Papers (1870), *Report of the Commissioners of Inland Revenue on the Duties under Their Management, for the Years 1856 to 1869 Inclusive; with Some Retrospective History, and Complete Tables of Accounts of the Duties from Their First Imposition*, Vols. I and II, Vol. 20.

Parliamentary Papers (1875), *Report from the Select Committee on Loans to Foreign States; Together with the Proceedings of the Committee, Minutes of Evidence, Appendix and Index*, Vol. 11.

Parliamentary Papers (1903), *Memorandum on the Excess of Imports into the United Kingdom*, in *Memoranda, Statistical Tables, and Charts Prepared in the Board of Trade with Reference to Various Matters Bearing on British and Foreign Trade and Industrial Conditions*, Vol. 67.

Parliamentary Papers (1919), *Report of the American Dollar Securities Committee*, Vol. 13.

Parliamentary Papers (1920), *Report of the Royal Commission on the Income Tax*, Vol. 18.

Parliamentary Papers (1930-31), *Committee on Finance and Industry (Macmillan Report)*, Vol. 13.

Parliamentary Papers, *Annual Statement of the Trade and Navigation of the United Kingdom with Foreign Countries and British Possessions*, published between 1853 and 1870. From the year 1871 it is divided into: *The Annual Statement of the Navigation and Shipping of the United Kingdom* and *The Annual Statement of the Trade of the United Kingdom with Foreign Countries and British Possessions*.

Parliamentary Papers, *Report of the Commissioners of His (Her) Majesty's Inland Revenue*, published annually from 1857 onwards.

Parliamentary Papers, *Statistical Abstract for the United Kingdom*, published annually from 1854 in Parliamentary Papers.

Trade Figures Committee (1926), *Report of 28th April*, not published but available, together with relative correspondence, in the Public Records Office of London (reference T. 160/244/F. 9390).

International Organizations

League of Nations (1922), *Records of the Third Assembly. Plenary Meetings, Vol. I, Text of the Debates*, Geneva.

League of Nations (1924), *Memorandum on Balance of Payments and Foreign Trade Balances,1910-1923,Vol. I, Balance of Payments and Summary Trade Tables*, Geneva.

League of Nations (1929), *Proceedings of the International Conference Relating to Economic Statistics*, Geneva.

Statistical Office of the European Communities (1983), *Balance of Payments Methodology of the United Kingdom*, Luxembourg.

United Nations, Department of Economic Affairs (1949), *International Capital Movements during the Inter-War Period*, New York.

Author Index

Subject Index

For Product Safety Concerns and Information please contact our EU representative GPSR@taylorandfrancis.com Taylor & Francis Verlag GmbH, Kaufingerstraße 24, 80331 München, Germany

Printed and bound by CPI Group (UK) Ltd, Croydon, CR0 4YY
01/05/2025
01858456-0001